THE UNITED NATIONS AND THE HUMAN RIGHTS

THE UNITED NATIONS AND THE HUMAN RIGHTS

Patanjali Nandan Chaturvedi

MD PUBLICATIONS PVT LTD
NEW DELHI
www.mdppl.com

Published by :

MD Publications Pvt Ltd
"MD House", 11, Darya Ganj,
New Delhi - 110 002
Phone : +91-11-45355555
E-mail : contact@mdppl.com
Website: www.mdppl.com

ISBN: 978-81-7533-259-1

Published and Printed by Mr. Pranav Gupta on behalf of **MD Publications Pvt Ltd** at Mohit Enterprises, Delhi.

PREFACE

In 1945, in the aftermath of a bloody and destructive war of unprecedented cruelty, 51 countries, led by the winner nations, decided to launch a project, both ambitious and tough, to protect peace in the world. Sixty years later, 191 countries still struggle to achieve the goals set out in the first lines of the United Nations Charter: to prevent the scourge of war; to reaffirm faith in the fundamental human rights, in the dignity and worth of the human person, in the equal rights of men and women and of nations large and small; to respect treaties; and to promote progress and freedom.

The pursuit of human rights was one of the central reasons for creating the United Nations. World War II atrocities and genocide led to a ready consensus that the new organisation must work to prevent any similar tragedies in the future. An early objective was creating a legal framework for considering and acting on complaints about human rights violations.

The UN Charter obliges all member nations to promote "universal respect for, and observance of, human rights" and to take "joint and separate action" to that end. The U.S. considers the United Nations to be a first line of defense of the principles enshrined in the Universal Declaration of Human Rights. It is also a means by which those principles can be applied more broadly around the world. A case in point is support by the United Nations for countries in transition to democracy. Technical assistance in providing free and fair elections, improving judicial structures, drafting constitutions, training human rights officials, and transforming armed movements into political parties have contributed significantly to democratisation worldwide.

The United Nations is also a forum in which to support the right of women to participate fully in the political, economic, and social life of their countries. QUNO works to strengthen the promotion and protection of human rights through the United Nations system, with particular reference to the interface between human rights and armed conflicts, the protection of refugees and other Quaker concerns. The questions of the rights of indigenous peoples, gender, violence against children and the impact of the "war on terror" are included in all programme areas.

QUNO also organises informal, off-the-record meetings to promote and enhance dialogue, networking and the building of relationships on human rights and refugee issues between government representatives across the regional groups of the UN, amongst the key Non-Governmental Organisations and across the government, NGO, UN secretariat and independent expert spectrum in order to further the promotion and protection of human rights.

I am very grateful to Mr. Pranav Gupta, Director of MD Publications Pvt Ltd, New Delhi, for his kind cooperation and support for this book.

Patanjali Nandan Chaturvedi

Contents

1

The United Nations and the Struggle for Human Rights

There have been numerous calls for UN reform over the years. The Oil-for Food fiasco has tarnished the reputation of the organization. The United Nations' performance in human rights has been especially suspected. Its lack of proper action in the former Yugoslavia and Rwanda is scandalous. History appears to be repeating itself in Darfur, Sudan.

The U.S. administration of President George W. Bush continues to push to make democracy a reality in Iraq. American authorities have been widely criticized for allegedly torturing some of those in their custody. Meanwhile, Slobodan Milosevic has died in prison before a verdict on his alleged war crimes could be reached and the trial of Saddam Hussein, full of theatrics, goes on and on. The Middle East remains a powder keg filled with charges and countercharges of human rights transgressions.

Incapacitation of former Prime Minister Ariel Sharon combined with the ascendance to power of Hamas greatly clouds the Arab-Israeli picture. When Chinese leader Hu Jintao is greeted on the White House lawn, he is heckled by a spectator regarding treatment of the Falun Gong in China. Throngs of people throughout the world protest the publication of cartoons in Denmark said to be blasphemous to Islam. Italy shelters a former-Muslim-turned-Christian while many in his native Afghanistan say his execution is mandated by their faith. It is clear that human rights concerns dominate our world now and will do so in the future. It is also apparent that the United Nations will continue to be linked to many of the world's most intractable human rights dilemmas.

The Charter upon which the United Nations rests makes frequent mention of "human rights". As we approach the 5th anniversary of September 11th and the 61st anniversary of the United Nations, it is entirely fitting to assess the role played by this collective security institution in protecting human rights. Such a review is serious business and will help exhibit the strengths and weaknesses of this universal intergovernmental organization. A word of caution is in order. The United Nations as a whole is an extremely complex organization. Those parts of the UN which deal with human rights per se form an intricate labyrinth. Since its inception the UN system for promoting human rights has grown "like topsy".

Charter-based organs dealing with human rights include the General Assembly (with its Third Committee), the Economic and Social Council (ECOSOC), the Security Council, the Commission on Human Rights (replaced in 2006 by the Human Rights Council), the Sub-Commission on Prevention of Discrimination and Protection of Minorities, the Commission on the Status of Women and, perhaps most notably, the UN High Commissioner for Human Rights. Certain human rights treaties (concerning racial discrimination; political and civil rights; discrimination against women; economic, social and cultural rights; torture; rights of children; and migrant workers) created under the auspices of the UN have mandated still other organs to monitor compliance.

Moreover, over the years several working groups have been founded to confront issues as varied as contemporary forms of slavery and the plight of indigenous populations. In addition, Special Rapporteurs have been entrusted to study and report on a whole host of issues ranging from the right to a fair trial to discrimination against peoples with AIDS to human rights and the environment. The UN Secretariat may also play a role in promoting and implementing human rights. Specialized agencies, such as the International Labor

Organization (ILO) and the United Nations Educational, Scientific and Cultural Organization (UNESCO), have conducted human rights programs. The UN High Commissioner for Refugees has also done human rights work.

EVALUATING THE UN VIS A VIS HUMAN RIGHTS

Assessing the performance of the United Nations with respect to human rights is difficult because observers tend to emphasize different things under the rubric of "human rights". For example, some are mostly concerned with political and civil rights. Others concentrate on economic, social and cultural rights. Furthermore, some individuals evaluate the United Nations' performance in terms of a relatively short time span. Other people take a long-range perspective.

Also, certain observers evaluate the UN primarily in terms of its role in incrementally establishing or promoting human rights criteria in international law. But, others measure the UN according to how well it has actually implemented and enforced existing human rights standards. Finally, some evaluators of the UN, when all is said and done, do not expect too much of the organization. Others have lofty aspirations. The aforementioned observations help to explain in part why scholars sharply differ in their views of the United Nations concerning human rights.

The new UN Human Rights Council is controversial before it becomes an operational reality. The Council was created on March 15, 2006 by the UN General Assembly. One hundred seventy countries voted for the entity. Four nations voted against the resolution: Israel, Marshall Islands, Palau, and the United States. Three countries abstained: Belarus, Iran and Venezuela. The United States has decided not to run for a seat during the May 9, 2006 election.

THE CONVENTIONAL WISDOM

On the first page of the Introduction to his popular book on Argentina's Dirty War, human rights and the United Nations, Iain Guest writes:

During the 1980s, it has been an article of faith... that the U.N. is "politicized", its human rights machinery "selective"... Whether or not this is true of 1990 lies beyond the scope of this study, but it was certainly not the case in 1980.

This chapter contends that Mr. Guest is incorrect in his major assertion that in 1980 the United Nations human rights machinery was neither selective nor politicized. Facts suggest otherwise. The history of the United Nations with respect to human rights, particularly their actual protection and implementation, was decidedly checkered and lackluster in the 1980s. Moreover, the UN's human rights performance was extremely weak in the 1970s and remains poor to this day. To understand why this is so, it is important to concentrate on more than just one case study. The Perspective of the Reagan Administration.

This chapter will explain how key players within the administration of President Ronald Reagan-most notably, Ambassador Jeane J. Kirkpatrick, his permanent representative to the UN perceived and analyzed the United Nations with respect to its human rights mandate. First, Kirkpatrick's view of the UN as a political system will be explored. Subsequently, her ideas on human rights and US foreign policy and the United Nations will be examined. Then, empirical evidence will be cited in an attempt to learn whether there is support for her major contentions.

During the Reagan era the UN came under very sharp attack from the government of the United States. Reagan, claiming parts of the UN were being used for anti-American purposes, cut off millions of dollars normally targeted for the international organization. Many people who championed the cause of human rights were (and are) extremely critical of the President's posture vis a vis the United Nations as well as of his human rights policy.

Reagan's support of the contras in Nicaragua was especially scorned. Indeed, some commentators believed Reagan's policy on human rights was so abysmal that members of his administration could not possibly have anything worthwhile to say about that subject or about the United

Nations. One of the purposes of this chapter is to assess whether or not this is true.

THE KIRKPATRICK CRITIQUE

It is both appropriate and useful to study the ideas of Dr. Jeane J. Kirkpatrick relating to the United Nations and human rights. As a professional political scientist and member of both the Cabinet and the National Security Council, Reagan's ambassador to the UN was the administration's most articulate spokesperson regarding these matters. The Kirkpatrick Doctrine on dictatorships and double standards has been cited as guiding US human rights policy between 1981 and 1985. More generally, it has been suggested that Dr. Kirkpatrick initiated a debate over the value of the United Nations that would become a constant in American politics.

ON THE UN AS A POLITICAL SYSTEM

Kirkpatrick viewed the United Nations in the early 1980s as a political system in which the United States frequently had virtually no influence. It was a place that bred "conflict extension, exacerbation and polarization" and where the United States was recklessly insulted. Unlike some conservatives who favored a US withdrawal from the organization, Kirkpatrick argued that the UN was important and that possible constructive outcomes made the UN worthy of American participation. For example, she valued the United Nations Development Program.

What happened at Turtle Bay, particularly in the long run, might influence important events. However, she lamented that her country had "progressively acquiesced in a notion that it was a normal part of U.N. for us to be essentially isolated and lacking in influence". Past American feather touch diplomacy had prevented the United States from achieving its goals. Thus, she disdained State Department bureaucracy, championed forthright rebuttal and spoke bluntly.

The UN was seen by Kirkpatrick as a special type of representative body that represented governmental rulers.

However, the latter did not necessarily represent own people. That the UN had not in her opinion even remotely fulfilled the expectations of its founders was in no small measure attributable to its system of voting blocs and US lack of participation in same.

Blocs could be geographical, political, economic, ideological, cultural, etc. They could be large or small, loose or cohesive, disciplined or non-disciplined, heterogeneous or homogenous. Whatever their configuration, blocs were the key to the main political decisions in the General Assembly, the Economic and Social Council, and, to a larger extent than commonly realized, in the Security Council.

The more cohesive a bloc, the more likely it would be effective. According to Kirkpatrick, in the General Assembly radical views often dominated because of bloc politics. Thus, the 1975 resolution of that body equating Zionism with racism was a result of an African bloc-Arab bloc alliance. The former gave its support to this resolution in exchange for the latter's help on South African issues.

Dr. Kirkpatrick referred to UN blocs as "happy hunting ground" for radical factions such as the Soviets, Libyans, Syrians, and Cubans. She noted a dynamic of extremism whereby people supporting the wildest positions in the UN appeared to gain disproportionate influence. The largest bloc, the non-aligned, was never cohesive unless it united to foster a position acceptable to the USSR. Furthermore, the politically astute Soviets encouraged client states, like Cuba, to join the non-aligned movement.

Hence, the Soviet Union, in marked contrast to the USA, was very successful in various UN bodies in the 1980s. In comparison, the United States was not a member of any bloc and paid the price in the form of impotence. Only when the bloc system failed could it exercise power. It was forced to scramble to form new coalitions for every issue.

The lack of power was symbolized by evermore frequent American vetoes in the Security Councila sure sign that the

US did not have sufficient clout to stop adverse resolutions by mustering the requisite votes. Regarding the General Assembly Kirkpatrick complained that "those who pay the bill don't have the votes, and those who have the votes don't pay the bill".

ON HUMAN RIGHTS AND THE UNITED STATES

Kirkpatrick's critique of President Jimmy Carter's human rights policy first brought her to the attention of Ronald Reagan. Dr. Kirkpatrick believed the much publicized Carter stance was flawed because of its:

- Failure to recognize that human rights must rest on specific institutions stabilized patterns of human behavior
- Consideration of human rights violations independently of context
- Nearly exclusive focus on human rights violations by governments while tending to exclude atrocities by terrorists and guerrilla groups
- Emphasis on social and economic "rights" as opposed to "aspirations"
- Universal human rights rhetoric which was almost invariably anti-Western in its application
- Overwhelming concern with purity of intentions rather than actual consequences
- Attempt to invoke universal moral rules as justification for a policy which will necessarily be selectively applied
- Disinclination to single out communist countries (e.g. USSR, Cambodia, Rumania, Yugoslavia) for human rights transgressions
- Public criticism of countries such as South Korea and the Philippines which helped to delegitimize them while simultaneously rendering them less susceptible to American views
- Tendency to attempt to influence other governments by publicly humiliating them rather than by using quiet persuasion and diplomacy

In a statement before the Third Committee of the UN General Assembly, Dr. Kirkpatrick summarized her views on the UN's track record on human rights. She said that the UN had no more important charge than the protection and expansion of the rights of persons.

These rights of individuals, in turn, were most effectively promoted through democratic political institutions insuring inter alia periodic, meaningful, competitive elections and freedom of press and assembly. She added: "There would be no serious human rights abuses if all peoples enjoyed self-government and democracy".

Since human rights can be violated by private violence as well as public coercion, the protection of human rights should have a double focus: working against both forms of abuse. Most importantly, said Kirkpatrick, reasonable human rights judgments, must depend on both standards and contexts:

All infringements of the rights of citizens must be judged by the same standard, and the concrete circumstances in which they occur must always be taken into account.

Thus, Kirkpatrick argued it was unreasonable to expect weak governments in strife-torn societies to maintain order and justice on the same level as strong well-established governments. It was likewise unwise to dilute the special meaning to "human rights" by including under that rubric a proliferating list of virtually all objects of human desire. Most importantly, it was wrong to single out for harsh criticism some members of the UN while completely ignoring others with worse records. Her evaluation of the United Nations stood in sharp contrast to the aforementioned ideas of Iain Guest. The latter wrote:

... the U.N. was never more effective in promoting human rights than on the eve of Mr. Reagan's accession, and that this was largely due to its vigorous if belated response to the disappearances in Latin America.

Kirkpatrick countered:

No aspect of the United Nations affairs has been more perverted by the politicization of the last decade than have its human rights activities.

The main targets of scorn in the UN had for years been South Africa, Israel and certain noncommunist Latin American countries. But other regimes had "more brutally repressed and slaughtered their citizens". Yet, the human rights agencies of the United Nations were silent on the abuses of regimes like Pol Pot's Kampuchea, Idi Amin's Uganda, Leonid Brezhnev's Soviet Union, and Fidel Castro's Cuba. Clearly some persons and governments in the UN utilized human rights as a political weapon-wielded by the mighty against the weak, by the majority against the isolated, and by the blocs against the unorganized.

THE DONNELLY STUDY

In 1988 Professor Jack Donnelly published an important quantitative study of the question of UN bias pertaining to human rights. Through analysis of meeting times in both ECOSOC's Commission on Human Rights and the General Assembly's Third (Social, Humanitarian and Cultural) Committee, he concluded bias was "one of the most important impediments to increasing the effectiveness of the United Nation's human rights work".

Hence, Donnelly's study gives strong support to those, such as Jeane Kirkpatrick and Senator Daniel Patrick Moynihan (also a former U.S. Permanent Representative to the UN), that have accused the United Nations of double standards and bias. Between 1965 and 1985 the Third World, with Soviet bloc backing, shifted the bulk of the human rights discussion at the UN to self determination, racial discrimination, and economic and social rights. The Commission, especially between 1980 and 1985, seriously shortchanged the discussion of civil liberties such as freedoms of speech, press, assembly, and association-those rights people use to shape their governments.

The professor found a similar pattern of priorities in the

Third Committee of the General Assembly. While certain "pariah" regimes (South Africa, Chile, and Israel) received superabundant attention, partisan politics sheltered some states, equally bad or worse, from any scrutiny whatsoever. The Uganda of Amin escaped public pressure by the Commission as did the second Obote regime and Mengistu's Ethiopia. Indonesian human right violations in East Timor were largely ignored as were transgressions in Kampuchea and Equatorial Guinea.

African countries other than South Africa were rarely rebuked by the Commission. In Asia, Vietnam, both Koreas, and the Philippines escaped censure as did all Arab countries in the Middle East. Afghanistan and Poland were the only Soviet client states to receive Commission study. Latin America's Argentina, Cuba, and Uruguay were similarly neglected.

In the General Assembly, Donnelly discovered a very disappointing record of resolutions for human rights violations. Aside from the pariahs, General Assembly activity concentrated primarily on El Salvador, Guatemala, and revolutionary Iran. Donnelly concludes:

> ... only politics can explain why resolutions have been adopted on these countries but not on dozens... with records as bad or worse...comparably repressive Soviet-backed regimes have not been subjected to comparable scrutiny.

As stated above, the machinery at the United Nations for developing, promoting, and implementing human rights is exceedingly complex. Therefore, it is not easy to fairly evaluate. How one grades the UN is a function of one's expectations of it as well as many other factors.

This chapter has detailed the major criticisms of the UN's work on human rights as propounded by Ronald Reagan's UN ambassador, Jeane Kirkpatrick. Many people feel it is curious, or even scandalous, to link Reagan (or his top advisers) and human rights because of his support for the contrast in Nicaragua, other policies in Latin America, suspicion of international organization, alleged neglect of economic and social rights, and the supposed lack of support for human rights in past Republican presidencies, etc.

Nevertheless, the empirical evidence presented by scholars, including Kirkpatrick herself, in no small measure supports the key contentions of members of Reagan's foreign policy brain trust. Despite Mr. Guest's protestations to the contrary, the simple fact is that for most of its sixty plus years the UN has been extremely "political" and "selective" vis a vis human rights issues.

These shortcomings are nothing new. Former US Ambassador to Burundi, Thomas Patrick Melady, has lamented, for example, the double standard operating at the UN in the 1970s. This permitted too much attention to be focused on South African apartheid at the expense of any attention on Uganda, Burundi, and the former East Pakistan-three cases in which tens of thousands were massacred.

Professor of Law Philip Alston has written:

It is easy to cite a string of situations during the 1970s... which involved egregious violations but which failed to attract any specific UN sanction... review of the 1980s... will yield an infinitely more favourable balance sheet....

Nevertheless, this chapter has demonstrated that the UN's human rights record even in the 1980s was extremely suspect. Kirkpatrick was correct in her major assertions on this score. Although her ideas were anathema to those holding naive "irrational exuberance" in international organizations, she made a major contribution to the cause of worldwide human rights by accurately describing the duplicity of the United Nations in these matters.

It may be that the end of the Cold War and the collapse of the Soviet bloc may lead to a UN system in which human rights abuses are considered more evenhandedly. This has not yet come to pass. Other blocs remain. Countries of special status, such as China-despite Tiananmen Square are likely to remain unchecked by the UN. It is equally probable that, as in the past, some of the worst violators of human rights will from time to time sit on UN human rights bodies.

In 2002, the United States, for the first time, did not receive the votes necessary to be reelected to the UN Human Rights Commission. The Commission affirmed "the legitimate right of the Palestinian people to resist Israeli occupation"; but, it did nothing to condemn groups like Hamas which had just sent a suicide bomber to kill Israelis celebrating Passover.

The following year, Dr. Kirkpatrick headed the American delegation to the annual 6-week session in Geneva. Libya was elected chair and the group was "filled with an assortment of world-class rights abusers, including Syria, Sudan, Sierra Leone, and Uganda." Kirkpatrick was dismayed that "Russia voted almost exactly as it had during the Cold War"- siding with dictatorships represented on the Commission. She was encouraged, on the other hand, that democratic states displayed considerable solidarity -with the notable exception of matters involving Israel.

As the Commission was meeting, Fidel Castro's government was sentencing scores of "Cuban teachers, doctors, journalists and librarians to prison terms of 12 to 26 years, at trials lasting less than a day each". The Commission took no immediate action to register its disapproval. Neither did the Commission reprimand Russia for repression in Chechnya, the Sudan for slavery, and Zimbabwe for murder, nor China for victimizing the Falun Gong.

Joshua Muravchik argues persuasively that much of the rank hypocrisy concerning human rights in the United Nations stems from the influence of the Non-Aligned Movement. He claims NAM's spirit of "developing world versus the West" infuses various UN caucuses and regional blocs. One result was that in 2004 the UN refused to make any significant criticism of ethnic cleansing in Darfur. This is eerily reminiscent of the United Nations' intransigence in Bosnia and Rwanda.

Much optimism over the new Human Rights Council has been expressed by UN Secretary-General Kofi Annan, General

Assembly President Jan Eliasson and High Commissioner for Human Rights Louise Arbour. The latter, for example, has stated that candidates for Council membership will have to make commitments on human rights. Election to the Council (for a three year renewable term) requires approval via secret ballot of 96 of 191 UN members. The human rights records of elected members are first in line to be scrutinized. Council members guilty of gross and systematic human rights violations may be suspended by a 2/3 majority vote of the General Assembly. The Council will meet for at least 10 weeks per year and can under certain circumstances hold special sessions.

But, the aforementioned optimism seems ill-placed. According to UN documents, no substantive eligibility criterion re human rights is required for membership. As of late April 2006, the following list of candidates for the Human Rights Council has emerged: Algeria, China, Cuba, Iran, Pakistan and Saudi Arabia. This is hardly a group to inspire confidence in the new system. Furthermore, membership on the Council is determined by geographical distribution rules. This means that Africa and Asia are each allotted 13 seats; Eastern Europe, 6; and Latin America/Caribbean, 8. The remaining 7 seats are left for the Western European and Others Group, of which the United States is a member. As a result, the new 47-member Human Rights Council can easily be dominated by autocracies.

If such spectacles continue, they will surely gravely detract from the splendid work of countless dedicated people within the UN system who endeavor to build a more humane world. Those individuals and the people they seek to protect deserve better.

TOTALITARIANISM

The specter which has truly haunted much of mankind for a large part of this century has been the specter of totalitarianism. Not only was it a totalitarian government which unleashed World War II, but totalitarian systems have both in times of peace and times of war been responsible for millions of deaths and for enormous human suffering.

The phenomenon of twentieth century totalitarianism is the product of the marriage of tyrannical government, as practiced since ancient times, with modern technology, with ways and means under which the tyrant can indeed exercise total control over his subjects. George Orwell, in his famous novel 1984, has described the frightful extremes to which a totalitarian system could go in degrading human beings, in depriving them of every vestige of what we call human rights and then, we have never descended to the nightmare existence envisaged by Orwell, but we must not overlook the fact that in some situations we have come frightfully close.

As there has been discussion in recent years, of the distinction that can and should be made between authoritarianism and totalitarianism and the treatment of these phenomena in the United Nations system. Article 21 of the Universal Declaration of Human Rights provides that citizens shall have the right to choose their governments in free elections. Authoritarian systems act in violation of that article by depriving their subjects of that right, by imposing a government on them which is not a government of their choice.

They accomplish that end either by a coup, which is followed by the issuance of appropriate edicts, or through rigged elections, or both. Authoritarian systems also impose other limitations on freedom, such as on freedom of speech, of the press, or of assembly, so as to inhibit criticism of the government and prevent any concerted activity from changing the government. Inevitably, under such authoritarian systems, opposition movements form and engage the ruling group in a struggle for power. Depending on the nature of the authoritarian system and the character of the struggle, the rulers will retaliate with various forms of punishment, which can even take the extreme form of killing opponents of the regime, either under color of law or extra-legally.

Totalitarian systems resort to all the deprivations of human rights that characterize authoritarian systems, but go far beyond them. The authoritarian ruler, as already noted, wants the citizenry to leave government to him, is prepared to come down hard on the citizen who wants to effect governmental change, but will, generally speaking, not seek to interfere with the life of the citizen who decides not to intervene actively in governmental affairs. Private lives and private institutions can exist side by side with a rigidly controlled authoritarian government and can remain substantially unaffected by government.

The situation is, however, radically different in a totalitarian state. There government claims the right to and seeks to affect all aspects of life. Not only is the economy placed under total governmental control, but the same is true of all other social institutions, all aspects of culture, and most aspects of the interrelationship between individuals. To make the system function in this manner, to counter the innate human instinct to be free, the totalitarian government relies on a vast secret police apparatus, augmented by volunteer spies and informers, whose task it is to monitor the population and, to simplify the task of monitoring, to instill fear.

Fear is indeed one of the significant hallmarks of life in a totalitarian system, fear of being denounced for committing an act of disloyalty against the regime, which can result in various forms of punishment, ranging from demotion or loss of a job to incarceration and possibly death. Alexander Solzhenitsyn, in his novel The First Circle, vividly describes the cycle of fear that existed under one specific totalitarian system. The zek, the prisoner, he notes, is least fearful. He is, after all, already in prison and does not have much hope for the future. He does not have much to lose.

His jail guard is somewhat fearful, but because he does not have as much at stake, he is not as fearful as is the prison warden, who most certainly does not want to risk losing his job and all the privileges associated with it. But the warden is by far not as fearful as is his superior, the police chief who has more to lose than his job if the minister of state security turns against him. And the minister, in turn, trembles at the thought that something might happen which might cause the supreme leader to think ill of him. The supreme leader, finally, is totally paranoid, afraid of sleeping in the same bed every night, afraid that one of his loyal subjects might assassinate him.

Fear, massive fear, fear of being watched, of being denounced, fear of being punished for alleged violations of even the most unjust and absurd rules, fear is the all-pervasive emotion that paralyzes the people's political will in a totalitarian state. It establishes an attitude of self-control and self-censorship that requires the secret police service to subject the general population to only occasional surveillance to reinforce the feeling of fear, and allows the secret policemen to concentrate their attention on the few hardy souls who are willing to speak up in spite of the inevitably harsh consequences which follow their assertion of their human rights.

Adolf Hitler and Joseph Stalin, the twin scourges of our century, have now been dead for decades. The peculiar totalitarian systems of despotism which they spawned, driven, to use Nikita Khrushchev's term, by a cult of personality, are no more. But the scheme of government organizations which made their rise to total power possible lives on. Millions of people continue to be deprived of liberty and often also of human dignity through the assertion of power by an all-controlling state apparatus. That is why it is indeed appropriate for this commission to deal in a generic manner with the phenomenon of totalitarianism and the whole range of human rights violations engendered by it.

There is a litmus test which can be used most effectively if we try to determine whether a state is totalitarian or merely authoritarian. All we need to do is examine the responsibilities of its border guards as they relate to the action they take against their fellow countrymen. If the guards' function is to keep some of their fellow citizens from returning to their homeland, the country is merely authoritarian. If the guards' responsibility is also to keep fellow citizens from leaving their country it is totalitarian. The question to be determined in each case is whether the state seeks to fence people out or whether it seeks to fence them in.

The existence of an all-pervasive secret police, the engendering of a climate of fear and rigid controls on emigration are not the only characteristics which identify a totalitarian regime. Here a few others:

- Total control by the state of all print and electronic media. In other words, as distinct from the authoritarian state, the totalitarian state does not depend on censorship of the media. It sees to it that all those involved in media work are agents of the all-powerful state.
- Severe punishment for the expression of verbal or written politically dissenting views. While the authoritarian state seeks to inhibit organized activity by groups who seek through speech or the printed word to express criticism of the government, the totalitarian state will punish a single person, even though he acts merely as an individual and not in concert with anyone else, for the expression of political dissent. It was Lenin who in urging a program of revolutionary propaganda instead of terrorism once said "words are more powerful than bombs." Latter-day totalitarians believe that this principle is as valid when they are at the receiving end as it was in the past, when their predecessors were at the giving end.
- Rigid control not only over travel to foreign countries but also over domestic travel. Severe limitations on the right to move from one locality to another.
- Rigid control over the right to work, as exercised by assignment of persons to specific jobs, with severe limitations on the right to move from job to job.
- State control of scientific endeavor. This can have significant long range implications, which reach beyond the laboratory. Ironically, Hitler's decision not to authorize nuclear research proved to be a boon for humankind. By the same token, Stalin's support of Trofim Lysenko severely retarded Soviet progress in genetic research for a great many years.
- State control of art, literature, and all other forms of cultural endeavor. Totalitarian states, let me add, have the unique distinction of incarcerating poets for the writing of poetry which is deemed subversive.

- Toleration of only a single state ideology. That ideology, elevated to the place of a state religion, is preached incessantly and is paid lip service at all public occasions, often by leaders who long ago lost faith in this or any other ideology.
- Falsification of history. Historical facts may often disprove the validity of the authorized state ideology. In that case, or for any other reason deemed suitable by the leadership, history is simply rewritten to fit the ideology.
- Use of the schools in support of the state ideology. Instead of allowing the education system to be a place where young people can develop their ability to think independently, the totalitarian state, through its control over teaching faculty and curriculum, makes every effort to use the schools to inculcate state-authorized thinking in young people, including all the falsifications of history which are an integral part of such thinking.
- Incitement of hatred of a special enemy. To unify the people, to raise their emotions to a fever pitch of frenzy, the totalitarian state selects an enemy, to whom all evil is ascribed and against whose machinations the loyal citizen must at all times be on the alert. As many, if not all, allegations are totally false; this aspect of totalitarian state activity often dovetails with the rewriting of history and the undermining of the integrity of the educational system.

A pattern of consistent and massive violations of all generally accepted standards of human rights, violations deliberately designed to turn human beings into automatons totally subservient to the state. Has it worked? Have the totalitarians succeeded in remolding human nature, in extirpating the spark of freedom? The answer, fortunately, is "no." Permit me to cite a few examples, some of them based on personal experience, in support of this conclusion.

Adolf Hitler had been dead then for, perhaps, forty-eight hours. The system which he had said would last a thousand years was crumbling after twelve. And twelve years of indoctrination with a totalitarian ideology had quickly rubbed off as far as these two young women were concerned. It turned out to rub off just as quickly on tens of millions of their countrymen.

Stalin's remains have long ago been removed from the mausoleum on Red Square. And Stalingrad and Stalinsk and all the other cities named after the dictator have had their names changed. The cult of personality has been significantly attenuated. The fact that the systems to which I have referred are now part of a bygone age should not cause us to lose sight of the fact that while they lasted they caused a great deal of suffering. Nor should it cause us to overlook totalitarian features of governments wherever they exist today. As I have said earlier, this commission should indeed deal with the phenomenon of totalitarianism in all its aspects and should direct attention to the serious violations of human rights in states in which totalitarian forms of government exist.

SOVIET ANTI-SEMITISM

Earlier in this session the commission dealt at some length with the phenomenon of discrimination and deprivation of rights on grounds of ancestry practiced in South Africa and known as apartheid. Though this extreme form of discrimination based on ancestry may very well be unique in today's world, similar practices can nevertheless be identified elsewhere around the globe. One such place is the Soviet Union, and, we regret to say, that discrimination and persecution based solely on ancestry has been on the increase in the Soviet Union. In fact, 1984 has been one of the worst years in recent memory.

Singled out for such discrimination and persecution are the Soviet Union's Jews. It is because of the increasing virulence of Soviet anti-Semitism, harking back to the days of Konstantin Pobedonostsev and of the last Romanov czars, Alexander III and Nicholas II, that we have identified this issue for this expression of special concern.

As we all know, all printing in the Soviet Union, of newspapers, periodicals, books and other publications, as well as all productions of the electronic media are under state control. It follows that whatever material is distributed to the general public through these print and electronic media is officially authorized. It constitutes information or a point of view with which the government wants to indoctrinate the people. It is because the Soviet media reflect the government's point of view that the further increase, in 1984, of anti-Semitic propaganda is of particularly serious concern.

Soviet anti-Semitism, as promulgated in official materials, has, over the years, been served up under differing labels. It was once known as anti-cosmopolitanism. But in recent years it has been offered to the public under the label of anti-Zionism. These semantic veils do not hide the purpose and effect: to stir up hatred of the Jews. Neither the theme nor the method is new. The theme, alleging a world-wide Jewish conspiracy, is taken from "The Protocols of the Elders of Zion," a forgery dating back to the days of the czars. Furthermore, as I have heretofore had reason to observe in this commission, caricatures of Jews in Soviet publications have a frightening resemblance to the caricatures which once appeared in the Nazi publication "Der Stuermer," published by the notorius Julius Streicher, who was sentenced to death and executed as a war criminal.

The consequences of this officially sanctioned anti-Semitic propaganda campaign are felt throughout Soviet society. The campaign has the effect of causing members of the general public to subject Jews to verbal and sometimes physical abuse, for children to suffer opprobrium in school. It also has the effect of passing the word to all government institutions that Jews are not entitled to the same rights as the rest of the population. As government controls all aspects of economic life and education, Jews increasingly find themselves passed over for promotions, shut out from certain types of employment, and discriminated against when they seek admission to particularly desirable educational institutions.

I want to emphasize that these forms of discrimination are applied to persons not because of their attitudes or political beliefs, but solely because of their ancestry. The persons so affected are, in the first instance, the approximately two million persons who are classified in their internal passports as persons of Jewish nationality. In addition, persecution and discrimination extend to persons of partially Jewish ancestry, their origin being surmised from their names, their mothers' maiden names (which sometimes is required to be furnished), or their looks. The Soviet Union thus has the equivalent of the "coloreds" of South Africa.

Many of the people who today are the victims of this kind of discrimination and persecution are the descendants of persons who helped create the Soviet state or enthusiastically supported it. It is not surprising that the enthusiasm of the third generation is greatly diminished. A good many Jews of the Soviet Union have turned inward, have accepted their fate, and simply want to get by in life with a minimum of difficulty. Others, however, have reacted by turning to their religion, becoming interested in their culture, and identifying themselves with their nationality. In other words, if they have to suffer for it anyway, they are seeking to derive something positive from their heritage. These are the people on whom the Soviet state has now come down particularly hard.

The focus in 1984 has been on cultural activists, with particular emphasis on teachers of the Hebrew language. A number of them have, in accord with the concept of so-called socialist legality, been tried and convicted. In some instances, the alleged crime was what is known as slander of the Soviet Union. In a good many cases the slander in question was telling the truth about how the Soviet Union treats its Jewish citizens. Others have been convicted on such trumped-up charges as hooliganism, illegal possession of a weapon, possession of drugs, or resisting the militia. The sentences handed down in these cases have been in the range of two to four years.

Formal trials and long-term prison sentences are not the only punishment levied against Jewish cultural activists. Other forms of harassment include administrative jailing for fifteen day periods, sentences to several months of corrective labor, commitment to psychiatric hospitals, and severe beatings by plainclothes policemen for persons outside prisons and by jailers and fellow inmates within prisons. One such prisoner, Iosif Berenshtein, a Hebrew teacher who is serving a sentence for resisting the militia, had one of his eyes gouged out in prison and the other one seriously damaged.

This campaign of threats, intimidation, beatings, and imprisonment has the result of only increasing the bitterness and enlarging the number of activists. It is, of course, also understandable that the number of Jews eager to leave the Soviet Union is once again growing by leaps and bounds. It has been made clear to them that they are not wanted in the country and they, in turn, have drawn the conclusion that it is indeed in their best interest to depart.

And so, we would indeed be witnessing a vast exodus from the Soviet Union, similar to the exodus from Russia which began about a hundred years ago and lasted until the beginning of World War I. But now the gates are shut and the Jewish citizens of the Soviet Union find themselves beleaguered in the country of their birth, yet unable to leave.

It is difficult to understand what the Soviet government seeks to achieve by the policy it is now following. Its decisions are normally the result of reasoning rather than being based on emotion. In this case, what is the result to be achieved? If the intention is to drive the Jews out of the country, why not let them emigrate? If the goal is to show certain foreign countries such as the United States that tense foreign relations will result in Jews being victimized, the result is the opposite of what is intended: Any set of violations of human rights by the Soviet Union serves only to aggravate international tension. As indicated, the Soviet Union's motivation for this recent further step-up in anti-Semitic propaganda and activity is both troublesome and puzzling.

Because of the deep shadow which this phenomenon casts over the international scene, particularly over relations between the Soviet Union and the United States, we consider it important to draw international attention to this matter in the sincere hope that those who have it in their power to help solve this problem will begin to do so.

HUMAN RIGHTS CONDITIONS THROUGHOUT THE WORLD

In recent years, we have been happy to begin our speeches on the general state of human rights in the world with a few optimistic observations about further progress toward democracy in Latin America. This year is no exception. Free elections and respect for human rights are becoming increasingly the norm rather than the exception throughout Latin America. In the period ahead we look for further progress in the same direction among our neighbors to the south, progress which we find indeed most welcome. Progress toward democracy and increased respect for human rights in Latin America has, to be sure, not deterred this commission from focusing disproportionately on that part of the world in its deliberations. We note that in the course of our further proceedings, we shall consider three resolutions dealing with Latin American countries, namely with El Salvador, Guatemala, and Chile.

Concerning El Salvador, we are pleased to note that the report of the special representative and the resolution which has been tabled have taken due note of the significant progress made in the field of human rights in recent times by the government of El Salvador, now under the leadership of a man with a direct mandate from his people, President José Napoleon Duarte. It is, at long last, becoming clear that El Salvador's democratic forces, deeply committed to human rights and to economic reform, are gaining strength and are leaving their imprint on the institutions of the country. They are doing so, however, under the most difficult set of circumstances.

This, it should be remembered, is the sixth year in which the government of El Salvador is battling an insurrection financed, supplied, and organized from across the country's borders. That democratic roots have nevertheless remained alive in the country and now are able to sustain new growth is indeed a matter for which the Salvadoran people and its elected leadership deserve a great deal of credit. Let me add that in our opinion the special representative has not exhibited sufficient understanding of this facet of recent developments in El Salvador, nor does he, in our view, pay appropriate attention to the fact that Article 21, calling for free elections, is an integral part of the Universal Declaration of Human Rights.

An armed struggle against the government also paid for and led from abroad retards progress toward democracy in Guatemala. Nevertheless, there, too, we should take note of the significant improvements in conditions described in the report of the special rapporteur. Although we are prepared to support the continued mandate of Lord Colville, we made it clear last year that we cannot support a resolution which, in describing conditions in Guatemala, bases itself on unsubstantiated allegations and deals inadequately with the fact that an armed rebel group supported from abroad is at work there, attempting to overthrow the government.

If the present schedule is adhered to, as we have every reason to believe it will be, Guatemala will have an elected president the next time the commission meets. We would hope that in the interim the commission and its representative will make every effort to assist Guatemala in this process of democratization. The matter of progress toward democracy in Chile is of deep concern to us. Our specific reasons for concern are set forth in detail in the report of the United States Department of State on the subject of human rights practices, which was transmitted to the Congress a few weeks ago.

The State Department's report on Chile, which we are prepared to make available to anyone interested in it, deals with conditions in Chile in an evenhanded manner, as part of a description of human rights conditions throughout the world. As I have indicated, our discussion of Chile reflects our deep concerns. But when we look at the resolutions adopted by this commission on the subject of Chile, resolutions which lack all sense of proportion, and which are adopted without considering that worse offenders exist in the region and elsewhere, we must say they have a hollow ring to them.

Let us, for instance, compare the number of political prisoners in Chile with those of Cuba. At the end of 1984, 274 persons were reported to be in prison in Chile for politically motivated acts, some of which were violent acts. The comparable number in Cuba is generally assumed to be in excess of 1000. While Chile is an authoritarian state, of the type I described in a speech earlier in this session, there is in Chile a clear consensus that there must be a return to democracy, in spite of occasional set-backs. The issue in Chile is not "whether," but "when" and "how." While we deeply hope that a return to democracy will come earlier, we do note that the present constitution provides for a plebiscite on the presidency in 1989.

No such plebiscite, no such hope is offered to the people of Cuba. Cuba is now a totalitarian state, totally controlled by a single group which holds all facets of life in the country in an iron grip, thereby retarding all chances to move toward political democracy or, for that matter, to improve the increasingly miserable economic conditions of the country. Let me offer a few illustrations of the state of affairs in that country: In Cuba, during 1984, five young people, ranging in age sixteen to nineteen, were sentenced for terms up to five years in jail for writing such slogans as "Viva Reagan" and "Viva USA" on school walls. An American citizen who expressed himself on the subject of Cuba's activities in Grenada was sentenced to six years for spreading "enemy propaganda."

During 1984, twenty-six long-term political prisoners were released by Cuba in a highly theatrical gesture. Most of them had been in jail for twenty years or more. They reported a variety of physical and psychological torture, to which they had been subjected over the years, such as playing of high decibel tapes, continuous threats of death, and withholding of food, water, and medical assistance.

The average citizen's life in Cuba is under continuous surveillance by big brother. Telephones are monitored, mail is opened, and life in one's own home is monitored by block wardens who form part of the neighborhood committee for the defense of the revolution. A country which with all its drawbacks was once a place of joy and cheerfulness has been turned into a drab and dreary police state. A country which before the accession to leadership by Fidel Castro was one of the most economically advanced countries in Latin America has dropped to a relatively lower position on the regional economic ladder, subsisting to a significant extent on the Soviet dole which totals about four billion dollars annually.

In recent years, this commission has expressed its deep concern about human rights conditions in Iran. While a good many of even the most serious human rights violators throughout the world pay lip service to the human rights principles which have evolved during the last forty years under the auspices of the United Nations, Iran does not even do that. It rejects these principles and the concepts of the rights of the individual on which they rest. The amount of human suffering created thereby is enormous. Many people are arrested for such offenses as expressing dissenting political views. Once a person has been arrested, there is no real chance of a fair trial.

Many persons are detained for a long time prior to trial. Torture and other mistreatment of prisoners is commonplace. There continue to be a significant number of summary executions. In light of our recent action in approving a declaration against religious intolerance, we must again draw attention to the terrible fate of Iran's Baha'is, a group of people who are persecuted for nothing other than their religious convictions. Over seven hundred Baha'is are now in prison. During 1984 at least twenty-nine Baha'is were executed for no reason other than their religious belief. We must again emphasize the desperate need for the international community to come to the rescue of these completely inoffensive people.

While we regret that the special representative on Iran has not as yet been able to furnish the commission with an initial report of his findings, we note that a major service to humanity has been performed by Professor Ermacora in his thorough and extraordinarily well-documented report on the tragedy that is Afghanistan. There is no point to my recapitulating Professor Ermacora's findings. The report speaks for itself. It will in the period ahead be the principal reference work for all those who want to familiarize themselves with present-day conditions in Afghanistan and the circumstances from which they stem.

Principal leaders of a nation are sometimes shielded against information that reveals unpleasant truths. It is to be hoped that the Ermacora report will be read at the highest levels of the government of the Soviet Union, that it will produce a fuller understanding of the damage done not only to Afghanistan but also to the Soviet Union, in terms of its reputation in the world and the suffering and the brutalization of its own troops. One would hope that the result will be a willingness to end this colonialist adventure. A country, on which we have not been furnished a report this year, is Poland. To be sure, given the quality of the report which was distributed to us last year, we may not be the worse off for it.

What we failed to do, however, has been compensated for by the International Labor Organization. The comprehensive report filed last June, identified as GB. 227/3/6 of the 227th session, contained all the information that would have been made available to this commission if the persons charged with the task of reporting to the commission had paid due attention to their responsibilities. At any rate, through the conscientious work of the ILO, the international community is now in possession of a full report on the repressive measures taken by the government of Poland from December 13, 1981, onward to crush the Solidarity movement and all the efforts toward freedom associated with it.

Shortly after the issuance of the ILO report Poland proclaimed a comprehensive amnesty for political prisoners, a step which was welcomed throughout the free world. However, it should be understood that the people who were released from prison were not released into a Poland that resembled the Poland of the summer of 1981. They were released into a tightly-controlled state that would watch their every move.

The recent re-arrest of Bogdan Lis, Adam Michnik and Wladyslaw Frasyniuk demonstrates the tightness of the leash on which the people of Poland are being held. Let me add, that I am not certain whether the Polish authorities are inclined to follow events at this commission closely. Yet, it may not be a matter of coincidence that within hours after our deadline for filing resolutions had closed without a resolution and Poland having been tabled, Lech Walesa was called in by the Polish police, was questioned, and was ordered not to leave his home city of Gdansk without receiving special police permission.

The tightness of the leash by which people are being held in Poland is, of course, also demonstrated by the Popieluszko case and all circumstances surrounding it. The question which will continue to be asked is whether the case would have ever come to trial if Father Popieluszko's chauffeur had not escaped and had not reported the abduction. Note should also be taken of the fact that both defense and prosecution united in the case during the second half of the trial in a chorus of criticism directed at free speech, free assembly, and, above all the Catholic church in Poland.

Someone had obviously given the order that the mere fact of the trial had to be compensated for by a campaign of verbal violence against those whom the government had identified as its principal opponents. That very point was made in an important commentary on Poland which appeared in the issue of the Neue Zuercher Zeitung of February 16/17, 1985:

It appears that the very top of the Polish government decided (in agreement with the Kremlin) that the judgments rendered in Torun must not lead to any weakening of the military and police dictatorship in Poland. In this context the former Kor-committee member, the sociologist Jozef Sreniowski was sentenced in Lodz on February 12 to two and a half years in prison for the dissemination of false information.

This sentence is alleged to set a frightening example because of Sreniowski's close contacts with the workers of the textile city Lodz. Another example is the measures ordered by the authorities against the vice chairman of Solidarnosc, Andrzei Gwiazda.

The latter was amnestied last summer, and then imprisoned once more for participation at the memorial service for the victims of the workers' revolt in Danzig in the year 1970.

He was sentenced on December 17, 1984, to a number of months imprisonments. Since then further harassment against him was ordered. Polish oppositionists regard all these events, together with the expulsion of Sewerin Blumsztajn as a sign of a hardening of domestic policy. One can obviously not speak of any liberalization of the system. It appears that Jaruzelski is not only required to rebuild the frustrated secret police apparatus, he must also fulfill the demands posed by the Kremlin and other allies as compensation for holding the trial at Torun.

Nor does the Popieluszko case stand alone. There have been other deaths, such as the death in 1984 of Piotr Bartoszcze, which are assumed to be politically motivated. In other parts of the world one would speak of the operation of death squads, and, let me say that if Poland were in South America, we can be certain that this commission would have appointed a rapporteur, who would have subjected the events which I have mentioned to most careful scrutiny.

But the people of Poland will survive as a nation without the benefit of a rapporteur. "Poland is not lost yet, as long as we live" are the beginning words of the Polish national anthem. The people of Poland have over the centuries demonstrated an extraordinary commitment to freedom and to their national identity. There are few places in the world in which the gulf between the governing and the governed is as wide and deep as it is in Poland. The will of the Polish people will undoubtedly ultimately triumph over the country's present adversity.

Because the Soviet Union and its attitude toward human rights sets the tone for a large portion of the world, our general discussions of human rights conditions have consistently included a discussion of human rights conditions in the USSR. This year, we have given separate and special emphasis to one very serious problem, that of persecution of the Jews.

There are a few other concerns to which we want to draw attention. Let me say at the outset, that while we hope that some day the Soviet Union will turn itself into an open society; we do not expect that to happen in the near future. But we do believe that the Soviet Union could take certain steps, without causing a basic change in its system that would significantly improve its human rights conditions and thereby also contribute to the relaxation of international tensions.

One important area is that of religious freedom. The Soviet system would not be at risk if it allowed full freedom of conscience by permitting the Ukrainian Catholic church and the Lituanian Catholic church, as well as Baptists, Jehovah's Witnesses, Seventh Day Adventists, and Pentecostals to exercise their religion in peace and if it were to end the repressive measures and harassment which now characterize the actions of the state against these religious groups.

Second, there is the problem of deliberate steps at Russification of areas in which persons of a different nationality constitute the majority of the population. Thus, the colonial rule of the Baltic states, Estonia, Latvia, and Lithuania, has continued apace. Russian settlers are increasingly gaining dominance in the states in question and persons who speak up for their national integrity continue to be severely persecuted, with a good many activists arrested, tried, and sentenced to long prison terms. Again, may I ask, are these oppressive measures truly needed to maintain the Soviet state?

Another problem, which continues to be a serious blot on the Soviet Union's human rights record is the practice of committing persons who are no threat to society or themselves to mental institutions and torturing them thereafter with drug injections. This practice did not stop during 1984. This continued abuse of psychiatry has not only shocked the psychiatric profession throughout the world, causing the Soviet Union ultimately to resign from the World Psychiatric Association, but is looked upon by a great many laymen as a particularly heinous kind of human rights violation.

Here one must once more ask oneself: Is this practice really needed to maintain the Soviet state? Can't the Soviet system survive without resorting to this particularly abhorrent system of punishment?

Finally, in speaking of the steps the Soviet Union can take to warm the international climate, let me mention again the case of Andrei Sakharov. This world-renowned scientist has now spent five years in exile, deprived of contacts with his friends and of any opportunity to engage in discussions on scientific topics. It is because of Dr. Sakharov's unusual qualifications as a scientist that not only the Soviet Union, but the whole world has lost as a result of the decision of the Soviet leadership to send him into banishment.

It is obvious, that no symbolic act on the part of the Soviet Union could do more to signal to the world that we are indeed entering a period of thaw than would a relaxation of the restrictions imposed on Dr. Sakharov. We can, of course, already anticipate the replies that will be offered by the representatives whose countries I have mentioned. There will be another prepared Soviet speech attacking the United States for all its imagined faults and there will be the customary ad lib attacks from others, remarks specially designed to win friends and influence people in the United States. As usual, the replies will mix a few facts with a great deal of fiction and a great deal of venom. But none of these replies will make the commentary which I have offered any less true.

Those who hear our presentations or might read reports thereof might ask themselves what these exchanges of words are intended to accomplish, what good they will really do. It is a good question. Let me seek to answer it from our point of view. In the case of the United Nations Human Rights Commission and the procedures which have evolved over the years, we are dealing, speaking from a historical perspective, with a relatively young institution, with relatively recent history.

The notion that governments may comment on the manner in which governments of other countries deal with their own citizens is fairly new. What is hoped is that through such comments, through such discussions, governments can be made aware of the fact that the rest of the world takes notice of the human rights violations they are committing and disapproves of them.

But for the entire process to work, to be taken seriously, there is need for a high standard of intellectual honesty to be applied, a sense of fairness, of objectivity, and a commitment by those who make presentations to the notion that the facts should speak for themselves, with a minimum of hyperbole and emendations. At the risk of being accused of blowing our own horn, that our annual country reports on human rights practices qualify on that count. In our presentations here we have sought to follow that model.

2

The United Nations and Human Rights Institutions

There is a new and significant development in the field of human rights: the U.N. led proliferation of national human rights institutions (NHRIs). NHRIs are government agencies whose purported aim is to implement international norms domestically. These institutions have expanded considerably since the early 1990s, quadrupling in number and appearing in almost 100 countries. What explains the diffusion of such similar institutions across diverse national contexts? The entry of this actor onto the world stage cannot be understood without examining the role of international organizations, especially the United Nations.

Whereas international support for NHRIs in the past merely defined appropriate institutional structures and functions, today international actors are directly engaged in creating and strengthening these institutions. Support from the UN and other international organizations, both governmental and non-governmental alike, has allowed NHRIs to take the unprecedented step of forging trans-governmental alliances and to even begin acquiring formal international standing.

While students of international relations have overlooked these developments, NHRIs do signal an important innovation in global governance. The emergence of these institutions marks a potentially significant step in the implementation of international human rights law. In the words of the Canadian government, NHRIs may be "the practical link between international standards and their concrete application, the bridge between the ideal and its implementation." Given this transformative agenda, we need a much better understanding of how international actors like the UN, which has been at the forefront of these human rights activities, actually engage in national institution building. At the same time, as long as states remain the principal "makers" and "breakers" of international law, support for NHRIs may be a double-edged phenomenon, presenting both opportunities and challenges for the local protection of human rights norms.

Other actors-including government agencies, human rights non-governmental organizations (NGOs), and international organizations like the Organization for Security and Cooperation in Europe (OSCE)-have contributed to these activities, especially in terms of capacity building; but only the UN has been equipped to coordinate and legitimate the global diffusion of these national institutions. Second, drawing on the nascent experience of NHRIs, while the creation of NHRIs is a welcome development, insofar as it serves to embed international norms in local structures, it also can have perverse consequences. National human rights institutions can have the unintended effect of heightening social expectations, which governments are then unwilling or unable to meet; in some instances, this could lead to less rather than more human rights protection.

DOMESTIC IMPLEMENTATION OF INTERNATIONAL NORMS

The stated objective of all governmental human rights institutions is to implement international norms domestically. Put differently, NHRJs are intended to be the permanent, local "infrastructure" upon which international human rights norms are built; they are not to be confused with ad hoc truth commissions or other temporary crisis-driven institutional arrangements.

Implementation itself requires that states desist from violating international norms and, in the event of such violations, that these abuses be redressed. In implementing human rights norms, moreover, NHRIs are to complement rather than replace international or regional mechanisms for monitoring and investigating human rights abuses. These basic principles are the cornerstone of today's leading NHRIs, including, for example, India's National Human Rights Commission, Canada's Human Rights Commission, the National Human Rights Commission of Mexico, the South African Human Rights Commission, and the Human Rights and Equal Opportunity Commission of Australia.

While the purpose of all NHRIs is to implement international norms, these institutions vary in terms of their specific organizational features. According to the UN, there are two principal types of NHRIs: national commissions and national ombudsmen. The key difference between the two types of institutions is one of substantive focus. National commissions, which number almost 100, address primarily issues of human rights violations and discrimination, regardless of whether abuses are committed by government or non-government agents. National ombudsmen, also edging close to 100, emphasize questions of "fairness and legality in public administration."

Additionally, some institutions are hybrid brands that combine characteristics of national ombudsmen and human rights commissions, such as Ghana's Commission on Human Rights and Administrative Justice or Russia's Plenipotentiary for Human Rights. All NHRIs, however, can be part of either the executive or legislature, or they can even be mandated by an internationally brokered peace agreement (e.g., Afghanistan, Bosnia, Guatemala, Northern Ireland, and Sierra Leone). The principal requirement is that they be independent bodies, autonomous in both decision-making and organizational resources.

The potential significance of NHRJs for human rights reform also is evident in their scope, particularly their broad and flexible mandate. In fact, a survey of UN and other documents reveals that their functions can be classified according to whether they are regulative or constitutive.

Regulative functions are those focused on eliciting conformance with international norms and rules. Constitutive functions are those intended to transform the identity of state or societal actors.

On the regulative side, all national institutions undertake multiple and often overlapping functions in three important spheres: government compliance, relations with the judiciary, and independent activities. For example, in terms of eliciting government compliance, NHRIs can offer general advice on human rights issues, encourage ratification of treaties, and review proposed legislation. NHRIs also assist governments in preparing state reports for treaty bodies. Rather than drafting these reports directly, which would undermine their basic independence, NHRIs tend to share their own reports and expertise with governments. Still more broadly, NHRIs often cooperate with governments in devising comprehensive national human rights action plans.

A related and often vital task of national institutions is to complement the role of the courts in protecting human rights norms. Accordingly, NHRIs can assist human rights victims in seeking legal redress, refer human rights cases to national tribunals, and contribute to the overall development of human rights jurisprudence. In some cases, NHRIs may receive evidence in affidavits and participate in legal proceedings, including litigation. When NHRIs take the form of equal opportunity commissions, which have a more limited mandate and focus on issues of discrimination, they can play an explicit role in issuing codes with statutory force and in submitting amicus briefs. While not all NHRIs perform all of these functions, they all help to supplement the work of the judiciary in implementing international norms.

In addition to its relations with the government and the judiciary, NHRIs themselves can play an independent role in regulating compliance. Most national institutions review state practices and compile this information regularly in annual and other reports. Another key independent function of NHRIs is to investigate complaints or allegations of human rights abuse.

In the course of an investigation, NHRIs can be empowered to inspect facilities, compel documents or information to be turned over, and examine witnesses. When broader types of abuse, such as those involving economic and social rights are at stake, NHRIs sometimes may initiate a general public inquiry in lieu of a specific investigation.

Following an investigation, moreover, NHRIs can mediate between parties in a human rights conflict or perhaps submit the dispute to arbitration. Finally, a few national institutions can issue binding resolutions (e.g., Uganda Human Rights Commission) and award victims compensation (e.g., the Australian Human Rights and Equal Opportunities Commission).

On the constitutive side, NHRIs perform two fundamental sets of activities. The first arena involves socialization, namely attempts to diffuse international human rights norms domestically by means of the media, grassroots campaigning, and educational reform. Socialization also consists of establishing and strengthening ties with domestic NGOs, an increasingly important but often challenging task for many NHRIs. A second set of constitutive activities moves beyond socialization to address issues of international cooperation.

The objective in this area is to forge common interests with and links to other NHRIs around the world. Both sets of constitutive functions are premised on the assumption that socially sanctioned NHRIs, and the human rights culture they help engender, are a prerequisite for any sustainable human rights reform. Consequently, implementing international human rights norms successfully may require overcoming a key challenge: closing existing gaps between the constitutive and regulative functions-or the promotion and protection-of NHRIs.

THE ROLE OF THE UNITED NATIONS

It may seem surprising, given the pervasiveness of human rights issues today, that NHRIs are a relatively new phenomenon in international relations. Several factors may explain the sharp and significant growth of these institutions in recent decades. Internationally, the rise in national institutions coincided with the end of the Cold War and the strengthening of international human rights mechanisms what Thomas Risse and Kathryn Sikkink refer to as a change in "world time."

Domestically, the rise in NHRIs also overlapped with a global wave of democratization. While both international and domestic structural conditions surely facilitated the vast increase in NHRIs, and the diffusion of NHRIs would not have been possible without the active support provided by international organizations like the UN.

STANDARD SETTING

Despite the fact that NHRIs did not appear dramatically on the international scene until the 1990s, UN activism in this area has been longstanding and essential for their subsequent proliferation. UN support for NHRIs consisted historically of defining and demarcating the boundaries of these institutions. In establishing universal criteria for NHRIs, or engaging in standard setting, UN involvement has gone through several important stages. Initial UN standards for NHRIs were vague and treated national institutions as subsidiary organizations.

The UN first addressed the topic in 1946, when the Economic and Social Council issued a resolution calling for the general creation of NHRIs. Most early UN statements emphasized how national institutions should merely supplement the work of the UN Commission on

Human Rights. With the exception of a few resolutions in the 1960s, little attention was paid to enhancing the independent role of NHRIs. Yet in the late 1970s, UN standard setting began to consolidate. International norms for NHRIs were detailed in a September 1978 seminar, "National and Local Institutions for the Promotion and Protection of Human Rights," held in Geneva. It is noteworthy that even the name of this early seminar reflected the dual functions of NHRIs to regulate and constitute human rights practices.

These standards remained in place throughout the 1980s. Several possible reasons explain why UN activism vis-a-vis NHRIs increased notably in the 1970s. Institutionally, international human rights mechanisms themselves were quickly gaining ground, making the creation of parallel domestic bodies a natural organizational complement. National human rights institutions could serve as local counterparts to international human rights commissions.

Functionally, moreover, the work of the UN Human Rights Commission was coming under increasing strain, resulting in both a heavy workload and a widening array of state targets. Creating national institutions may have seemed a particularly viable long-term solution to these twin problems. Politically, these institutions generated a unique degree of international consensus, overcoming both East-West and North-South divisions.

As human rights issues became politicized internationally and transnational activist networks solidified, it became increasingly likely that any state (whether newly independent, Cold War proxy, or even hegemonic power) could come under assault for its human rights practices. Thus, the United States itself supported the creation of national advisory committees on human rights as early as the 1960s, a period when it resisted both UN pressure for its civil rights record and the creation of a UN Commissioner for Human Rights. According to the U.S. representative to the UN Commission on Human Rights, Judging from the interest evoked in the Commission by the US report on its national advisory committees on human rights (national and state Civil Rights Committees...) and the comparative lack of government... committees on human rights in all other countries... our Government could profitably elucidate this point-especially for the benefit of African and Asian states.

For any state that was subject (or feared being subject) to international human rights pressure, national institutions may have offered a way to avoid greater international institutionalization. By the 1970s, then, promoting the idea of an NHRI within the UN was a strategy that achieved a consensus precisely because it promised to shield state sovereignty while satisfying rising demands for human rights reform. The political climate of the time made it amply clear that states could hope at best to control, but not stop, the institutionalization of human rights. It is not surprising that, against this political backdrop, states enhanced their support for NHRIs within the UN.

Building on the guidelines that were issued in Geneva in 1978, the UN transformed its standard setting in the 1990s, as NHRIs went from relative obscurity to playing a leading role in the human rights program of the UN. This sea of change was launched at a workshop in Paris in 1991, where a "common charter" for NHRIs emerged. The Paris Principles, as they came to be called, developed into the touchstone of all NHRIs. While not differing significantly in content from the rules agreed to in earlier decades, the Paris Principles began to outline a more ambitious role for NHRIs as autonomous and pluralistic institutions.

This expanded agenda was echoed in the Vienna Declaration (1993), which confirmed the growing significance of NHRIs: "The World Conference on Human Rights reaffirms the important and constructive role played by national institutions for the promotion and protection of human rights." The Vienna Declaration, however, also addressed "the right of each State to choose the framework which is best suited to its particular needs." Never mind that these states might also be routinely violating human rights norms. Despite vast improvements, UN standards have yet to specify how states are to perform the delicate balancing act of implementing universal standards while meeting local needs effectively.

CAPACITY BUILDING

A second way in which the UN has bolstered the growth of NHRIs is by providing governments with concrete forms of assistance, including offering expertise and training, organizing workshops, and helping to draft legislation. In principle, such assistance can be indispensable to a government that is interested in creating or strengthening a national institution but lacks the requisite resources. Recent UN assistance illustrates this influence. In a period of just under two years, the UN Office of the High Commissioner for Human Rights, sometimes in collaboration with the UN Development Programme, assisted approximately twenty-five countries around the world in creating or reinforcing an NHRI.

For example, experts sent to Rwanda helped that country's Human Rights Commission develop a documentation center and strengthen its educational component. Such assistance was essential in sustaining and deepening the autonomy of Rwanda's NHRI. Likewise, an earlier technical cooperation project had facilitated the very creation of Rwanda's Commission in 1999, a condition stipulated in the 1993 Arusha Accords.

All evidence indicates that providing early international assistance to an NHRI can be critical for getting it off the ground and launching it in the right direction. According to an OSCE report, "Early in a new institution's history, the most difficult problems are in learning how to organize the office and conduct the investigations.... Mistakes made early in the history of Ombudsman [or other NHRI] can be difficult to reverse."

While extensive data isolating UN assistance to NHRIs remain incomplete, the focus in the remainder of this section on broader UN advisory and technical support in the field of human rights. This kind of aid can serve as a relatively reliable proxy for UN assistance to NHRIs. Support for national institutions, after all, falls under the larger umbrella of human rights services provided by the UN. Human rights capacity building, including that destined exclusively for NHRIs, has increased gradually over time. Dating to the mid-1950s, UN human rights assistance was spearheaded by a program on advisory services.

This program provided experts, funded fellowships, and organized human rights seminars. Yet it was not until the mid-1980s, and especially the early 1990s, that UN assistance to human rights projects skyrocketed, particularly in the form of advisory services and technical assistance. The creation of the Voluntary Fund for Technical Cooperation in the Field of Human Rights in 1987 part and parcel of a global trend toward democratic governance-propelled activities in this area.

Most, though not all, future NHRI projects would be supported by this fund. A decade later, additional progress was made when both the UN General Assembly and the UN Commission on Human Rights requested that the nascent Office of the High Commissioner for Human Rights devote a major component of it s technical cooperation program to the creation and strengthening of NHRIs. International attention and assistance to NHRIs increased almost immediately.

It is true that governments must initiate a request for UN human rights assistance, but once provided, such aid may make possible the otherwise infeasible establishment and improvement of national institutions. In fact, UN efforts appear to be going precisely where they are most needed. UN capacity-building initiatives, for example, have been strongest where regional human rights mechanisms have been weakest. The UN has been most active in Asia, the only major area of the world lacking a regional human rights treaty or commission.

UN human rights assistance has been highest to Africa, Asia, Latin America, and Eastern Europe, areas of the world with relatively stronger regional human rights institutions. The one exception to this is the Middle East and North Africa (MENA), where both NHRIs and UN human rights assistance are lowest, a phenomenon that might be explained by relatively weak patterns of democratization rather than conventionally favored explanations of cultural relativism. If the appeal of NHRIs is in fact culturally specific, then we should not have seen a high concentration of NHRIs in both Asia and Africa, two regions where cultural relativist debates have been fiercest. And yet, that is precisely what has occurred.

Clearly, much more research will have to be done to clarify the dynamics mediating the relationship between UN assistance and NHRIs, including compiling a comprehensive dataset. What is now apparent is that rising UN support has facilitated the global diffusion of NHRIs, especially in areas lacking strong regional human rights mechanisms. By providing expert advisers, holding national seminars, and helping to draft relevant legislation, the UN is equipping governments with the capacity to create and strengthen national institutions that are consistent with international standards.

NETWORK FACILITATING

The practice of forging organizational links among national institutions or network facilitating-has been a third way in which the UN has shaped the rise of NHRIs and, more generally, of trans-governmental networks. This is a recent strategy dating largely to the 1990s. In promoting the formation of both international and regional networks of NHRIs, the UN has supported international meetings of NHRIs, established a special post within the UN, and overseen the creation of a coordinating committee.

Following the first International Workshop on National Institutions for the Promotion and Protection of Human Rights in Paris, five similar UN-sponsored international workshops were held in the last decade: Tunis, Manila, Merida, Mexico, and Marrakesh. The sixth and most recent of these international conferences took place in Copenhagen and Lund, Denmark, in April 2002. Additionally, there has been an increase in UN-facilitated regional and sub regional meetings devoted to NHRIs. In 1994, for example, the first European Workshop on National Institutions was hosted by France. Africa likewise held a series of regional workshops, beginning with a meeting in Yaounde, Cameroon, in 1995.

The Asia Pacific region also has seen a significant increase in activities devoted to NHRIs since the mid-1990s, including several regional meetings and the creation of a permanent region wide network (the Asia Pacific Forum of National Human Rights Institutions). Most recently, a network of NHRIs in the Americas has also been formed. Transnational activities soared following the creation in the early 1990s of new mechanisms for facilitating cooperation among NHRIs.

First, a special post devoted to NHRIs was created under the Office of the High Commissioner for Human Rights.

Originally labeled the Coordinator for National Institutions, the UN head of NHRI activities is now known as the Special Adviser on National Institutions, Regional Arrangements, and Preventive Strategies. The broader title reflects growing attention to issues of regionalization and prevention in the human rights field, as well as the adoption of more comprehensive mandates. Second, a coordinating committee for NHRIs was proposed in the Paris Principles of 1991 and established in 1994. The International Coordination Committee of National Institutions currently organizes and oversees all international and regional links between NHRIs. Together, these developments demonstrate how the UN has been instrumental in facilitating the formation of trans-governmental networks of NHRIs.

MEMBERSHIP GRANTING

In addition to supporting the formation of NHRIs and facilitating the links among them, the UN has begun granting these institutions official international status, that is, the UN has given NHRIs formal participatory rights within certain UN meetings. This new privilege raises practical questions about the scope of NHRI rights in international forums, especially relative to the existing rights of states and NGOs. National human rights institutions took their first steps in acquiring formal international status, a possibility initially envisaged in the Paris Principles, when they participated as a group at the 1993 World Conference on Human Rights in Vienna.

Discussions continued throughout the decade as to the exact status of these institutions. In 1999, some of the controversy was resolved when the UN Commission on Human Rights decided that NHRIs could participate in relevant meetings from a special section of the floor devoted to "national institutions." Eighteen NHRIs from a cross section of regions would participate in meetings and have seven minutes of speaking time on items of special concern to them.

More important than the actual scope of NHRI participation is the fact that international organizations now are treating these institutions as autonomous and enduring actors, as evidenced by the visible participation of NHRIs at the 2001 World Conference Against Racism in Durban.

Debates nonetheless continue to be waged over the exact nature of NHRI membership in the UN. Specific disputes exist over whether NHRIs should be direct participants in international bodies, enjoy observer status, or have a status comparable to that of specialized agencies. Regardless of the details that evolve, NHRIs are emerging as global actors that are embedded formally in both domestic and international structures. The advantages of this expanded membership, along with newly acquired participatory rights, could help national institutions practice more effective governance.

REDEFINING STATE INTERESTS

Through a multifaceted process of standard setting, capacity building, network facilitating, and membership granting, the UN has helped to create and strengthen NHRIs. Skeptics might argue, however, that the UN has been largely inconsequential in this process. Rather, the rise of NHRIs could be explained more persuasively by the end of the Cold War, global attention to human rights issues, and a resurgence of democratic governance. At best, from this perspective, the UN has merely enabled the creation of institutions that states already desired for other reasons.

This depiction is inaccurate and that the UN in fact has shaped states' interests in creating NHRIs. Consider the following counterfactual: Would the overall level of NHRIs be the same in the absence of UN support? While broader structural conditions clearly have been significant and a "contagion" effect may help to explain the rapid spread of NHRIs, and the initial impetus for the global rise of these institutions came from the UN.

The UN devised the very concept of an NHRI as part of its human rights foundations as far back as the 1940s. Standard setting especially that resulting from the 1978 seminar in Geneva and the 1991 Paris Principles preceded rather than followed the dramatic rise in NHRIs. The recent increase in NHRIs in Asia, for example, also occurred only after UN-sponsored regional workshops were held and international assistance was provided. These efforts served to define and diffuse global standards for NHRIs as well as to transfer valuable knowledge and resources to individual NHRIs.

In the absence of such UN assistance, it is unlikely that there would be as many NHRIs in the world today. Other actors might have taken the lead in promoting NHRIs, but few if any could have done so on both a global scale and in a coordinative capacity. And as an intergovernmental organization, the UN has been uniquely situated to promote national governmental institutions. Networks of NHRIs and their international allies do thrive, but the UN remains the hub of their activities.

Furthermore, the UN has succeeded in diffusing these institutions partly because of how it has defined the concept of an NHRI: the UN has cast it broadly and on multiple levels as a democratic institution, a sign of commitment to international norms, and the emblem of membership in a liberal community of states. Indeed, NHRIs may be so popular precisely because they tap into a cross section of more basic state interests. First, NHRIs appeal to states that are undergoing regime change and seeking to create democratic institutions (transitional states).

Second, NHRIs appeal to states that violate international human rights norms but want to portray themselves as committed to these norms, perhaps going so far as to assert a leadership role (hypocritical states). Third, NHRIs entice even states with long-standing and relatively good human rights records but that face claims of discrimination at home or pressures from abroad to join the NHRI bandwagon (late bloomers). The broad-gauged manner in which the UN has framed NHRIs may therefore have contributed to their rapid proliferation. Beyond defining NHRIs as a desirable goal for states, the UN has played a more straightforward, though no less active, role in equipping states with the tools to create and reinforce their national institutions.

It has accomplished this through an intensive set of activities that include providing experts, organizing seminars, and offering training in several related areas (e.g., human rights investigation, conflict resolution, and the preparation of studies and evaluations). More recently, the UN role has expanded to include facilitating trans-governmental cooperation and membership in international organizations. All of these forms of support have involved the provision of financial, technical, and organizational skills, or the exact resources that countries seeking to create NHRIs often lack.

In short, the UN has defined NHRIs as a viable goal and provided states with the means to realize this goal. This extensive role is reminiscent of how, according to Martha Finnemore, national science policies were "supplied" by the UN Educational, Scientific, and Cultural Organization (UNESCO) more than they were "demanded" by domestic constituencies. National human rights institutions may therefore be the product of UN involvement as much as domestic initiative. While broader changes in international and domestic systems (i.e., the end of the Cold War and the spread of democracy) may have been necessary factors in the proliferation of NHRIs, they alone have been insufficient. The UN has defined and promoted the concept of an NHRI, provided states with the technical capacities needed to build these institutions, facilitated the networking of these new actors, and offered them the benefits of membership in international organizations. Without this web of UN activities, the global rise of NHRI s may not have been possible in the first place.

PERVERSE IMPLICATIONS FOR GLOBAL GOVERNANCE

Like other institutions in a globalizing world, NHRIs can have both beneficial and perverse consequences. I highlight three of these unintended side effects: NHRIs could exacerbate tensions between opponents and supporters of international norms; lead to a reassertion of state authority and a dampening of the role of civil society; and fail to satisfy the very human rights demands they help to create, perhaps paving the way for greater if less visible abuses. Whether an NHRI will have these side effects may depend on the degree to which it is politically independent, inclusive of civil society, and adequately funded. The UN certainly supports these goals, but it may not be doing enough to challenge domestic political authorities whose NHRIs fall short of international guidelines.

First, the worldwide diffusion of NHRIs could lead in some cases, especially where insufficient attention is paid to the local context, to ineffective institutions and concomitant social tensions. UN documents emphasize that there is no particular "model" for an NHRI and that the stated advantage of an NHRI is precisely that it can be tailored to meet national circumstances.

In practice, however, international actors have paid relatively short shrift to how existing local institutions might constrain the effectiveness of an NHRI. For example, as the nongovernmental Asian Legal Resource Centre recently communicated to the UN Commission on Human Rights, "When a juridical system is fundamentally flawed national human rights institutions cannot do their work effectively." Thus, NHRIs as diverse as those in Malaysia, Latvia, and Senegal have failed to meet popular expectations and thereby alienated important segments of civil society.

Even in countries where human rights issues already are institutionalized, national debates have surfaced over the compatibility of different local institutions. The UK, for instance, rejected a proposal in the late 1990s to create a broad-based NHRI. Concerns there revolved around who would bear the costs of a national human rights commission and what would happen to well-established national institutions like the Equal Opportunities Commission and the Commission for Racial Equality. Insofar as NHRIs are therefore created over an incompatible or "crowded" national landscape, they may be pathologically incapacitated.

Second, in cases where governments are using NHRIs primarily to improve their international images and co-opt local human rights groups, there is a danger that the state will move to displace non state actors. This would explain why national governments might agree to create institutions that monitor the very international norms they violate. Likewise, as NHRIs acquire more formal international powers, they may begin to compete directly with nongovernmental groups for resources as mundane but as important as speaking time in international forums.

Domestically, NHRIs could help states occupy the "space" now filled by societal groups, thereby controlling the human rights agenda and silencing calls for accountability. These dynamics are evident across diverse regions. For example, critics of Mexico's National Human Rights Commission, created on the heels of the North American Free Trade Agreement (NAFTA), have noted the perverse effects of this internationally popular NHRI, especially in Chiapas: "Federal and state officials... appear less concerned with investigating and prosecuting complaints of human rights violations by government security forces and their paramilitary allies (although they have made recommendations in such matters), than with limiting the powers of indigenous authorities."

This commission, like too many others, is accused of undermining the very rights of those it purports to protect. Similar issues have arisen in Africa, where "in a number of cases, including Cameroon, Chad, and Togo, commissions have become less outspoken over time in response to government pressure." And in India, whose National Human Rights Commission plays a leadership role globally but lacks internal jurisdiction over its security forces, NGOs have virtually stopped filing cases with the commission, learning relatively quickly that it is better to go directly to the courts or to launch a political human rights campaign.

These distortions paint a somewhat disturbing picture: states with NHRIs may appear to be conceding some of their domestic sovereignty or control over national authority structures only to gain a firmer grip on it. To ensure that this does not occur, it will be necessary to create NHRIs that are more fully independent, perhaps funded partly by non state sources, and have full jurisdiction, including over members of the security forces and the entire state apparatus. International rules also will have to be devised to regulate relations between these new institutions, on the one hand, and traditional state agencies and non state groups on the other.

As it stands, the UN may not be doing as much as it could to pressure governments into moving beyond nominal frameworks and symbolic gestures to forge credible and effective NHRIs. Third, NHRIs may not be able to accommodate the social expectations they help to generate. For governments that seek to use NHRIs mainly for appeasement purposes, they may be surprised at how quickly human rights demands can rise. Even where these institutions are longstanding and influential, social expectations may become paradoxically high. After all, many NHRIs are relatively successful in promoting human rights norms domestically; and as social awareness rises, so do demands for actual protection, which NHRIs are not always willing or able to meet.

Across Africa, including countries like Benin and Senegal that have "a certain degree of democratic openness, the human rights commissions have paradoxically not achieved as strong a record of activity as expected." Even in the case of highly effective NHRIs, such as Canada's Human Rights Commission, problems of funding threaten the capacity of these institutions to supply the human rights protection increasingly demanded of them. In the end, these institutions could replicate what already is evident in international human rights institutions: if NHRIs are not independent, representative, and organizationally powerful, they could be more adept at promoting rather than protecting human rights norms.

Despite a dramatic rise in NHRIs in recent years and their broad implications for global governance, the role of the UN and other international actors in promoting these institutions has not yet been studied systematically. An overview of

NHRIs, including these institutions' dual regulative and constitutive functions and the activities of the UN in creating and strengthening NHRIs, a role that it has executed by means of standard setting, capacity building, network facilitating, and membership granting and not only has the global rise in NHRIs coincided with an overall increase in UN human rights support, but UN assistance has corresponded most closely with a regional increase in NHRIs in Asia and Africa.

The UN has exerted two kinds of influence: it has defined the establishment of NHRIs as a valuable goal for a wide range of states, and it has helped to equip states with the necessary means to create and strengthen NHRIs. These benefits aside in the absence of concerted attention to several factors-the particularities of the local context, organizational independence from the government, clear rules delimiting the relationship of NHRIs to other actors, and an adequate base of sustainable resources-national institutions could have negative effects, ranging from ineffectiveness to complicity with government violations.

The UN itself has played a critical role in the proliferation of NHRIs, or the incorporation of international norms into domestic structures. For the first time, moreover, a trans-governmental human rights network is emerging, a partnership characterized by regular meetings and close linkages. These NHRIs are also beginning to obtain formal international status, permitting them to act as new participants in international forums. It remains to be seen whether these developments will translate into deeper political change so that state behavior increasingly is aligned with international norms.

What is certain is that the active role played by the UN challenges conventional views about the way international norms is diffused into domestic settings. Contrary to common assumptions, international organizations can be key players in this process; they can shape the interests of states and may even create a new class of global actors. Ironically, however, the long-term success of these state actors may depend on the extent to which they are organizationally empowered to meet social demands.

In the United Nations and the International Court of Justice (ICJ), peace law is slowly emerging, just as military law emerged centuries ago. In this United Nations Decade of International Law, following the 1998 celebration of the Fiftieth Anniversary of the Universal Declaration of Human Rights, people all over the world are looking back to the founding of the United Nations, and forward to its operation in the twenty-first century. This is a propitious moment to consider methods of enforcing human rights by actions of UN organs and agencies and World Court opinions, and by initiatives at the local and national levels. And it is the moment to consider the emergence and definition of peace law.

Peace law starts with individuals, their organizations and Governments. Like all basic law, it emerged from horrors and necessities: the Great Depression, the Holocaust, the Second World War and the atomic age. Albert Einstein warned that the atomic bomb has changed everything except our way of thinking, and thus we drift toward unparalleled disaster. Peace law is part of the new way of thinking and acting to stem this drift. It breaks through the traditional separation of law into a State's domestic law, international law and the law in transnational agreements.

It requires all of us - voters, lawyers, litigants, non-governmental organizations (NGOs), transnational corporations, Governments and armies - to realize that there is a cohesive body of law at the center of all law, which must be included in consideration of every issue. Peace law is an enormous, magnificent tapestry. At its centre is the UN Charter, in which each nation pledged to settle its international disputes by peaceful means and established the United Nations to work unceasingly toward this goal through its organs and agencies. At the very core of peace law are the Nuremberg principles, setting forth the duty of each Government and each individual not to commit crimes against peace, crimes against humanity or war crimes, and not to be complicit in their commission.

The memories of Nuremberg, Dresden, Bataan, Soweto, Hiroshima and other tragic regions have led Governments to sign more international and regional treaties on non-proliferation of nuclear weapons, against other specific kinds of weapons, and for regional peace and human rights. These actions and resolutions by the General Assembly, the Security Council, the Economic and Social Council, and other organs and agencies of the United Nations comprise the continuously expanding central portion of peace law.

It is found in the peaceful customs of ethnic, racial, cultural, religious and national groups, and has traditionally been especially close to the minds and hearts of women who, with their children, are mostly the victims of its violation. It encompasses portions of existing law: international, human rights, civil rights, constitutional, criminal, property, contracts, conflict of laws, environmental, administrative, commercial, tort, legislative, immigration, labour, military, municipal and tax.

The almost 200 smaller areas in the peace law tapestry dude the peace law of each State in the United Nations: laws passed by governmental bodies from cities to nation States. For example, United States peace law includes the First Amendment protection of the fight to be a conscientious objector to war, the requirement that only Congress can declare war, the excess profit tax on war production in the Second World War, the War Powers Act, statutes enforcing neutrality, and Executive Order 13107. Peace law includes laws at the city level, establishing nuclear-free zones and incorporating Articles 55 and 56 of the UN Charter on human rights into dry ordinances. Peace law inspires actions for peace and protects peaceful activists who fed responsible. It rejects much traditional military law and ideology.

The UN system of governance relies in part on agencies created by UN bodies requiring States to make periodic reports on compliance with treaties, conduct dialogues, and report back to the major UN organs. These reports lead to action. While the United States media emphasize changes in the law resulting from litigation and acts of Congress, in fact, reports lead to action in the United States system as well.

On the governmental side, the Commissioner of Immigration and Naturalization Service reports to the

Department of Justice, which then reports to the President who reports to the Congress, suggesting new laws or changes in existing laws. The Hate Crimes Reporting Act now calls for collection of statistics from each State. The Department of Health reports on the number of people with HIV to plan scientific studies. On the economic side, the free market system relies absolutely on accurate minute-by-minute reports on stock sales from the New York Stock Exchange and other stock exchanges so that investors can make decisions.

These examples in the United States have parallels in other countries. Most recently, reports on deaths of Spaniards in Chile under Pinochet led to litigation, and these reports led to the collection of additional reports on Pinochet's actions against other targeted groups. We are each trained in the governing system in our own State and take pride in the enforcement of our national laws. So it comes as something of a surprise to many trained in the United States' legal system to realize that such system of enforcing hard-won human rights through litigation and legislation is no more effective than the UN system through reporting and resolutions.

The United States Federal Government did not start enforcing the Civil War's civil rights amendments of the 1860s until 1954, when the Supreme Court issued its opinion in Brown v. Board of Education, or even later when the Civil Rights Acts were passed by Congress in the 1960s. The adoption of the Woman's Suffrage Amendment in 1920 was just the beginning of a long effort to achieve equal treatment of women, including the collection of statistics and making reports demanding affirmative action by Federal and State Governments and private employers.

Now the Meiklejohn Civil Liberties Institute in Berkeley, like a few NGOs, has initiated a project to provide information for United States Government reports under the three ratified treaties. In preparing their first report to the United Nations Human Rights Committee in 1994, law school interns at the Meiklejohn Institute used information from other NGOs and the media and from obscure government reports to prepare Issue

Sheets on violations and enforcement of many specific articles in the International Covenant on Civil and Political Rights.

Both United States and UN officials indicated that the materials were very useful in supplementing the official government report. Now the Institute is preparing Issue Sheets for reports under the other two treaties and for the second United States report to the Human Rights Committee. In 1996, the National Lawyers Guild convinced the State Bar of California to support legislation to collect information at the State level for reporting under the three ratified treaties. A similar proposal is pending in the City of Berkeley to implement the new Executive Order at the city level.

As we approach the year 2000, people in the United States, from City Councils to the White House, are moving toward implementation of the peace law and human rights enunciated in the UN Charter, treaties and World Court opinions.

CASE IN POINT: THE UNITED STATES PRESIDENTIAL EXECUTIVE ORDER

On 10 December 1998, the Fiftieth Anniversary of the Universal Declaration of Human Rights, United States President Bill Clinton issued Executive Order 13107 on the implementation of human rights treaties ratified by the United States: the International Covenant on Civil and Political Rights; the International Convention on the Elimination of All Forms of Racial Discrimination; and the Convention Against Torture and Other Inhuman or Degrading Treatment or Punishment. For people in the United States, this Executive Order is in the tradition of President Franklin D. Roosevelt's Executive Order 8802, issued in 1941 to establish the first Fair Employment Practices Committee.

Executive Order 13107 established an Inter-agency Working Group to:

- Inform all federal agencies about the commitments in the three treaties and their responsibility to select someone to receive complaints and collect information on violations of treaty rights;

- Make periodic reports to United Nations committees;
- Provide information on the treaties and their reporting requirements to all American States, possessions and Native American reservations;
- Study all legislation proposed by the President to ensure that they do not violate these treaties;
- Reconsider each year whether to remove some reservations, understandings and declarations attached to the treaties on ratification.

As a result of Executive Order 13107, two Bay Area coalitions, in the State of California, are transforming themselves in 1999 into Universal Declaration on Human Rights 50th-Plus committees, to join the peoples of all nations in demanding that Governments publicize the United Nations treaty law, report on enforcement and its failures, and step up education at all levels of government and among trans-nationals and non-governmental organizations. For the United States, this marks a tremendous step forward for human rights and peace law.

THE QUESTION OF LEGALITY OF NUCLEAR WEAPONS

Peace law is rooted in the opinions of the International Court of Justice (IGJ), the judicial organ of the United Nations, which hears cases involving violations of peace law and writes opinions in which it digests existing peace law and elaborates on the historic contributions from every region. One of the strongest tenets in peace law today is found in the 1996 decision of the World Court on the Legality of the Threat or Use of Nuclear Weapons, that is: "There exists an obligation to pursue in good faith and bring to a conclusion negotiations leading to nuclear disarmament in all its aspects under strict and effective international control" (1052.F).

The need for people in the United States to think about this opinion is clear from one stark figure: the Government is spending $67.4 million per day on nuclear weapons, including their maintenance, improvement, storage, handling, transportation and testing, experimenting on new forms of tests and controlling the existing arsenal. In 1996, no major newspaper in the Bay Area in San Francisco or in other United States cities mentioned this advisory opinion. This is one lasting result of the cold war in the United States: a quiet shift in coverage by the media away from the activities of UN organs and the decisions of the Court.

One Bay Area legal newspaper rejected a short article on the Opinion and told the author that it did not intend to publish anything on that subject. And in December 1998 someone in the Legal Advisor's office in the State Department indicated that he had never heard of the Opinion in the Washington media (nor had he received a State Department memorandum or briefing on it). Yet, the Opinion directly affects the human right to life by placing on Heads of State and their top advisers the specific duty to negotiate for nuclear disarmament.

By this formulation, the Court took a conceptual step forward in enunciating peace law. The judges acknowledged that the judicial branch of the UN system does not have the power to enforce its decisions. Like the United States Supreme Court Justices who issued the decision in Brown v. Board of Education, they have no court staff at their command armed with weapons for enforcement, even in adversarial cases, let alone Generals and armed forces. For this reason, the judges stated the reality that the burden of enforcing the law as to nuclear weapons lies on Heads of State and legislators with power to negotiate treaties and administer their enforcement.

But the strength of peace law and the mobilization of shame do affect governmental actions. In Northern California, everyone is well aware of the University of California laboratories' continuing work on nuclear weapons. The World Court opinion was discussed by the Berkeley City Commission on Peace and Justice, established in 1986 by popular initiative vote to administer the city's nuclear-free-zone ordinance. The Opinion was quoted in a public forum called by the City to discuss a new contract by the Department of Energy with the University of California Lawrence Berkeley Laboratory to conduct simulated tests of nuclear weapons. The City Council voted to notify the University that it opposes this kind of work on the Berkeley campus.

Executive Order 13107 to implement the three human rights treaties brings into prominence the General Comment issued by the UN Human Rights Committee, after listening to distinguished jurists from Japan, that Article 6 of the International Covenant on Civil and Political Rights, enunciating the inherent right to life, includes the right to be free from nuclear weapons. These efforts are leading some United States litigants and lawyers to take seriously the ICJ decisions and to consult and follow the General Comments of the Human Rights Committee and authoritative documents of other UN committees, commissions, rapporteurs and specialized agencies.

3

The UN and the Fighting of Racism and Racial Discrimination

From its inception in 1945, the United Nations has led an unrelenting fight against racism and racial discrimination. The framework for the Organization's work in that area was the declaration in the preamble to its Charter on the question of human rights: "We the peoples of the United Nations determined... to reaffirm faith in fundamental human rights, in the dignity and worth of the human person, in the equal rights of men and women and of nations large and small, and... to practice tolerance and live together in peace with one another as good neighbours."

Hardly had the ink dried on the Charter when the United Nations was called upon to live up to that declared intent by having to address the issue of racism, one of the first human rights questions to be dealt with by the world body. On 22 June 1946, almost a year after the signing of the Charter and nine months after its coming into force, India drew the UN General Assembly's attention to the treatment of the people of Indian origin in South Africa and requested that the subject be placed on the Assembly's agenda of its first session. South Africa strongly objected to that request, asserting that under Article 2 of the UN Charter the matter was a purely domestic one, but the Assembly voted to retain the item.

On 7 December 1946, the debate on the Indian complaint began. In resolution 44 (I), its first on the subject, the Assembly affirmed that the treatment of Indians in South Africa should be in conformity with the UN Charter. However, in 1947, it failed to adopt any resolution on the matter for lack of a two-thirds majority, forcing India in 1948 to again request that the matter be brought before the Assembly. From that time and for the next 43 years, until 23 June 1994 when the item was removed from its agenda, the Assembly considered the matter annually, expanding it on 17 October 1952 to the study of the whole question of apartheid in South Africa.

In December 1948, it gave substance to the declaration on human rights in the preamble to the Charter by adopting the Universal Declaration on Human Rights, a clear statement of common standards of behaviour for the entire world, in which it recognized that "all human beings are born free and equal in dignity and rights". The Declaration, as well as the Convention on the Prevention and Punishment of the Crime of Genocide, also adopted in December, opened the conscience of people worldwide to the need to work for the respect of those rights and freedoms. In March 1948, the UN Economic and Social Council had asked the United Nations Educational, Scientific and Cultural Organization (UNESCO) to collect and disseminate data concerning racial questions throughout the world and to prepare an educational campaign based on the information gathered.

Although the situation in South Africa was the catalyst for consideration of the issue of racism by the General Assembly and would dominate that debate for decades, it was not the only race-related issue to come before the world body. At its third session in 1948, the Soviet Union asked that the situation of the aboriginal populations, especially in the Americas, be studied within the general framework of the fight against racial discrimination and the protection of national minorities. In resolution 275 (III) of December 1948, the Assembly recommended that the situation of those populations and underdeveloped social groups of the States of the American continent be studied, at the request of the countries concerned.

In 1952, the Assembly widened consideration of the issue to include complaints by several Member States, organizations and individuals against racial discrimination in non-self-governing territories. Based on the annual reports of the UN Committee on Information, the Assembly also considered annually the question of racial discrimination in these territories. On 2 December 1950, under resolution 395 (V), it declared that "a policy of 'racial segregation' (apartheid) is necessarily based on doctrines of racial discrimination" and established a three-member United Nations Commission on the Racial Situation in the Union of South Africa.

Meanwhile, dissatisfied by the pressure being brought to bear on it over its racial policies, South Africa withdrew in protest from membership in UNESCO, and from 27 November 1956 downgraded its representation at Assembly meetings. While the Universal Declaration on Human Rights was not binding on Member States, the Assembly, recognizing the necessity for firmer action, requested the Economic and Social Council, in resolution 1780 (XVII) of 7 December 1962, to ask the Commission on Human Rights to prepare a draft declaration and a draft convention on the elimination of all forms of racial discrimination.

The entire UN system continued to put pressure on South Africa and the Security Council in its resolution 123 (1960) of 1 April, called upon the Government to abandon its policies of apartheid and racial discrimination. It asked Secretary-General Dag Hammarskjold to make arrangements for the country to uphold the purposes and principles of the UN Charter. The Secretary-General visited South Africa in January 1961. On 29 June 1962, the International Labour Organization voted in favour of a resolution calling for South Africa's withdrawal from that Organization. In resolution 1761 (XII) of 1962, the Assembly requested Member States to take specific measures to bring about the abandonment of apartheid, including the breaking of diplomatic, trade and transport relations with South Africa.

It also established the Special Committee on the Policies on Apartheid of the Government of the Republic of South

Africa (later renamed the Special Committee against Apartheid). In 1968, the Assembly requested all States and organizations to "suspend cultural, educational, sporting and other exchanges with the racist regime and with organizations or institutions" in the country. In November 1971, in resolution 2775D (XXVI), it called for a boycott of sports teams selected in violation of the Olympic principle of non-discrimination. The Security Council, for its part, adopted resolutions 181 (1963) and 182 (1963) imposing a mandatory arms embargo on South Africa.

Action against racism, racial discrimination, apartheid, Nazism and racial intolerance continued to intensify. On 20 November 1963, the General Assembly adopted the United Nations Declaration on the Elimination of All Forms of Racial Discrimination, by which it "solemnly affirmed the necessity of speedily eliminating racial discrimination throughout the world, in all forms and manifestations, and of securing understanding of and respect for the dignity of the human person". On 21 December 1965, the Assembly unanimously adopted, under resolution 2106A (XX), the International Convention on the Elimination of All Forms of Racial Discrimination, which described the nature of racial discrimination, set out ways States parties could eliminate it and established the Committee on the Elimination of Racial Discrimination to oversee its implementation.

On 26 October 1966, by resolution 2142 (XXI), the Assembly proclaimed 21 March-the anniversary of the 1960 Sharpeville massacre in South Africa-as the International Day for the Elimination of Racial Discrimination, to be observed annually. On 11 December 1969, it designated 1971 as the International Year for Action to Combat Racism and Racial Discrimination, and the ten-year period 1973-1983 as the Decade for Action to Combat Racism and Racial Discrimination, and approved the Programme of Action for the Decade. On 30 November 1973, the Assembly designated apartheid as a crime by adopting the International Convention on the Suppression and Punishment of the Crime of Apartheid, which had been ratified or acceded to by 75 States or territories by December of that year.

However, the most controversial issue arising under the auspices of the Decade was the adoption on 10 November 1975 of resolution 3379 (XXX), which determined that "Zionism is a form of racial discrimination". As a consequence of that action, several States withdrew their support for the activities to be undertaken in the context of the Decade, including financial support for the convening of a world conference. That action notwithstanding, the First World Conference to Combat Racism and Racial Discrimination was held in Geneva from 14 to 25 August 1978 and attended by 125 States and a number of international organizations and observers.

The Conference adopted the Programme of Action to further the objectives of the Decade. The Programme was a further source of controversy as it contained a number of references unacceptable to many Member States and regional groupings, especially the provision condemning the "existing and increasing relations between the Zionist State of Israel and the racist regime of South Africa". It also referred to the "expulsion of Palestinians from their homeland, the practice of racial discrimination against them and their right to self-determination". There was also a growing connection between considering the question of racism and that of the self-determination of peoples.

In Africa, in particular, these two issues were inseparable in relation not only to South Africa, but also to Namibia, Northern Rhodesia and other (Portuguese) territories. Despite several concerted actions by UN bodies, the Special Committee on Apartheid reported in 1982 that 30 years after the General Assembly began consideration of the question of the race conflict in South Africa, the oppression had increased: more than 3 million blacks had been rooted out of their homes and 13 million arrested under the "pass laws", which restricted movement outside reserved areas, and the Government had sought to deprive 7 million persons of citizenship through its policy of Bantustans, or homelands confining blacks to certain "independent areas".

Not only did the Assembly declare 1982 the International Year of Mobilization for Sanctions against South Africa but, with the Security Council, also appealed for the clemency for the leaders of the African National Congress sentenced to death. On 10 December 1985, the Assembly adopted and opened for signature the International Convention against Apartheid in Sports. In 1983, the United Nations held in New York from 21 to 25 March the Second World Conference to Combat Racism and Racial Discrimination, to evaluate the work accomplished during the first Decade and chart new measures, where necessary.

The Conference adopted a Declaration and Programme of Action, which the Assembly approved in resolution 38/14, setting the stage for the Second Decade to Combat Racism and Racial Discrimination (1983-1993). In addition, based on the work of the Commission on Human Rights, it considered and adopted a resolution on measures to be taken against Nazi fascist and neo-fascist activities, as well as all other forms of totalitarian ideologies and practices based on racial intolerance, hatred and terror.

However, in 1993, at the end of the Second Decade, many of the activities envisaged to implement the Programme of Action were not accomplished because of a lack of financial resources. The Assembly, in adopting the Third Decade (1993-2003), noted that despite the efforts of the international community, the principal objectives of the first two Decades had not been attained and that millions of people continued to be victims of racism, racial discrimination and apartheid.

The Programme emphasized measures to be taken for the complete elimination of apartheid and support for the establishment of a united, non-racial and democratic South Africa. Notably absent from it were the issue of Zionism and reference to the Palestinian question, which had caused serious disagreements at the time of the adoption of the Second Decade. On 16 December 1991, in resolution 46/86, the Assembly voted to revoke the determination that Zionism was a form of racism and racial discrimination, as declared in 1975.

The vigorous and sustained efforts by the UN system and the international community bore fruit when in 1994 apartheid South Africa was transformed into a united, democratic and non-racial society, with the coming into force of the new interim constitution, which guaranteed universal adult suffrage to all South Africans. The country held its first democratic general elections in April, which were won by the African National Congress, whose leader, Nelson Mandela, became the first President of a new, non-racial South Africa.

The question of the elimination of apartheid, which had been on the General Assembly's agenda since 1946, was removed and the Special Committee against Apartheid dissolved. The Security Council removed the mandatory arms embargo and ended all measures it had imposed against South Africa. It also terminated the mandate of the United Nations Mission in South Africa.

The end of apartheid in South Africa, however, was not the end of the consideration of racism by the United Nations. Through its Special Rapporteur, the world Organization continued to examine contemporary forms of racism, racial discrimination and any form of discrimination against Blacks, Arabs and Muslims, xenophobia, Negrophobia, anti-Semitism and related intolerance, as well as governmental measures to overcome them. From 31 August to 8 September 2001, the third World Conference against Racism, Racial Discrimination, Xenophobia and Related Intolerance was held in Durban, South Africa. The Durban Declaration and Programme of Action committed States to combating those forms of racism and also acknowledged that slavery and the slave trade were a crime against humanity and contributed to racism.

The Programme was devoted to prevention, education and protection measures, including the establishment of a follow-up arrangement comprising a five-member panel of eminent independent experts to help implement the Declaration. In 2003, the Assembly closed the Third Decade and emphasized the implementation of the Durban Declaration and Programme of Action as a solid foundation for a broad-based consensus for further action to eliminate racism.

Despite the advancements made, the issue of racial discrimination continues to be a major preoccupation of the

United Nations, especially its human rights bodies, as it seeks new ways to reverse the trend towards intolerance and to fight racial hatred as they manifest themselves in new ways.

INTERNATIONAL HUMAN RIGHTS INSTRUMENTS

Education rests at the core of success and progress for children worldwide. By providing access to information and creating a gateway to opportunity, education permits the full and complete development of young minds. Even more, it is meant to serve as "the great equalizer" within and among nations. This is especially profound in light of the historical misuse of education as a device for separation and oppression. For generations, "well-educated" members of society have reaped the benefits of enhanced knowledge and advanced skills, while the "undereducated" and "uneducated" have suffered financially and politically. Today, select groups continue to enjoy the simultaneous acquisition of financial and political power to the exclusion of others, due, in large part, to disparate educational opportunities.

The legacy of education in the United States consists of the outright denial of educational opportunity for women and blacks during antebellum slavery, the perpetuation of inequality via segregated schooling during the Jim Crow era, and the continued provision of disproportionate education for minorities and poor students in under-funded school districts. Notwithstanding its turbulent past, the United States, like most countries, acknowledges the critical importance of education for all citizens.

The landmark Brown decision served as judicial confirmation of this notion, hailing education as vital to the promotion of democratic ideals, essential to the exercise of constitutional guarantees, and critical to the creation and maintenance of a harmonious society. Educators and scholars from a range of professional disciplines espouse various theories that further elucidate the integral nature of education. Moreover, the international community heralds the importance of education for all. Yet, the United States exists as one of two countries that have persistently declined to outwardly recognize a federal "right to education."

The United States' first open refusal to recognize a fundamental right to education surfaced within the Supreme Court decision San Antonio Independent School District v. Rodriguez. Specifically, the Court held that "[e]ducation... is not among the rights afforded explicit protection under our Federal Constitution." From a strict textualist perspective, the Court was correct in its assertion. However, the Court also refused to "find any basis for saying [education] is implicitly so protected." It is this refusal that represents the critical error of Rodriguez, and it is this error that requires a significant remedial response to ensure that all children are afforded equal educational opportunities.

The profoundly negative implications of Rodriguez linger, and its fruits continue to pervade American society today. The United States' failure to recognize education as a fundamental right has caused a host of unwieldy ramifications including, the prolonged provision of substandard education for racial minorities and the urban poor. This failure also has hampered the United States' ability to function as a democratic society-one in which citizens can fully exercise fundamental rights and liberties. Furthermore, it has reduced the influence of the United States as a global leader, and as a byproduct, has contributed to the decline of America's image as an ultimate sovereign state. Stated more aptly, failure to recognize such a right has placed the United States "out of step with the rest of the world."

It proposes judicial reexamination of Rodriguez in light of the prevailing international consensus supporting the right to education and based upon the recent trends reflected in Roper v. Simmons. Specifically, this section recommends that the Court employ the analytical framework provided by Roper in order to recognize education as a fundamental right. This section also articulates the need for uniformity with respect to legislative efforts to "federalize" education. Furthermore, it advocates congressional ratification of both the International

Covenant on Economic, Social, and Cultural Rights as well as the Convention on the Rights of the Child. Ultimately, this Note urges the United States to join the rest of the international community by recognizing a federal right to education.

DISCERNING THE MEANING, PURPOSE, AND FUNCTION OF EDUCATION

Education is the act or process whereby individuals develop innate capacities, obtain knowledge or training in a particular area, and access information to achieve a level of understanding. The educational process is also designed to stimulate mental and moral growth and the refinement of character. Although the right to education affects people of all ages, Lawrence LeBlanc has stated that,

[f]or all practical purposes, to speak of a right to education is to speak of a right of the child. Adults too may be said to have a right to education, since the eradication of illiteracy has been a goal of many governments and organizations for many years. But ensuring that children have a right to education is the best place to begin.

Essentially, "it is the business of education to perfect the mind." Yet, a true education also requires a tangible, value-added experience: "[u]nless it makes a difference, a very real difference, in the systematic procedure of human nature, it is not education." Two divergent schools of thought exist regarding the purpose of education: 1. that education provides a communal benefit; and 2. that education is an individual's primary means of achieving personal autonomy. The first view contends that education civilizes children and helps cultivate "common cultural goals."

Under this premise, education is intended to benefit the student as well as society. The second theory argues that "the educational system must respect [a child's] inherent value and instill socially responsible self-determination." It shifts the goal from one intended to yield a societal benefit to one focused primarily on arousing independence and self-sufficiency.

While each view possesses a certain level of merit, a blend of the two approaches provides a more accurate picture of the overall purpose of education. Rev. Dr. Martin Luther King, Jr. blurred the distinction between the two theories quite well. According to Dr. King, "education has a two-fold function to perform in the life of man and in society: the one is utility and the other is culture." He further asserted that education is designed to promote efficient behavior and to permit the achievement of personal goals "with increasing facility." Thus, education yields a dual benefit to society and to self. Based on this theory, the advantages of education for all are undeniable.

SELECT THEORIES ON THE IMPORTANCE OF EDUCATION

Education undoubtedly entails a socialization process. Children interact with peers and learn to function as competent and productive members of society. However, the right to education entails much more than the mere right to be socialized. This section briefly outlines four theoretical models that highlight the importance of education, namely: 1. the empowerment model; 2. the citizenship model; 3. the multicultural democracy model; and 4. the economic benefits model.

THE EMPOWERMENT MODEL

Education promotes the development of one's "intellectual capacity... to think seriously and critically about his or her place in society and the world at large," and, as such, exemplifies an "empowerment right." According to the empowerment theory, "[p]eople must not simply be protected against attacks by the state or other citizens; they must be empowered to act and to lead autonomous lives."

Education encourages individual success and breeds confidence by providing an escape from poverty and enabling one to participate actively in his community as an informed citizen. Furthermore, it plays "a vital role in empowering women, safeguarding children from exploitative and hazardous labour and sexual exploitation, promoting human rights and democracy, protecting the environment, and controlling population growth."

Beyond its practical importance, education serves as a platform for enlightenment and freedom of thought. It opens young minds and allows students to expand their horizons. Education also provides a sense of personal accomplishment and exists as "one of the joys and rewards of human existence." Mastery of various skills and topics typically evokes feelings of personal accomplishment. Consequently, education functions as a harbinger of individual empowerment.

THE CITIZENSHIP MODEL

The founding fathers envisioned an educational system that would serve civic and moral purposes. Under the citizenship model, education embodies a platform for the development of knowledgeable citizens and future political leaders. According to proponents of this view, the classroom is a place in which individuals come to understand the functions of government as well as their unique role as citizens in a free nation. Furthermore, advocates of this model believe education prepares young people for a variety of citizenship duties including, but not limited to, voting, allegiance, patriotism, knowledge of history, and "an interest in good government."

Accordingly, the success of America's "great experiment in government 'by the people, for the people"' remains inextricably linked with education. Focusing primarily on the need for leaders "who have the power to see a little farther, to imagine a little better life than the present," the citizenship model seeks to create "a vast army of men and women capable of understanding and following these leaders intelligently." This model advocates an all-encompassing education that ensures a certain level of knowledge while cultivating a sense of collective responsibility.

Schools provide the perfect venue to achieve this goal, because "the conditions and problems of the larger society are more easily reproduced and met and solved" within the four walls of the classroom. Yet, this theory also acknowledges the need for supplementation in the home. Ultimately, the citizenship model envisages an education whereby students, as a direct consequence of learning to be good citizens, discover ways to live and achieve at their maximum capacity. Naturally, education facilitates the type of preparation needed to produce well-qualified leaders as well as an informed community of supporters.

THE MULTICULTURAL DEMOCRACY MODEL

The multicultural democracy model favors an education that promotes democratic ideals to accommodate "the growing diversity of the citizens of this nation." Created in response to demographic shifts, this model calls for the revamping of educational systems in order to remedy the history of hegemony that has vexed learning institutions in the United States. Under this model, education is meant "to prepare our young people for citizenship in an America which fully includes in its self-definition women as well as men, all races and all ethnic groups." Furthermore, multicultural education is designed to embody "visions of the future."

Proponents of the multicultural democracy model insist that "if a democracy which includes all of America's people is to be fostered and prefigured in this nation's educational system, then multicultural education must be at the heart, and not on the margins." They seek "to re-vision America, to redefine American life and culture, and to develop metaphors, narratives, practices, and social and power relations consonant with this new definition."

Because "the history of education in this country is a story of two competing and contradictory traditions-education for full citizenship and education for second-class citizenship," this model accounts for the flaws of the citizenship model of education. Schools designed in accordance with this model are "informed by the social realities of the communities they serve and representative of the vision of the society in which they exist."

THE ECONOMIC BENEFITS MODEL

The global economy benefits from knowledgeable, skilled individuals. To that end, some theorists push for the inclusion of economic considerations in the debate surrounding the importance of education and reform efforts. These scholars tout the importance of incentives and efficiency goals as a means of achieving favorable results. The "economic benefits perspective" is based on the reality that "students coming out of America's elementary and secondary schools fare poorly in head-to-head competition with students from many other parts of the world."

Supporters claim that "the schools have been unable to bring all students up to acceptable levels of achievement, leaving a long-term disadvantaged group that most likely will be unable to participate in the American dream of enjoying an ever improving standard of living." Therefore, by focusing on outcomes, the economic benefits model links education with prospects of future success, financial gain, and a thriving economy.

Whereas the other models are widely accepted, the economic benefits perspective has been critiqued extensively. According to some, "the human rights dimension of education need[s] to be strengthened without looking at education from a utilitarian perspective that guarantees an economic result." Opponents reject the technocratic notion of education as a mere means of ushering young people into defined roles within the economy.

They see education as much more than a precursor to gainful employment and caution against the dangers of "preoccupation with receiving 'value for the education dollar' and with bottom line concerns that are 'cost-effective' and 'outcome oriented.'" Furthermore, they reject the view that education is only vital to maintaining the United States' ability to compete internationally or that it is merely a tool to prepare the future workforce. However, the economic benefits model uniquely acknowledges the unquestionable correlation between education and the strength of the economy.

EXCLUSION AND MARGINALIZATION

Exclusion has weakened the true function of education within the United States. A unique, albeit subtle, form of oppression was accomplished through the separation of certain groups in schools. Specious justifications for these divisions were based primarily on gender, race, and class. Denial of access to education for some enabled others to hold their post in the upper echelons of society. As demonstrated below, this denial ultimately shaped the lives of many of the individuals who were marginalized.

Traditionally, education was designed to prepare males for survival in the world. With respect to the curriculum, teaching methods, and structure of schools, women were not given due consideration. Prior to the 1950's, education bred a culture of separation and schools were characterized by sex segregation.

For example, separate entrances were maintained for males and females. In fact, the entire country has been operating separate systems for boys and girls despite the fact that they usually share classrooms. Not only are classes always lined up in two lines with boys in one and girls in the other, but teachers and other educators also have different expectations about the interests and abilities of individual children based largely on the sex of the child.

Even today, women continue to be stigmatized and victimized by sexism in education. "As part of the system of patriarchy, education plays an active role in perpetuating the status quo of unequal social and economic roles of women and men within our society." Schools also have consistently reinforced rigid, uneven gender roles. "Discrimination in education is one of the most damaging injustices women suffer. It denies them equal education and equal employment opportunity, contributing to a second class self image."

Historically, the effects of such discrimination spilled over into other aspects of life for women. As early as 1873, the Supreme Court upheld a state law barring women from the practice of law. Prior to the Equal Pay Act of 1963, it was legal for employers to pay a woman less than what a man would receive for the same job. Congress took specific action to remedy the disparities between men and women by enacting Title IX of the Education Amendments of 1972 and the Women's Educational Equity Act. In spite of these legislative efforts, "many girls still do not receive an education that prepares them adequately for a world of work and economic independence."

RACE

"Free public schooling in the United States began at a time when it was illegal in many states for Black people to learn how to read and write." During the Jim Crow era, American public schools were segregated, and the facilities for blacks were substandard. However, in 1954, the Court abolished this practice in the landmark decision Brown v. Board of Education. Specifically, the Court held that "the doctrine of 'separate but equal' has no place" in the field of public education, since "[s]eparate educational facilities are inherently unequal."

In addition to establishing the unconstitutionality of separate but equal, Brown "gave the importance of education a constitutional dimension." Likewise, the context of the Brown decision was built upon a concern for the standard of education that children received. In the years following Brown, small numbers of "qualified" black students entered the academy of higher education. Many children were forced to travel unearthly distances in order to get to school after mandates of busing as a remedy.

However, desegregation decrees and the rules of Brown and its progeny were not merely about racial-mixing; they were also intended to eliminate the inferior learning experiences of those who had long been subjected to second-rate education and anything less "would be an incomplete if not perverse, realization of Brown's import." Slavery and segregation were major components in the social, political, and economic development of America as a nation. In the words of W.E.B. DuBois, "the problem of the Twentieth Century [was] the problem of the color-line."

This statement continues to hold great significance for minorities today, particularly within the realm of public education, because the color line has a tendency to dictate educational opportunity in the United States. Centuries ago, African slaves fought long and hard to educate themselves in spite of adversity and oppression. Notwithstanding slavery's end, several negative thoughts and theories regarding the prospect of educational achievement and success for blacks in American society remain today. Many of these questionable ideas can be attributed to slavery and its influence. Sadly, persistent harmful attitudes toward the education of minorities are a clear example of this phenomenon.

CLASS

Following World War II, the United States strategically reorganized its economy, and, in doing so, "created a bifurcated labor market, locking poorly educated inner-city youth into low-wage jobs, despite the implementation of social policies designed to improve their life chances." This postwar transformation exacerbated the "longstanding racial divisions and economic inequities" that were characteristic of schools in the United States and further amplified obstacles to educational success for poor and minority students. The remnants of this process remain.

Even today, "the system of public education in reality perpetuates what it is ideologically committed to eradicate-class barriers which result in inequality in the social and economic life of the citizenry." Such miserable destitution will persist without an expedient increase in educational opportunity and economic power. There is also an undeniable correlation between race and poverty.

According to Katarina Tomasevski, former Special Rapporteur to the United Nations on the right to education, "efforts to eliminate racial discrimination have demonstrated that dissociating race from poverty has not led to desired outcomes." She further noted that "because economic exclusion has a visible racial and gender profile, revisiting the core concepts of equal and unequal rights seems timely."

This is because an invisible dividing line based on race and class has perpetuated a "class-based stratification" system in America. Julius Chambers provides a poignant description of this reality, stating that problems which plague minority students are not only a function of race but of class. As time passes, it becomes painfully obvious that three centuries of racial subjugation, *de jure* and *de facto* segregation, as well as overt and covert discrimination, have left black Americans disproportionately economically impoverished. Inadequate education, in turn, perpetuates economic caste distinctions.

As it stands, the fundamental problem is that "despite frequent good intentions and abundant rhetoric about 'equal educational opportunity,' schools have rarely taught the children of the poor effectively and this failure has been systematic, not idiosyncratic." Therefore, class-based distinctions further demonstrate the importance of a federal right to education.

INTERNATIONAL RECOGNITION OF THE RIGHT TO EDUCATION

Education is the single most popular topic of discussion concerning the international rights of a child. The international community's emphasis on this aspect of life underscores the need for a universal right to education. This section presents a synopsis of select international human rights instruments that contain provisions for a right to education. It also explains the significance of treaty ratification and discusses the United States' reluctance to ratify two of the most influential international treaties that include a right to education. Finally, it analyzes the strength of the international community's conviction on the issue of a fundamental right to education.

THE RIGHT AS REFLECTED IN MAJOR INTERNATIONAL HUMAN RIGHTS INSTRUMENTS

The international community possesses an unequivocal reverence for education. This is demonstrated by the presence of major provisions asserting a right to education in several key international human rights instruments. Although some international instruments only address the issue of education indirectly, others bear directly upon education as a substantive right. The three human rights instrument that address the rights explicitly are: 1. the Universal Declaration of Human Rights; 2. the International Covenant on Economic, Social, and Cultural Rights; and 3. the Convention on the Rights of the Child. These international instruments share a few basic ideas about education; that it should be free, compulsory for primary levels, equally accessible, and free from discrimination.

In addition, the International Convention on the Elimination of All Forms of Racial Discrimination is noteworthy for its considerable relation to the right to education. Notwithstanding the right to education as a common thread, these international instruments vary in purpose, content, and form.

THE UNIVERSAL DECLARATION OF HUMAN RIGHTS

The Universal Declaration of Human Rights (UDHR) was adopted by the United Nations General Assembly in 1948. According to drafting committee chairwoman and former United States First Lady, Eleanor Roosevelt, this Declaration was intended "to serve as a common standard of achievement for all peoples of all nations." The UDHR catalogues human rights for all individuals. Its basic framework consists of thirty articles that enumerate fundamental principles of equality, set out civil and political rights, and outline economic, social, and cultural rights.

Article 26 establishes the right to education. It summarizes the purpose and function of education and acknowledges the corresponding rights of parents with respect to the education of their child. Specifically, it provides:

Everyone has the right to education....

Education shall be directed to the full development of the human personality and to the strengthening of respect for human rights and fundamental freedoms. It shall promote understanding, tolerance and friendship among all nations, racial or religious groups, and shall further the activities of the United Nations for the maintenance of peace.

Parents have a prior right to choose the kind of education that shall be given to their children.

By making education a fundamental right, the UDHR substantiates the universal importance of education. Moreover, the UDHR breathes life into the right by clarifying the purpose of education and extending the liberty interest in education beyond a mere right to receive formal instruction. Instead, the right to education pursuant to the UDHR carries concomitant benefits to the individual and to society. Accordingly, the right to education under the UDHR is consistent with the aforementioned theories of education and their central purposes.

Unlike international covenants and treaties, the UDHR does not have signatories or ratifying parties. Furthermore, it arguably lacks any legally binding effect. However, there are three conflicting views regarding the legal status of this Declaration within the international community. The "minimalist approach" views the Declaration as non-binding. The "middle-ground" approach considers the Declaration "an authoritative interpretation... of the human rights provisions of the United Nations Charter." Finally, the "high ground approach" asserts that the Declaration is binding customary international law.

Notwithstanding apparent conflicts over interpretation, the UDHR is significant for two reasons. First, it is used to measure the compliance of U.N. member-states with human rights obligations. Second, and more importantly, the presence of a right to education in the UDHR prompted the ultimate creation of similar provisions in the International Covenant on Economic, Social, and Cultural Rights, a binding treaty which specifically incorporates the right to education.

THE INTERNATIONAL COVENANT ON ECONOMIC, SOCIAL, AND CULTURAL RIGHTS

The International Covenant on Economic, Social, and Cultural Rights (ICESCR) entered into force in 1976 after a long process of drafting, debate, and adoption. This treaty applies explicitly to men and women, and implicitly to children. The

ICESCR contains language almost identical to the UDHR, yet it has the benefits of legally binding effect on its parties. Moreover, the provisions that establish a right to education give state parties additional leeway to develop a plan of action in order to progressively implement the rights contained therein. Hence, the ICESCR offers a sense of flexibility for nations that may lack the resources necessary for successful and immediate compliance.

The right to education is defined explicitly in Articles 13 and 14 of the ICESCR. Article 13 requires states to provide education at varying levels, while Article 14 permits the gradual realization of educational goals. Although much of this Covenant's language mirrors the language of the UDHR, Article 131. of the ICESCR also provides that "education shall enable all persons to participate effectively in a free society, promote understanding, tolerance and friendship among all nations and all racial, ethnic or religious groups, and further the activities of the United Nations for the maintenance of peace."

Article 133 protects the liberty interest of parents by allowing them to choose schools "to ensure the religious and moral education of their children in conformity with their own convictions." Article 134 permits the establishment of educational institutions by individuals and bodies, provided that they adhere to the standards set forth by the Covenant. To bolster the guarantee of free and compulsory primary education, Article 14 permits noncompliant states "to work out and adopt a detailed plan of action for the progressive implementation, within a reasonable number of years, to be fixed in the plan, of the principle of compulsory education free of charge for all."

General Comment No. 13 of the ICESCR makes clear "the import of the right to education" and "elucidates the obligations of [each] State... to respect, protect and fulfill" the aims of the right to education provision. Member-states are required to provide an education comprised of four interrelated, critical features: availability, accessibility, acceptability, and adaptability.

According to the General Comment, an "available" education provides a safe learning environment fully-equipped with necessary facilities. An "accessible" education is one free from discrimination on the basis of race, physical disability, or socioeconomic status, while an "acceptable" education involves the teaching of relevant and culturally appropriate concepts. Finally, an "adaptable" education is flexible enough to respond to the needs of the students and of society.

THE CONVENTION ON THE RIGHTS OF THE CHILD

Adopted in 1989 and entered into force the following year, the Convention on the Rights of the Child (CRC) "defines the minimum standards of human rights for children and calls on governments to devote resources to implementing those rights." To date, it is the most widely ratified international human rights treaty in the history of the United Nations. In fact, the United States and Somalia are the only remaining countries that have not ratified the CRC. Characterized as a "universal benchmark on the rights of the child," the CRC is the only comprehensive international treaty that focuses extensively and exclusively on children's rights.

Article 28 outlines the right to education. Specifically, Article 281 recognizes "the right of the child to education... with a view to achieving this right progressively and on the basis of equal opportunity."

In addition to requiring free and compulsory primary education, Article 281 also enumerates a variety of educational areas that require special attention, including general and vocational secondary education, financial assistance for secondary students in need, access to higher education for children with the capacity to attend, educational and vocational information and guidance, and school attendance and drop-out rates.

Article 282 addresses the issue of school discipline and requires that it be "administered in a manner consistent with the child's human dignity." Finally, Article 283 "promotes and encourages international cooperation in matters relating to education." The CRC has been classified broadly in terms of "the four P's."

The CRC is concerned with "the participation of children in decisions affecting their own destiny; the protection of children against discrimination and all forms of neglect and exploitation; the prevention of harm to children; and the provision of assistance for their basic needs."

These fours tenets are enshrined in Article 29 of the CRC, which summarizes the primary goals of education. The goals are as follows:

- The development of the child's personality, talents and mental and physical abilities to their fullest potential;
- The development of respect for human rights and fundamental freedoms, and for the principles enshrined in the Charter of the United Nations;
- The development of respect for the child's parents, his or her own cultural identity, language and values, for the national values of the country in which the child is living, the country from which he or she may originate, and for civilizations different from his or her own;
- The preparation of the child for responsible life in a free society, in the spirit of understanding, peace, tolerance, equality of sexes, and friendship among all peoples, ethnic, national and religious groups and persons of indigenous origin; [and]
- The development of respect for the natural environment.

Much of the language of Articles 28 and 29 of the CRC parallels that contained within the Article 13 of the ICESCR. Yet, there are a few fundamental differences between the two treaties. First, more nation-states are parties to the CRC.

Second, contrary to the ICESCR, the CRC does not include a specific time frame within which states must progressively implement compulsory primary education. Finally, as demonstrated above, the CRC is "the most authoritative standard-setting international instrument on children's rights."

THE INTERNATIONAL CONVENTION ON THE ELIMINATION OF ALL FORMS OF RACIAL DISCRIMINATION

The International Convention on the Elimination of All Forms of Racial Discrimination (CERD) was entered into force in 1969. CERD proscribes discrimination by member-states and was designed "to promote and encourage universal respect for and observance of human rights and fundamental freedoms for all, without distinction as to race, sex, language, or religion." The treaty centers on the premise that "the existence of barriers is repugnant to the ideals of any human society." Notwithstanding its primary goals of eradicating and preventing various forms of discrimination, this treaty correlates with the right to education, particularly in Article 5. Under Article 5(e)(v), member states must guarantee the enjoyment of the right to education and training without discrimination.

RATIFICATION, RESERVATIONS, AND THE UNITED STATES' RELUCTANCE

Generally, treaty ratification occurs in two stages. First, an organized body-comprised of governmental delegates from nation states-negotiates the substance of the treaty and formally adopts the selected text. Next, each individual state decides whether to formally ratify the treaty. If a state approves ratification, it "specifically and explicitly accepts to be bound." However, this stage of the process is not always streamlined. Occasionally, an individual state may opt to include one or more reservations for provisions that "may not be deemed acceptable because the government does not wish to or cannot comply with their requirements."

A number of countries have made reservations in response to the provisions requiring a right to education in the international human rights instruments discussed above. For example, specific reservations to the ICESCR "range from acknowledgments that financial constraints to access to primary education were beyond the capacity of the state, to assertions that education should be treated as the monopoly of the state, or that parents should be allowed to educate their children themselves, in their own home." Thus, the reservation process offers a viable alternative for countries that prefer not to be bound in entirety by an international treaty.

The problem with extensive reservations is that "they diminish human rights obligations of the respective governments and human rights guarantees for the affected population." Furthermore, in some instances the reservations "are so wide-reaching that their compatibility with the spirit and wording of the treaties has frequently been challenged and their withdrawal urged." In the United States, ratified treaties are accorded the same weight as federal law. Despite its status as a leading nation, the United States' history of treaty ratification pales in comparison to that of other democratic states.

In fact, many authoritarian states that frequently violate fundamental human rights have a more impressive history of ratification. Interestingly, the United States ratified the International Convention on the Elimination of All Forms of Racial Discrimination on October 21, 1994, albeit with extensive reservations. The United States has not, however, ratified the International Covenant on Economic, Social, and Cultural Rights. More significantly, the United States is the only industrialized country that has not ratified the Convention on the Rights of the Child.

There are several underlying reasons behind the United States' failure to ratify the Convention on the Rights of the Child (CRC), including: 1. an unimpressive record of ratification of human rights treaties; 2. the federalist structure of the United States government; 3. the fact that United States law is "less protective" than the CRC; 4. conflict between treaty provisions and United States law; and 5. a lack of understanding and widespread misconception regarding the overall effect of the CRC upon national and state sovereignty. Some scholars have criticized the United States' failure to ratify major human rights instruments that directly relate to children, particularly the CRC.

They contend, based on its status as a world power, that the United States' feeble commitment to international human rights consequently weakens the human rights movement. Others maintain, however, that reluctance to ratify prevents the United States from engaging in hypocrisy. According to this view, since ratification signals compliance, failure to ratify necessarily exempts the United States from observing or implementing any human rights principles that conflict with American law.

Instead of ratification, a member-state may offer its "preliminary and general endorsement" by agreeing to sign the treaty. A signature "is not a legally binding step, but is an indication that the country intends to undertake a careful examination of the treaty in good faith to determine its position towards it."

The United States signed the CRC "subject to ratification," indicating general agreement with the treaty's objectives, but a desire to scrutinize all provisions thoroughly before submitting the treaty for final ratification. As a mere signatory, the United States is not formally bound, but is obligated to refrain from frustrating "the object and purpose" of this treaty. However, many argue that by signing the CRC, the United States signaled its clear intent to pursue ratification.

THE FORCE OF THE INTERNATIONAL COMMUNITY AND CUSTOMARY INTERNATIONAL LAW

Amidst an increasingly global economy, a growing sense of interdependence has emerged among nations around the world. To some extent, the international community has the power to influence the actions of its sister-nations. "If nations fail to respect standards, the international community typically encourages, pushes, prods, and ultimately embarrasses states into taking steps to guarantee the proper implementation of rights."

Typically, this influence amounts to pressure to do the right thing. Although this pressure is not determinative, it is significant. Yet, "[w]hile it is laudable that courts have found international human rights standards useful, that is not enough. Many of those standards have risen to the level of customary international law and should be considered as such by the courts."

The authority of customary international law is equally, if not more, significant than the moral peer pressure described above. "Customary international law 'results from a general and consistent practice of states followed by them from a sense of legal obligation,' and binds nations that have not dissented from the rule while it was developing." At the turn of the twentieth century, the Supreme Court held that customary law is "part of our law, and must be ascertained and administered by the courts of justice of appropriate jurisdiction, as often as questions of right depending upon it are duly presented for their determination." Therefore, in the United States customary international law typically has the status of federal law and supersedes contradictory state law.

Expressions of customary international law are also binding on all members of the international community. According to the International Court of Justice, any specific provisions that constitute customary international law "cannot therefore be the subject of any right of unilateral exclusion exercisable at will" by any state within the international community.

Some human rights advocates contend that "[t]he right to education and the right to enjoy it without discrimination are examples of economic, social and cultural rights that should be considered part of customary international law." In my view, the right to education is, in fact, a part of customary international law. Since the United States has declined to "manifest [its] dissent" to this general rule of customary international law, it does not qualify as a "persistent objector." Therefore, the United States has implicitly agreed to be bound by this international norm.

San Antonio Independent School District v. Rodriguez signaled the Supreme Court's first open refusal to recognize a federal right to education. The impetus for this suit was an equal protection challenge based upon Texas' school funding scheme. The Court issued a two-part holding, concluding that: 1. the Texas school funding scheme was constitutional and did not amount to systematic discrimination on the basis of wealth; and 2. education is not a fundamental Constitutional right. Hence, this decision directly implicated "the right to education" and led to the consequent lack thereof. Essentially, Rodriguez was responsible for putting an end to any further attempts to equalize the public education system through the federal courts.

Plaintiffs filed a class action suit on behalf of Demetrio Rodriguez and other similarly situated Mexican-American families, each of whom expressed immense dissatisfaction with the Texas school financing system. They alleged that the funding scheme was an unconstitutional violation of the Equal Protection Clause of the Fourteenth Amendment. The scheme permitted public schools to rely upon local property taxes in order to supplement per pupil expenditures. While the ultimate source of contention was the extreme difference in property tax values among the neighboring districts, the essential problem was simple: the poorer neighborhood, the poorer the school. Addressing the merits of the original complaint, the majority simultaneously issued a holding that has presented an everlasting challenge to quality public schooling in America.

In a sheer display of irony, the Court acknowledged the critical importance of education, yet contemporaneously refused to recognize education as a constitutional right. Justice Powell, writing for the majority, asserted that education does not fall within the limited category of rights explicitly or implicitly protected under the Constitution. To justify the Court's position, he further stated that "it is not the province of this Court to create substantive constitutional rights in the name of guaranteeing equal protection of the laws." However, by attempting to avoid judicial overstepping, the Court took a misstep.

The majority conveniently ignored the myriad contexts in which affirmative constitutional rights have been recognized. Generally, these rights are based upon flexible provisions of the Constitution in light of the framers' intent.

As one scholar notes, the Supreme Court has continually engaged in the selective incorporation of open-ended provisions of the Constitution in order to fashion numerous implied rights "by deeming there to be a nexus between them and the Constitution." A non-exhaustive list of these "scarcely at all specified" rights includes:

the right to interstate travel; the right to procreate; the right to vote in state elections; the right to appeal from a criminal conviction; the freedom of association; the right of privacy; the right of choice in marital relations; the right to choose to have an abortion; the right of free access to the courts; the right to an open criminal trial; and the right of married couples to use contraceptives.

Furthermore, certain rights "have been defined by judges' conscious value preferences, including their conceptions of justice, reasonableness, custom, fair procedure, and equality before the law." Arguably, this type of behavior amounts to unauthorized judicial overstepping or uncalled for judicial activism. The appropriateness of such activities, however, begs the question. What matters is the Court's focused decision to shy away from its traditional tendencies in this case. The Court's strategic choice in Rodriguez to remove education from the purview of federal enforcement bears an undeniable relation to the current state of public education in America. This, in turn, links with the limited ability of certain groups to exercise their basic rights today.

To refute this notion, the majority concluded that the Court "[has] never presumed to possess either the ability or the authority to guarantee to the citizenry the most effective speech or the most informed electoral choice." Stated otherwise, the Court hastened to reserve to the legislature what may properly belong to the judiciary. As a consequence, underprivileged Americans without access to an adequate education are now deprived of "their most basic right to seek redress." Thus, "[b]y abdicating their responsibility to provide a meaningful forum to address educational adequacy, the courts ensured this basic civil right will never be attained."

Justice Marshall was a keen advocate for equality of educational opportunity. This stance was apparent during his work with the NAACP, particularly his long, hard fight to abrogate the "separate but equal" doctrine that plagued the American school system in the pre-Brown era. Through advocacy and eventually through judicial pronouncements, Marshall has ardently and consistently opposed "practice[s] that would engrain second-class citizenship in children, and do so with respect to the social service most indispensable for an equal chance in life."

The Rodriguez majority opinion struck at the heart of Justice Marshall's greatest passion-education for all. Essentially, "two of his deepest convictions converged in Rodriguez: that all children ought to be afforded educational opportunities sufficient to reach their full potential, and that no one ought to be denied equal protection of the laws on account of his or her financial status." For that reason, Marshall vehemently opposed the majority's conclusion that education is not a fundamental right.

In dissent, Justice Marshall "categorically rejected the notion that the Constitution requires no more than the provision of a minimal level of education to children." He argued that "the right of every American to an equal start in life, so far as the provision of a state service as important as education is concerned, is far too vital to permit state discrimination on grounds as tenuous as those presented by this record." Marshall's powerful dissenting opinion articulated his diametric view with reason and lucidity. It chided the majority for engaging in "a retreat from our historic commitment to equality of educational opportunity and as unsupportable acquiescence in a system which deprives children in their earliest years of the chance to reach their full potential as citizens."

Marshall's opinion did not render mere visceral notions of the type of education American children deserve. Rather, it laid out, in a very compelling way, three key arguments in favor of the right to education: 1. education is essential to overcoming poverty and disadvantage; 2. education is inextricably linked with the First Amendment right to freedom of speech; and 3. education is integral to self-government. Marshall understood that equal educational opportunities would transform the inauspicious beginnings of undereducated, disenfranchised citizens into a life circumstance characterized by power, pride, and promise.

Justice Marshall's passionate disavowal of the majority stance is the natural consequence of his ultimate fear-the retrenchment of Brown. Susan Bitensky's description of the Rodriguez reflects this view. According to Bitensky:

The Rodriguez majority ruled that a positive fundamental right to education is not among the panoply of rights afforded implicit protection under the Constitution. This was the sleight of hand that broke Brown's promise of quality education; Rodriguez simply withdrew the promise without even mentioning that Brown had been in any way affected."

Bitensky continues, arguing that Rodriguez fails to comport with Brown. Specifically, she notes that "the consequence is that Brown has been sundered from its education context and substantially eviscerated." Marshall's apprehensions and Bitensky's assertions with respect to the Rodriguez decision are substantiated by the current state of public education in the United States, the blatant disparities, and the emergent national consensus supporting the right to education.

Rodriguez generated tremendous nationwide disparities with respect to the quality of education that children receive in the United States. As a direct response, individual states added constitutional provisions explicitly recognizing the right to education in a noble, yet insufficient, attempt to remedy the problem. This, in turn, has led to widespread inconsistency with respect to the quality of education that American children receive. Attorneys in school-finance litigation have turned to state constitutions in search of a practical remedy for those who are denied access to an adequate education. However, it remains apparent that "state-based education rights do not adequately safeguard the educational opportunities of the nation's school children."

Education is not the only area of United States law that has been riddled with variation and conflict. For example, the Supreme Court traditionally sanctioned the imposition of capital punishment for juvenile offenders. However, the Court recently changed its position on this issue in Roper v. Simmons, thereby abolishing the juvenile death penalty for offenders under the age of eighteen. In Roper, the Court found support for its conclusion based, in part, on the fact that capital punishment for juveniles is prohibited in 30 states. Here, the Court drew on the presence of a "national consensus" opposing the juvenile death penalty.

Dissenting Justice O'Connor was not persuaded by the majority's national consensus argument in this case, and, as a result, declined to assign a confirmatory role to the additional "international consensus" argument advanced by the Court. It is important to note, however, that O'Connor agreed with the overall analytical framework employed- i.e., international consensus may play a confirmatory role in the Court's analysis for decisions where a "genuine national consensus" exists. Justice Scalia, on the other hand, completely rejected the Court's national consensus argument, noting that "[w]ords have no meaning if the views of less than 50% of death penalty States can constitute a national consensus."

There is considerable foundation for the claim that a "genuine national consensus" exists with respect to the right to education in the United States. Currently, a total of forty-eight state constitutions explicitly recognize a right to education. Although varying permutations of the right exist, the right is still recognized by an overwhelming majority of states.

More importantly, unlike the debatable national consensus regarding the juvenile death penalty in Roper, the agreement among individual states that education should be considered a fundamental right is just short of unanimous. Therefore, the national consensus argument for the right to education does not suffer from the same uncertainties that troubled Justices O'Connor and Scalia in Roper. It follows then, that the presence of an international consensus regarding the right to education can and should play a confirmatory role in the United States' decision to recognize a federal right to education.

A tripartite problem continues to plague the American public education system, namely: 1. the error and judicial inconsistency of Rodriguez; 2. the marginalization of women, minorities, and poor students; and 3. the unresolved crisis despite legislative efforts to establish federal guidelines. Judicial recognition of education as a fundamental right would help alleviate this problem by ensuring equal access to the invaluable benefits of knowledge and by facilitating adequate educational preparation for the exercise of explicit constitutional guarantees.

As a corollary, a federal right to education would: give rise to increased personal empowerment, bolster good citizenship, teach students to succeed in a multicultural democracy, and generate a better-prepared workforce while simultaneously yielding economic benefits for society as a whole. The time has come for the United States to affirmatively recognize education as a fundamental right.

The unsuccessful attempts of the American courts, commentators, and policy makers to affirmatively decide who should control the right to education necessitate the consultation of international standards to begin resolving the educational crisis in the United States. First, the Supreme Court can and should continue its recent trend of consulting international norms, as in Roper, in order to recognize the right to education.

Second, the government's attempts to conform to the international community by "federalizing" education will continue to miss the mark without the firm establishment of a federal right to education. Finally, since global leadership demands accountability, the United States should follow through on its half-fulfilled commitment to the international community by ratifying the International Covenant on Economic, Social, and Cultural Rights and the almost universally accepted Convention on the Rights of the Child.

"The instinct to read international values into our domestic law dates back to the birth of our nation." Architects of the American judicial system anticipated the active pursuit and conscious incorporation of international law standards into our jurisprudence.

Consistent with this vision, there has been a recent shift in the Court's ideology regarding the use of "international consensus" as a factor during adjudication. A clear example is the case of Roper v. Simmons. In Roper, the Court held that the Eighth and Fourteenth Amendments forbid the imposition of the death penalty on offenders who were under the age of the eighteen at the time of the commission of the crime.

Writing for the majority, Justice Kennedy found "confirmation in the stark reality that the United States is the only country in the world that continues to give official sanction to the juvenile death penalty." The majority also concluded that "[t]he opinion of the world community, while not controlling our outcome, does provide respected and significant confirmation for our own conclusions." Accordingly, the international consensus opposing the juvenile death penalty was a decisive factor in the Court's ultimate conclusion. Moreover, Justice O'Connor's dissenting opinion also noted the Court's consistent reference to foreign and international law as germane factors in the assessment of "evolving standards of decency."

Roper has been the subject of intense criticism by scholars who believe the decision signals a dangerous retreat from the long-held principles of federalism and separation of powers. Many of these critics call for a strict interpretation of the Constitution. A stalwart of this view, Justice Scalia issued a scathing dissent, arguing that [t]he Court should either profess its willingness to reconsider all these matters in light of the views of foreigners, or else it should cease putting forth foreigners' views as part of the reasoned basis of its decisions. To invoke alien law when it agrees with one's own thinking, and ignore it otherwise, is not reasoned decision-making, but sophistry.

In their rejoinder, the majority stated that "it does not lessen our fidelity to the Constitution or our pride in its origins to acknowledge that the express affirmation of certain fundamental rights by other nations and peoples simply underscores the centrality of those same rights within our own heritage of freedom." Still, critics maintain that reliance on international law poses a threat to the very fabric of United States government. Despite these criticisms, the Court's consultation of international norms in Roper is not an isolated occurrence.

Additional decisions have been predicated upon the existence of norms housed in international human rights instruments. Justices also have consulted international norms in decisions implicating key educational issues. For example, Justice Ginsburg's concurrence in the groundbreaking Grutter v. Bollinger decision commented that the requirement of a time-limit on race-conscious University admissions policies "accords with the international understanding of the office of affirmative action." Using similar logic, there may be an occasion for overturning Rodriguez based on the existence of an "international consensus" regarding the right to education. This is feasible in spite of the Court's initial reluctance to consult international law on the issue of education as a fundamental right.

Simply put, the Rodriguez decision is problematic. The United States' failure to recognize a federal right to education vitiates the legacy of equal educational opportunity set forth by Brown. The Court's refusal to recognize education as an implicit right has led to the persistent exclusion of poor and minority students from access to an adequate education. In addition, education is a fundamental right implicitly protected by the Constitution.

Notwithstanding the absence of a federal right to education, the recognition of such a right to "is not precluded by Rodriguez." The Court made clear that "its limited ruling was not intended to foreclose future consideration of a claim alleging that a child had been denied an education on account of indigence." Furthermore, a national consensus supporting the right to education exists. By referencing the international consensus on this issue, a judicial decision recognizing education as an implicit constitutional right is possible and practical.

Although state and local governments have traditionally administered laws and policies that govern the education of their citizens, the increased federalization of education further justifies judicial recognition of education as a fundamental right. The most current educational reform efforts are embodied in the No Child Left Behind Act (NCLB). Likewise, the enactment of the Individuals with Disabilities Education Act (IDEA) exemplifies a congressional commitment tailored to students with special needs. These federal responses to the education crisis in the United States are laudable, but there can be no real action or realization of the goals of each without an established federal right.

While congressional policies make clear our political commitment to the education of America's children, the effective implementation of these policies will require exactly the type of legal commitment embodied in international treaties such as the Convention on the Rights of the Child. As in the CRC, the right to education must be formally recognized by the United States. In addition, cooperative action among each branch of government is vital in order to successfully remedy dominant problems associated with the current state of education in the United States.

NCLB is intended to address disparities reflected in the academic outcomes of poor, minority, disabled and limited-English proficiency students. Its primary objective is to close the achievement gap using four techniques: high stakes accountability measures, state and local flexibility, focus on proven educational methods, and improved educational choice. In reality, however, the goal of leaving no child behind amounts to mere fantasy without an underlying fundamental right to support it. Moreover, the secondary and tertiary roles of education to eliminate teen pregnancy, to promote self-sufficiency, and to minimize violence in the community, also demand the recognition of education as a federal right.

The bi-partisan enactment of NCLB proves that "the political capital for supporting many of the provisions of the CRC is evident in current domestic legislation." This is further underscored by the fact that the "countries in which the right to education is fully guaranteed experience improvements in some of the aforementioned problem areas. Establishment of a federal right to education therefore falls directly in line with America's recent decision to shift responsibility for education from individual states and localities to the federal government.

As noted previously, the overwhelming majority of international human rights instruments explicitly recognize the right to education. More significantly, the United States played a significant role in the development of human rights. For example, "the Universal Declaration of Human Rights emerged, with the unstinting support of the United States, as a pledge to remedy the previous absence of human rights safeguards-civil, political, economic, social and cultural."

It is difficult to reconcile the United States' direct involvement in drafting the UDHR with its subsequent refusal to ratify its offspring of treaties; specifically, the International Covenant international law in Roper and explaining the Court's suggestion that "international norms can play a confirmatory role" in constitutional adjudication) of Economic, Social, and Cultural Rights and the Convention on the Rights of the Child. This is particularly disturbing in light of the option to make reservations or to use other mechanisms that would give the United States a voice in determining the force of treaties and covenants within its borders.

Given the overwhelming recognition of the right to education in international treaties and human rights instruments, the United States' hesitancy to follow suit presents a distinct quandary. "This is a nation that has often been portrayed as the paragon of democracy and the leader in human rights reform. However, this enduring vision that other nations equate with America may slowly deteriorate as others see the United States fall behind on certain human rights' issues."

Recognizing the right to education by ratifying the ICESCR and the CRC would help avoid this consequence. Ratification would benefit children in the United States and throughout the world. Moreover, if the right to education amounts to customary international law, the United States should not continue to refuse to recognize that right within its borders.

In light of its traditional role in the development of human rights, the United States should abandon its wavering stance on the right to education and join its sister-nations by openly recognizing the right. Proponents of trans-nationalist jurisprudence maintain that,

The United States expresses its national sovereignty not by blocking out all foreign influence but by vigorous "participation in the various regimes that regulate and order the international system." The nationalists' suggestion that U.S. courts should disregard the rest of the civilized world by ignoring parallel foreign precedents only invites charges of parochialism, and undermines U.S. influence over the global development of human rights.

If the United States continues to ignore the needs of its own citizens, its image as a champion of human rights will fade away and become a mere facade. It follows then, that the right to education should exist as "the centerpiece of American efforts to build democracies around the world." To stand as a legitimate world leader and to promote and to protect freedom and democratic ideals in the distant lands of Latin America, Southeast Asia, and the Middle East, the United States must first recognize the right to education in its own backyard.

"Next in importance to freedom and justice is popular education, without which neither freedom, nor justice can be permanently maintained." Unfortunately, educational disparities represent one of this country's most pressing issues. Notwithstanding state-based constitutional provisions and federal legislative action, a solution is needed to reduce, and in time eradicate, the persistent, nationwide educational inequities that disproportionately affect minorities and poor children. Furthermore, due to the United States' reluctance, a universal belief in education as a fundamental right remains to be seen.

International law provides a potential avenue for judicial recognition of education as a fundamental right. The decisive use of an international consensus argument in overturning Rodriguez would be consistent with the Court's analysis in Roper. Moreover, recognition of education as a fundamental right would complement the current legislative efforts to remedy the education crisis via the No Child Left Behind Act and the Individuals With Disabilities Education Act.

This choice would not endanger the dual sovereignty characteristic of our nation's government. Rather, it would promote cohesion and ensure tangible results and progress in America's public schools. Ratification of the International Covenant on Economic, Social, and Cultural Rights and the Convention on the Rights of the Child would solidify our commitment to education, enhance accountability, and signal our cooperation with global peers on one of the most important issues facing young people today.

Establishing a federal right to education is an essential step if America ever hopes to resolve its public education crisis. More importantly, it is necessary in order to ensure that the nation's students are empowered, culturally aware, prepared to demonstrate good citizenship, and equipped to enter the workforce upon graduation. We have recognized international precedent for other pressing issues. Education should not be an exception to this practice. Recognition of education as a fundamental right through the use of international instruments will lead us one step closer to resolving the dissonant chords that have prevented this country from achieving harmony of opportunity for all students-male or female, rich or poor, white or black.

4

Reform of Lawmaking

The extent of the human rights lawmaking in the United Nations has been impressive, in terms of the quantity of both its output and the organs involved. Lawmaking, as a process by which organs of the United Nations adopt international human rights instruments, has naturally attracted the critical attention of governments and of scholars, for whom such processes have always held a special fascination. Recent studies have drawn attention to this process in the United Nations in general, and in the human rights area in particular. They point to deficiencies in both the process and the quality of the instruments that have been adopted.

These deficiencies are not always rooted in political factors, but often in incompetence, hasty consideration and approval, and lack of adequate research and editing. Therefore, they must not be viewed as inevitable and beyond reasonable prospects for reform. The important volume of essays on the International Covenant on Civil and Political Rights edited by Professor Henkin contains many examples of poorly drafted provisions, and worse, provisions that conflict with each other. It is not unusual to find that provisions drafted during a later session of the lawmaking organ conflict with those drafted earlier, and that no attempt was made subsequently to revise the conflicting texts.

Some of the unfortunate language involved in one of the major human rights instruments, the Convention on the

Elimination of All Forms of Racial Discrimination, was discussed in a recent article. Other instruments, e.g., the Convention on the Elimination of All Forms of Discrimination Against Women, pose equal or even greater problems, as demonstrated in an unusually candid memorandum of law by the Department of State. Inconsistencies and the potential for conflict between norms contained in different instruments have been observed. My own recent investigation of normative relationships between human rights instruments, now under preparation for publication, reveals that conflicts between such instruments are not mere hypothises *d'école*, but are real and immediate.

UN Secretariat studies have noted the lack of structure in human rights lawmaking processes and unhappiness with the present situation has been voiced openly by governments. The Government of the United States thus observed in the Third (Social, Humanitarian and Cultural Questions) Committee that much of the work in this area proceeds without planning, in a kind of haphazard manner, at a desultory pace and with overlapping jurisdictions. We have working groups in the Third Committee, in the Commission on Human Rights, and in the Sub-Commission. It is difficult to keep track of the different drafts. There is a lack of continuity and expertise among the persons working on the drafts. It makes no sense, for example, for a body of this size to attempt to draft a convention from its inception. As it is, one often has to reinvent the wheel each time a working group reconvenes. The result is neither fast nor fruitful.

The problem, however, cannot be attributed merely to a lack of coordination or of cost efficiency in the system; it also derives from the quality of the instruments themselves and has far-reaching impact on prospects for acceptance by states, respect for the norms stated and their interpretation. As the Government of Spain observed in the general context of UN treaty making, politicization of the negotiating process and inadequate preparation of the relevant texts help to explain "the legal inadequacies of many of the treaties adopted recently, a situation which in turn creates major problems in terms of the interpretation and application of such treaties."

A fresh look at the lawmaking structure of the United Nations is therefore needed. The recent beginning by the Sub-Commission on Prevention of Discrimination and Protection of Minorities (the Sub-Commission) of the examination of its role and its relationship with the Commission on Human Rights (the Commission) makes this inquiry particularly timely.

THE PRESENT STRUCTURE OF UN HUMAN RIGHTS LAWMAKING

In the United Nations, lawmaking in the human rights area is carried out by the General Assembly, the Economic and Social Council (ECOSOC) and the many subsidiary organs of these two principal organs, including the functional commissions of ECOSOC. The key provisions on human rights lawmaking are found in Articles 13 and 62 of the Charter of the United Nations, which suggest that the lawmaking powers of the General Assembly and ECOSOC are largely concurrent or shared, and, as regards the relationship between the General Assembly and ECOSOC, in Article 60. Although both the General Assembly and ECOSOC are mentioned in Article 7 as among the principal organs of the United Nations, ECOSOC's position is subordinate to that of the General Assembly.

The Charter empowers the General Assembly to exercise blanket authority over the lawmaking activities of the United Nations, but this power either has not been exercised or has not been exercised effectively. Rather than creating an effective infrastructure to carry out their lawmaking responsibilities, both the General Assembly, under Article 22 of the Charter, and ECOSOC, under Article 68, have established a plethora of standing and ad hoc bodies and entrusted them with the performance of human rights functions, including "legislative" activities.

Among those bodies, the Commission and the Sub-Commission enjoy particular importance in human rights lawmaking. The terms of reference of the Commission, as approved by ECOSOC in Resolution 5 (I) and amended by Resolution 9 (II), encompass the preparation of lawmaking human rights instruments. By Resolution 9 (II), ECOSOC authorized the Commission to call in ad hoc working groups of nongovernmental experts in specialized fields or individual experts, without further reference to the Council but with the approval of the Council's President and the Secretary General. While the Commission generally executes the directives of ECOSOC, on many occasions the General Assembly has addressed requests directly to the Commission, rather than through the Council. The Commission has been involved in the drafting of many human rights instruments. It is composed of 43 representatives of UN member states elected by ECOSOC on the basis of equitable geographical distribution.

ECOSOC resolutions provide that the Secretary-General shall consult with governments selected to serve on the Commission before the representatives are finally nominated by their governments and confirmed by the Council. The consultation with the Secretary-General, however, is routine. The original terms of reference of the Sub-Commission, as clarified and extended by the Commission in 1949, do not explicitly mention lawmaking. Yet both the Commission and ECOSOC may entrust the Sub Commission with lawmaking functions by specific resolutions. On many occasions the Commission has called on the Sub-Commission to prepare drafts of human rights instruments.

The Sub-Commission is composed of 26 members (and their alternates), who are elected by the Commission as individuals and not as representatives of states. Their selection is made in consultation with the Secretary-General and was originally subject to the consent of the governments of the states of which they were nationals. The latter requirement is now obsolete, however, since ECOSOC Resolution 1334 (XLIV) of May 31, 1968 provides for the nomination of experts by their governments.

The Commission and Sub-Commission perform other functions in addition to lawmaking, such as the preparation of studies and programs, and the consideration of violations. Thus, only part of their time, usually a small part, is devoted to lawmaking. Both bodies devote the major portion of their time to studying particular violations of human rights and situations prevailing in countries accused of infringing human rights.

However, the preponderance of studies of human rights violations over lawmaking does not appear to reflect a deliberate decision that, at the present stage of development of the law, the former are more important than the latter; rather, it is explained by their greater urgency, as well as by the time constraints on the Commission. Although the international community may have passed the zenith of its lawmaking activity, at least insofar as broadly oriented global instruments focusing on civil and political rights are concerned, work on such subjects as, among others, rights of the child is continuing and new subjects are coming to the fore, especially in the economic and social fields. The need for disciplined and informed lawmaking is thus as great as ever.

In addition to "standard setting," the Sub-Commission deals with various studies, considers gross violations of human rights in accordance with Resolution 8 (XXIII) of the Commission and ECOSOC Resolution 1235 (XXLII), and handles communications under the procedure established by ECOSOC Resolution 1503 (XLVIII). The Sub-Commission sends missions to various areas in which human rights are threatened. It adopts "rather hurriedly a large number of resolutions," particularly on the situation in countries where gross violations of human rights are occurring. Because so much of the Sub-Commission's work is related neither to discrimination nor to protection of minorities, it has been suggested that its name be changed to "Committee of Experts on Human Rights."

A perusal of the documents of the Sub-Commission, including the annotated agenda for its 1984 session, and my own observation of the Sub-Commission's work during that session reveal that little time and little priority are given to its lawmaking role. With the encouragement of the Commission, the Sub-Commission is now reviewing its role, decision-making processes, agenda, rationalization of work and relationship with the Commission. In acknowledgment of the low priority now accorded to lawmaking, suggestions "that the drafting of norms should be one of its priorities" have been advanced. In a candid and thoughtful statement before the Working Group on the Review of the Work of the Sub-Commission, Dr. Kurt Herndl, the Assistant Secretary-General for Human Rights, argued the need to consider the Sub-Commission's methods of preparing standards:

In the earlier years of the Sub-Commission standards were prepared with much deliberation. They usually were a direct follow-up to a study and were often based on the study's conclusions. Nowadays, draft standards may be proposed by one or more individual members of the Sub-Commission, appended to a resolution, sometimes discussed by a working group, and then sent by the Sub-Commission to the Commission. Would there not seem to be some need for better procedures and organization in this area? Dr. Herndl also called for rationalization of the Sub-Commission's procedure for selecting and preparing studies, a matter of importance in the present context since studies frequently lead to lawmaking projects.

The quality of the members of the Commission and Sub-Commission is a significant factor in the success or lack of success of their work. Alluding to the practice of many governments of designating as their representatives on the Commission persons possessing special competence in human rights, the United States Government observed, correctly, that "such representatives have been able to make the most significant contributions to the Commission's work." Clearly, the fact that the Commission initially had as members' persons of the caliber of René Cassin and Eleanor Roosevelt is an important reason for the speedy adoption of a truly remarkable instrument: the Universal Declaration of Human Rights. But the overall experience with regard to the quality of representatives on the Commission is not reassuring, since some states appoint representatives who lack the necessary expertise and standing.

The Commission is not only a political organ, composed of representatives of states, but also a politicized one. The Sub-

Commission, of course, is composed of experts, but their quality is uneven. There is some evidence of its growing politicization as well." One should not lose sight of the fact that human rights lawmaking is also carried out outside the Commission and the Sub-Commission. Thus, the important Convention on the Elimination of All Forms of Discrimination Against Women was elaborated largely by the Commission on the Status of Women, another functional commission of ECOSOC, composed of 32 representatives of member states.

Some lawmaking projects are undertaken by the General Assembly itself without any serious preparatory work by more expert organs. For example, the new UN Convention on the Protection of the Rights of All Migrant Workers and Their Families is being drafted by the General Assembly despite the greater expertise and considerable achievements of the International Labor Organization (ILO) in this area. Such work is carried out at the United Nations by an open-ended working group of delegates to the General Assembly; the process exemplifies the drafting of human rights instruments by generalists, rather than by experts. Through another open-ended working group, the General Assembly is also considering the elaboration of a declaration on the human rights of individuals who are not citizens of the country in which they live.

It should not be assumed, however, that a generalist governmental representative is necessarily incompetent. Talented academics, parliamentarians, lawyers and members of women's organizations, among others, have served on the Third Committee and other organs composed of representatives of governments; but this is not enough to guarantee the necessary "legislative" skill when the initial draft is not prepared by experts. While national lawmakers may not always be well qualified, they are usually assisted by governmental and legislative experts and function in a more structured setting.

Although the General Assembly often performs elaborate and complex drafting functions, such an organ is not well equipped to prepare a good text on the basis of many, sometimes conflicting proposals. For the most part, the General

Assembly can effectively deal with the adoption of multilateral instruments if the draft does not require much additional revision or negotiation before its adoption. Some topics, however, because of their highly political content, may require a greater degree of involvement by governments throughout the lawmaking process. In such cases, it might be necessary to call upon the General Assembly, which is an appropriate body for negotiation and the formation of a consensus.

While conferences of plenipotentiaries may also be hampered by the difficulty inherent in a broad membership, their rules of procedure, working methods and available time appear to be better suited to lawmaking than those of main committees of the General Assembly. Of course, the contents of the instruments reflect the parameters of political consensus. But the technical quality of the instruments often falls short even of the reach of political consensus (where there have been deficient drafting, inconsistencies as between different provisions of the same instrument, gaps, overlap or conflicts between instruments).

Problems of particular concern are the frequent lack of adequate research prior to the decision to initiate the lawmaking process and inadequate supporting research throughout that process. However, these problems are not limited to human rights. The Legal Counsel of the United Nations has complained that the time left to the Secretariat for study and research in the codification and progressive development of international law "has dwindled almost to a vanishing point."

Whether there is a need for an instrument and what form this instrument should take, i.e., a treaty or a declaration, are often insufficiently considered. Texts are frequently drawn up by representative organs with a large membership, without the benefit of a carefully formulated initial draft prepared by experts. There is inadequate resort to Special Rapporteurs, drafting committees and expert working groups.

The process suffers from lack of direction and structure. Authority is dispersed among many bodies. While several organs are involved in the drafting of human rights instruments, not a single organ is engaged exclusively in lawmaking. Organs that specialize in human rights devote the bulk of their time to "non-legislative" work. The center of gravity of the Sub-Commission as well as of the Commission has shifted from lawmaking to other activities, especially the consideration of gross violations of human rights.

ALTERNATIVE LAWMAKING MODELS

In considering possible reforms of lawmaking in the human rights field, it may be worthwhile to take a brief look at some other models of lawmaking. In the United Nations, three areas are particularly instructive: outer space treaties, international trade law and the general lawmaking activities of the International Law Commission. For the preparation of treaties regulating activities in outer space, a structured procedure has been developed by the Committee on the Peaceful Uses of Outer Space and its Legal Sub-Committee.

This process is characterized by the successive consideration of texts by a working group of the Legal Sub-Committee, the Legal Sub-Committee itself and the committee, all of which are composed of members from the same 53 states, and finally by a main committee of the General Assembly (at present, the Special Political Committee). The report of each organ to the next senior one record problems and progress. The treaty is eventually adopted and opened for signature by the General Assembly. In the drafting process, the working group is sometimes assisted by a drafting committee, as is the committee itself when completing preparation of a particular text.

The procedures of the United Nations Commission on International Trade Law (UNCITRAL) are regular and relatively structured. The usual practice is to request the Secretariat to prepare studies on the issues pertaining to the adoption of a proposed convention. UNCITRAL has adopted the salutary policy of referring a subject matter to a working group only "after preparatory studies... have been made by the Secretariat and the consideration of these studies by the

Commission have indicated not only that the subject-matter is a suitable one in the context of the unification and harmonization of a law, but that the preparatory work is sufficiently advanced."

When UNCITRAL decides that a particular subject merits further study, possibly with a view to the preparation of a treaty, it assigns the subject to a working group. While UNCITRAL is composed of representatives of 36 governments, not of experts elected in their individual capacities, states are encouraged to send representatives who are experts in the field to each working group. Working groups are central to UNCITRAL's functioning. They benefit from the constant input of research by the Secretariat and comments by governments.

The Secretariat's background studies analyze various questions, as requested by the working group, examine the existing law, highlight problems and suggest ways of harmonizing or unifying the law. They often contain draft provisions intended to facilitate the efforts of the working group. At various stages of the working group's endeavors, the Secretariat circulates questionnaires to all states and interested organizations soliciting comments and suggestions for consideration by the working group. In addition, working groups establish drafting committees to recommend the text of the draft provisions and their place in the draft treaty.

When the draft treaty reaches an advanced stage, the working group often requests the Secretariat to prepare an explanatory memorandum on the draft treaty, which is intended to aid the working group but not to constitute an official commentary. A careful editorial review is undertaken and a final text is prepared for submission to UNCITRAL. The draft text as approved by the working group is circulated to governments and interested organizations, together with a commentary. At the final stages, it is considered by UNCITRAL with the assistance of a drafting committee.

The revised text is submitted by UNCITRAL to the General Assembly with the recommendation that a diplomatic conference be convened to adopt the draft convention.

Lawmaking by the International Law Commission (ILC), a body of 34 experts elected by the General Assembly upon nomination by governments, is characterized by the recourse to one expert for the basic preparatory work through the use of a special rapporteur, the subsequent careful scrutiny of the successive drafts, the progressive and gradual elaboration of texts with constant input from governments and organizations until the texts are ready for adoption, and the careful recording of the preparatory work, which is crucial to the proper study of the legislative histories and interpretation of the text.

Normally, the principal stages in the ILC's work are: the appointment of a special rapporteur; the preparation of a special report or series of reports (which contain analyses, draft articles and commentaries); the consideration of these reports by the ILC at several readings; the formulation and emendation of texts by drafting committees, which play a central role; the assignment of various tasks to the Secretariat; the input of governmental comments on the evolving texts, through written observations and debate in the Sixth Committee of the General Assembly; and the convening by the General Assembly of a diplomatic conference that would use the articles adopted by the ILC as the basis for discussion, or the adoption of the articles by the Assembly itself.

When the ILC submits final articles on a given subject to the General Assembly, it also submits a commentary on them and a recommendation on whether they should form the basis of a convention. The General Assembly is thus called upon to decide whether or not such a convention should be concluded, and, if so, what organ should be entrusted with the task. The General Assembly, through the Sixth (Legal) Committee, has adopted several conventions on the basis of articles adopted by the ILC, but far more have been adopted by conferences convened by the Assembly.

The primary reasons for the success of the ILC drafts lie in the procedure followed and, as one commentary has suggested, in the independent expert character as well as in the superior scholarship of its members. The fact that the ILC has included some of the leading international lawyers and has benefited from the services of several outstanding Special Rapporteurs has helped to build up support for the drafts it has prepared. "Negotiations between states which were based on a draft prepared by the Commission have been... more successful than those which began without a first draft, or where the first draft was negotiated by state representatives."

Outside the United Nations, the ILO procedure for the adoption of conventions and recommendations by the International Labor Conference deserves interest because of its proven effectiveness and highly structured character. Although this procedure is rooted in the statutory provisions of the ILO and in its tripartite character, there is no reason why some of its features could not inspire appropriate reforms in UN human rights lawmaking.

The lawmaking experience of the Council of Europe, which is characterized by the formulation of draft texts by small committees of governmental experts with the assistance of the secretariat, also merits attention. The Council of Europe has taken a methodical approach towards carefully expanding the political and civil rights stated in the European Convention for the Protection of Human Rights and Fundamental Freedoms by a series of protocols, of which Protocols Nos. 6, 7 and 8 are the most recent. Through this process, some important protections, including those inspired by several substantive provisions of the International Covenant on Civil and Political Rights, have been incorporated in the additional protocols.

The Council of Europe has encountered greater difficulties, however, in trying to identify economic, social and cultural rights that might be included in another additional protocol to the European Convention. The United Nations should emulate the example of the Council of Europe and regard the task of human rights lawmaking not as an operation designed to produce a particular instrument, but as a continuing process, which includes extension, elaboration, consolidation and revision. The work begun on the possible elaboration of a Second Optional Protocol to the International

Covenant on Civil and Political Rights, aiming at the Abolition of the Death Penalty points in the right direction.

PROPOSED REFORMS

To rationalize the adoption of so called new rights, Philip Alston has recently proposed a set of procedures involving the Secretariat, the General Assembly and the Commission. Such procedures would indeed be useful and could also be applied to rights not regarded as new. It is far from certain, however, that the General Assembly would have the necessary incentive to adopt such procedures. It is even more doubtful whether the General Assembly and other organs would have the self-discipline to follow such a procedure as long as the existing framework for human rights lawmaking is not modified. Procedures operate best when they are tied to institutional arrangements, as in the area of outer space law or international trade law where lawmaking organs have been established.

What is needed is an organ that would devote its entire time to, and specialize exclusively in, human rights lawmaking. Future lawmaking activity should be concentrated in such an organ, a UN Human Rights Law Commission (UNHRLC), which would function according to well defined, structured processes particularly suitable for human rights, a broad, but nevertheless specialized, field. The lawmaking processes would gain in efficiency, and the instruments in quality.

The creation of a single expert body would not mean that that body would necessarily monopolize lawmaking activity in the field of human rights, any more than the ILC monopolizes lawmaking in other areas of international law. But the UNHRLC should be entrusted, at least, with the drafting of major instruments of general interest. It may be possible and even desirable from time to time to refer a particular subject to a different, perhaps ad hoc organ, especially where the subject requires particular expertise, or to a broadly representative political organ if it is politically very sensitive.

To paraphrase Professor Schachter's discussion of the ILC, when the objectives are not well agreed and the technical issues do not fall within the purview of the general international lawyer, there may be good reason to have recourse to a more specialized body in which the particular subject can be handled by technical experts, govern mental officials and lawyers knowledgeable in the field. In the present state of human rights law, much of the work of the UNHRLC would be devoted to progressive development rather than codification. However, the UNHRLC could also be charged with the preparation of drafts consolidating, improving and revising some of the instruments that have already been adopted.

This would include filling lacunae and improving the implementation clauses. When one considers how many instruments have already been adopted, the tasks of revision and consolidation, and in some cases of extending rights by drafting additional protocols to the major human rights treaties as in the Council of Europe, take on special importance. It might be possible to restructure the present Commission and Sub Commission and carve out the new lawmaking organ from them. But aside from the lawmaking activities of these organs, their present form and mandates might better be left unaltered.

Their agenda is demanding enough without lawmaking, especially if it is recalled that their mandate under resolutions adopted by the General Assembly and ECOSOC extends to all the member states of the United Nations and not only, as is the case with organs established by various human rights treaties, to state parties to particular instruments. Of course, the Commission and the Sub-Commission could also benefit from reform. The Sub-Commission has begun to review its role on an excessively timid note. Let us hope that this examination develops into a significant critique and, eventually, reform.

Leaving aside for a moment the question of the UNHRLC's composition, I will focus first on the process to be followed. There should be prior discussion at the political level, normally by the General Assembly, and sometimes possibly by ECOSOC, of the need to initiate the lawmaking process. Some general guidelines might be adopted at this time. To be well informed, the participants in the preliminary discussion should usually have at their disposal prior studies carried out by the Secretariat or outside experts. The preparatory work would include canvassing the membership and interested organizations by means of detailed questionnaires.

Before deciding to start working on an instrument, states should have a clear perception of the need for it and its feasibility. Another question that merits consideration at an early stage of the lawmaking process is the form appropriate to an instrument, i.e., whether it should be a binding agreement or a recommendation. In some circumstances, it might be desirable to start work on two parallel instruments, one binding, the other recommendatory, as in the ILO. The decision as to the type of instrument might have to be reconsidered as more is learned about the problems and the limits of state support for, and interest in, the new instrument.

In the elaboration of the instruments, the UNHRLC would be given constant research support by the Secretariat. The UNHRLC would model its work, mutatis mutandis, on the procedures of the ILC, and perhaps, when useful, would borrow some procedural ideas from UNCITRAL, or from other bodies. The UNHRLC should not, however, slavishly follow the ILC model. It should guard against such undesirable features as the undue fragmentation that results from discussing the draft articles over the course of many sessions, and the slow pace characteristic of the ILC.

There should be constant resort to rapporteurs, drafting committees, researchers and governments for comments. A single person, however, would have primary responsibility for preparing the first draft. The evolving texts would then be subjected to a fixed number of readings by the UNHRLC according to a predetermined timetable. When the drafting and editing are completed, the instrument would be submitted to a representative organ for adoption; it must be clear that the UNHRLC's role would be limited to formulating the text of the instrument.

As a general but not inflexible rule, major instruments would be submitted to conferences of plenipotentiaries for adoption, after a decision by the General Assembly. Such conferences would have more time, more expertise and more appropriate working methods than the General Assembly for the negotiation and adoption of human rights instruments. The General Assembly should be given the task of adopting a human rights instrument only if the draft approved by the UNHRLC, in view of both its content and the political context, seems likely to be adopted without prolonged negotiations and major revisions.

When a text is submitted to the General Assembly for adoption, the Sixth Committee could be involved usefully either by the referral of some matters to it by the Third Committee, or by the creation of a joint committee constituted of these two main committees or by the formation of a working group drawn from their members. The General Assembly ought to consider reviewing Annex II to its Rules of Procedure, "Methods and Procedures of the General Assembly for Dealing with Legal and Drafting Questions," which inadequately addresses human rights lawmaking, and drawing up more effective rules for its adoption of human rights instruments.

To ensure that the new scheme of things meets with success, adequate and efficient resources must be created in the Centre for Human Rights of the UN Secretariat. Such resources might make it possible to institute "pre-initiation" studies, as practiced by the ILO where they are statutorily required. The UNHRLC will also need strong support from the Secretariat when the preparatory studies are carried out by independent experts or Special Rapporteurs (unless they can call upon their national governments for help, a practice that is not always in the best interest of the international community). At present, it is unrealistic to expect the Centre for Human Rights to be able to respond to the proliferating requests for in-depth background research and studies.

One facet of the process that cries for improvement is the recording of the preparatory work for the instruments. A strengthened Secretariat could prepare analytical collections of records, as was done, inter alia, for the Vienna Convention on

Diplomatic Relations, the Vienna Convention on Consular Relations and the Vienna Convention on the Law of Treaties, but not for even the most important instruments in the human rights field. This is not to suggest that official explanatory memorandums on the various instruments should be prepared for adoption by the conferences that are to adopt the texts of the instruments, as this course of action would pose serious problems.

Rather, means for improving access to the records of preparatory work should be created. The UNHRLC should prepare commentaries on the draft articles that it adopts, following the pattern established by the ILC. Such commentaries would aid the plenipotentiary conferences or the General Assembly in considering the text for adoption and would constitute an important resource for the interpretation of the instruments. However, they would not be approved formally by these bodies and would not acquire the status of an authoritative commentary.

Let us now turn to the composition and character of the UNHRLC. The body should be relatively small, preferably smaller than the ILC. Like the Commission on Human Rights, it would be elected by ECOSOC and constitute another functional commission of that organ. The basic choice appears to be between an organ of representatives of states, such as the Legal Sub-Committee of the Committee on the Peaceful Uses of Outer Space or UNCITRAL, and a committee of experts elected in their individual capacity, such as the ILC, the Human Rights Committee established under Article 28 of the Political Covenant, the Committee on the Elimination of Racial Discrimination established under Article 8 of the International Convention on the Elimination of All Forms of Racial Discrimination, the Committee on the Elimination of Discrimination Against Women established under Article 17 of the Convention on the Elimination of All Forms of Discrimination Against Women, and the Committee Against Torture established under Article 17 of the recently adopted Convention Against Torture and Other Cruel, Inhuman or Degrading Treatment or Punishment.

While the latter pattern is clearly preferable because it creates better prospects for a high degree of expertise and continuity, and a lesser involvement in politics to regard the establishment of an organ composed of governmental experts as necessarily calamitous. The experience with UNCITRAL and the Council of Europe has shown that when governments are interested enough in influencing the formulation of an instrument they find important, they can and do appoint competent experts. Hence, the careful selection of experts is essential.

Moreover, any independent observer of the United Nations cannot avoid becoming increasingly cynical about the independence from their governments of individually elected experts from many member states, especially serving officials of government ministries and state institutions. Nor is the procedure of electing individual experts a guarantee of their professional competence. The crucial point, therefore, is not that members be elected in their individual capacity, but that they are genuine experts.

Those advocating that even the preliminary formulation of UN treaties should be entrusted to governmental representatives argue that this would ensure greater sensitivity to political consideration and a more reliable assessment of the support by states for a new instrument. Obviously, draft texts have to stand the test of acceptance by states. I am not suggesting that human rights lawmaking could or should be apolitical, for lawmaking is a political process. The Secretary-General of the United Nations himself has emphasized that the ILC does not stand aloof from political realities.

While excessive politicization of human rights lawmaking should be avoided, the prospects for de-politicizing United Nations human rights activities in general are unrealistic, as recently demonstrated by Professor Franck. What is needed urgently is a better balance between the participation of experts and of generalist diplomats. In any event, the political perspective would be provided constantly by governmental comments, guidelines and instructions from the political organs, and the knowledge of UNHRLC members that their drafts would be submitted for adoption to the political organs. The fact that human rights lawmaking occurs largely in the domain of progressive development should not make the preparation of drafts any less appropriate for a group of individual experts.

The Secretary-General's recent Report on the Work of the Organization calls upon member states to "give serious thought to the best way of doing business" and to examine "existing United Nations practices and consider ways and means to make them more effective in dealing with gross violations of human rights wherever they occur." This challenge also merits acceptance in the field of lawmaking. The proposal to establish the UNHRLC is likely to be greeted with skepticism, well justified no doubt, about the prospects for reform. It will be said that the United Nations already suffers from a proliferation of organs and that there is no guarantee that the UNHRLC would meet with our hopes and expectations if it were established.

Yet the subject of human rights lawmaking is crucial, the present system inadequate, and reforms needed. The academic community therefore has both the moral and the professional obligation to lead the way, to suggest reforms and to work for their adoption. Are human rights less important than the fields in which the United Nations has established better structures and procedures for lawmaking?

THE DECLARATION

Foremost in our minds was the knowledge that the tyranny of rulers and the technology of warfare can unleash an unprecedented capacity to hurt, maim and destroy. We vowed never to allow that to happen ever again. As one undivided and indivisible family, we vowed together to uphold the sanctity of the human person, to promote human rights, and to protect man and woman from every force that would violate their beings.

DRAFTING THE DECLARATION

Drafting the Universal Declaration on Human Rights was a difficult undertaking. As a member of the very first

Commission of Human Rights, the Philippines takes pride in its role in formulating the Universal Declaration. The Philippine delegation - led by General Carlos P. Romulo - explained the Draft Declaration thus:

"The primary purpose of the Declaration is not simply to achieve a moral success, but to enable man, all over the world to develop his rights and, in consequence, his personality. It is essential that he should feel confident that the executive, legislative and judicial powers could not impair his fundamental rights."

In the final debate before action was taken at the Plenary of the General Assembly, General Romulo noted:

"The United Nations has been on trial for its life, and it is at this very moment that it has justified its existence before an anxious world by producing the Declaration."

In the end, despite the divergence of views, the world acted with resolve, found common ground and adopted the Declaration during the 3rd General Assembly.

CONTINUING AND EMERGING CHALLENGES

Sixty years later, we find ourselves in a world drastically changed yet ironically the same in many respects. We have clearly advanced in upholding, protecting and promoting human rights. But we continue to face both traditional and new challenges to human rights. Non-state forces such as terrorist gangs -preying on ignorance and poverty-wreak havoc on innocent populations, violating their basic human right to live in peace. But our resolve remains firm: We must continue to move on in our common cause.

THE PHILIPPINE RESOLVE

We are proud that the Philippines itself has made steady progress in upholding, protecting, and promoting human rights. Our democracy - the oldest in Asia - was founded on the sanctity of human life and the dignity of the human person. We have abolished capital punishment. We protect the life of the unborn.

We have kept alive our tradition of political liberties by strengthening democratic institutions and processes that make our Government representative, limited and accountable.

We are working with our people - within Government and with civil society - and with the international community to advance human rights. Already, we have strengthened the capacities and capabilities of our agencies to protect and promote human rights. The Philippines is one of the few countries to have ratified all seven core international human-rights treaties. We also signed the Second Optional Protocol to the International Covenant on Civil and Political Rights. We completed and submitted our periodic reports under the Convention on Migrant Workers, the Convention Against Torture and the Convention on the Rights of the Child.

We are prepared for the Universal Periodic Review and the national human rights action plan. We are also prepared for the periodic review under the Optional Protocol on Children in Armed Conflict, the Convention of the Rights of the Child, as well as the Convention on Economic, Social and Cultural Rights.

TOGETHER, BROADENING HUMAN RIGHTS PROTECTION

Beyond our borders, we work with our partners in Southeast Asia to broaden the frontiers of human rights protection and to reinforce our shared commitment to uphold human rights. ASEAN signed its landmark Charter this year in Singapore. But before ASEAN could breathe life into this historic document, and give birth to a regional human rights mechanism, it is the Philippines' stand that protection and promotion of human rights should be at the heart of every member's commitment to the Charter.

The Philippines will continue to articulate this position. An area of particular interest to ASEAN - in the regional and global context - is the protection of the rights of vulnerable groups such as women, children and migrant workers. In our collective march to growth and development, we must not leave behind the weak and the defenseless.

We followed through this commitment during the 12th ASEAN Summit in Cebu:

ASEAN members agreed to extend assistance to ASEAN nationals in distress in third countries.

To bolster global efforts to give sustained attention to these vulnerable groups, the Philippines encourages the extension of the mandates of the Special Rapporteur on Trafficking in Persons, especially Women and Children, and the Special Rapporteur on the Human Rights of Migrants. We must also redouble our efforts to understand the impact of globalization on the individual human being.

As host of the 2nd Global Forum on Migration and Development this October, the Philippines take this opportunity to invite you all to attend. Another Philippine initiative, Interfaith Dialogue, is drawing wide and enthusiastic support from the international community. Even as we seek to promote dialogue between peoples of different creeds, faiths and religions, we underscore the commonalities that bind us into a single, indivisible human family.

Meaningful dialogue proceeds from awareness and understanding of what is inherent in all of us - our human rights. Our human rights are both our bond and our weapon against the extremism espoused by terrorists. We urge our partners to join us in this endeavor to promote Interfaith Dialogue.

TOWARDS A STRONGER, MORE RELEVANT HRC

The Human Rights Council is the most important international forum to breathe renewed life to the global efforts to protect, promote and uphold human rights. Membership in the Council is an honor and a responsibility. The Philippines is keenly aware of the confidence reposed on us by the community of nations. We thank you all for electing us to another term.

The Philippines is among the pioneer countries that will evaluate and be evaluated by the Universal Periodic Review. We repose great hope in the Universal Periodic Review or UPR. In its success, we hope to find the basis for international cooperation in promoting and protecting human rights. The UPR and its recommendations should prove crucial in enhancing the capacities of nations to fulfill their human rights obligations.

The process will prepare a national human rights action plan that sets standards for achieving human rights objectives and identifying the means of accomplishing them. Hence the UPR should be an instrument for cohesion and not a device for increasing tensions between member-countries. The full development of the human person is the main objective for our human rights efforts.

Six decades after the Universal Declaration was adopted, our world continues to face challenges to the universal protection and promotion of human rights. We have made significant strides-yet we have a great deal more to do. The Human Rights Council should bring us together, as one global community engaged in a common cause. To commemorate and promote the Universal Declaration, the Philippine Government pledges to donate to the Special Fund of the Office of the High Commissioner for Human Rights.

Sixty years ago, we responded to the challenge of protecting human rights with our collective resolve in adopting the Universal Declaration. That same passion and resolve we carry in our hearts and minds today. With human rights at the center of our synergy of interaction, we should not-we shall not-fail.

OMBUDSPERSON FOR THE UNITED NATIONS

In recent years, the UN has assumed a widening scope of responsibilities and has gradually been transformed from an intergovernmental organization to a global governance mechanism with an ever greater direct impact on individuals. This entails that the UN is also, in principle, capable of violating human rights and occasionally does so in different operational contexts. While this has raised demands for greater UN accountability, Hoffmann and Megret argue that the existing institutional mechanisms do not allow the UN to respond to these adequately.

They then explore the contribution that a UN-wide ombudsperson could make to the objective of fostering UN accountability. Ombudspersons have become recognized almost universally as an indispensable good governance mechanism, and the creation of ombudsperson institutions in peacekeeping contexts, which may theoretically scrutinize the UN's own actions, shows that the time may be ripe for a more ambitious proposal. They conclude by outlining a few concrete suggestions as to how a UN-wide ombudsperson could work and how such an institution could be created.

The UN is involved in more activities than it ever has been. By and large, it is probably fair to say that its engagement has helped to improve many often intractable situations around the world. However, the UN has certainly not been immune to failures. Of course, some of these are bound to arise when it comes to an organization that is, after all, expected to deal with a wide range of the world's problems. Yet there is an increasing number of such failures that cannot easily be blamed on the imperfect structure of international society and that would seem to exceed the limits of the UN's political and operational fallibility, properly understood. These are failures that are directly attributable to incapacity on the part of the UN to live up to its own standards, particularly those standards that have been at the heart of its activities, namely human rights.

This occasional incapacity is in itself potentially very damaging to the UN's credibility. But it has only been made worse by the UN's failure to respond adequately to the question of accountability. In this chapter, we propose to examine the contribution that the creation of a UN system-wide ombudsperson could make to improve the UN's human rights accountability record.

THE ACCOUNTABILITY PROBLEMATIQUE

Before we address some of the specific institutional forms that accountability might take, it is important to understand that accountability is essentially a demand, made by civil society in general, for the UN to be more responsive to complaints about the consequences of its actions. This demand covers a wide range of alleged UN shortcomings. At one end are some of the UN's "structural failings." Srebrenica and Rwanda, in particular, stand out as striking cases where the UN's lack of political will and its operational meekness led to catastrophic consequences for entire populations. In situations where the UN had effectively undertaken to protect civilians, its incapacity to back promises by force led to what are arguably some of the worst stains on the organization's record.

However, the UN's accountability problems are not confined to the structural level. On a much smaller scale, the UN has not escaped criticism for some of the more significant negative side effects of its activities. Peace operations, because of their breadth and because they involve the use of force, were an early case in point. Already during the UN operation in the Republic of Congo, for example, concerns were raised about the possibility that troops operating under UN command had violated international humanitarian law.

Even in the context of lower-key peacekeeping missions, and aside from routine problems concerning compensation for use or destruction of property or accusations of drug trafficking and black marketeering, UN Blue Helmets have not escaped accusations of occasional grave wrongdoing. In one notorious case, three members of an elite Canadian paratroopers regiment were photographed smiling next to the blood-drenched body of a tied-up Somali, leading to charges of acts of barbarity and torture. Similar accusations later surfaced concerning Italian and Belgian troops.

UN Protection Force (UNPROFOR) peacekeepers were also reported to have gravely misbehaved in a hospital they were guarding in central Bosnia. After a string of incidents in Cambodia, Bosnia, Macedonia, Mozambique, West Africa, the Democratic Republic of Congo, and Eritrea, and following the publication of several UN reports, it has emerged that rape, child prostitution, and the trafficking of women are a common consequence of the deployment of peacekeeping troops and civilian police forces in many operational theaters. The problem has assumed even wider proportions in cases where the UN is entrusted with the administration of entire territories. Indeed, in both Kosovo and East Timor, despite UN international administrations' remarkable achievements there, UN police forces, for example, have been accused of brutality and illegal detention.

The UN Mission in Kosovo (UNMIK) administration, in particular, has been accused of authoritarian behavior and of ignoring the decisions of courts, an attitude that prompted the Organization for Security and Cooperation in Europe (OSCE) to note that the applicable domestic and international law "is almost universally ignored in Kosovo." Moreover, UN international administrations have generally been described as unresponsive to calls for participation by the local population in decisions affecting its future.

However, peace operations are probably only the tip of the iceberg, the most obvious manifestation of a growing accountability problem at the UN. There are many less prominent operational areas in which previously "submerged" accountability shortcomings have recently been brought to the surface. One example is the management of international criminal tribunals. Here, the UN International Criminal Tribunal for Rwanda has, in particular, come under substantial criticism for repeated failures to respect the rights of the accused and to compensate adequately when such abuses became clear.

Another instance of an unexpected accountability void is the international refugee regime. Although the recent "sex-for-aid" scandal in Sierra Leone now appears to have been exaggerated, concerns about the failure of the UN High Commissioner for Refugees (UNHCR) to guarantee human rights in the refugee camps under its control are not new and raise similar questions of UN accountability. Finally, there have also been complaints, even if on a smaller scale, in a number of other areas of UN activity, including humanitarian assistance, development aid, and health administration.

It is apparent that the accountability problematique applies to a wide range of UN activities and covers a variety of problems, from political negligence to outright human rights violations.

These are normally treated as distinct issues in what is, on the whole, a very scarce literature on the topic. Yet, following a more ambitious approach that we sketched out in a previous publication, we propose to deal here with the UN's various accountability incidents as part of a larger genus of problems.

Indeed, the emergence of the UN's accountability problem may be seen more generally as a consequence of the gradual transformation of the UN from a predominantly intergovernmental organization into a global governance institution, a transformation that, in a context of crumbling or fragilized state institutions, is making the UN come increasingly face to face with the people it is ultimately meant to benefit. Therefore, at the heart of this problematique lies the issue of the UN's responsiveness.

THE UN'S RESPONSE

Traditionally, diplomatic immunity bestowed on many UN employees and special arrangements with troop- and personnel-contributing states, not to mention mere indifference, have been seen as a barrier to a more proactive engagement on the part of the UN. The UN's typical response to the problems mentioned above has been to call for improved and broader training, to issue codes of conduct and guidelines, or to carry out lessons-learned exercises.

For example, after the refugee scandal in western Africa, the Inter-Agency Standing Committee (IASC) went so far as to set up a task force that adopted a Plan of Action on Protection from Sexual Exploitation and Abuse in Humanitarian Crises.

Although all these steps may represent significant progress toward mainstreaming human rights into the UN, they have essentially been soft, preventive measures. As such, although they might trigger awareness of potential human rights problems, they are insufficient in terms of ensuring human rights compliance by UN personnel in future missions and of providing concrete and effective remedies for past abuses. As one report put it, in the context of the protection of children in peace operations, "Codes of conduct and specialized training do not seem to address the problem adequately.... Perceptions based on an eroded status... for children will not be erased by a few hours or even days of human rights training. This suggests that... stricter preventive and punitive measures may be the only solution."

Admittedly, since episodes such as those in Somalia, the UN has become more sensitive to the need to show signs that it is responsive to demands for accountability in the particular context of peace operations. Both the Security Council and the General Assembly have directly addressed such issues as the special vulnerability of women, children, and refugees in peacekeeping contexts. In recent cases of sexual misconduct by the UN Transitional Administration in East Timor (UNTAET) police officers and the UN-sanctioned International Force for East Timor (INTERFET) soldiers, UN officials have made it clear that the perpetrators will not enjoy immunity. The UN has repeatedly called on troop-contributing states to vigorously investigate and prosecute all allegations of human rights violations by peacekeepers and to report their findings back to the UN.

Still, the fact that new incidents have occurred since Somalia shows that the problem is likely to persist. The UN, for its part, has continued to display a somewhat ambiguous attitude toward its own accountability. For instance, often it has acted as if sending soldiers home or expelling staff-assuming such minimal measures are taken are an effective substitute for a proper accountability policy. The logic behind such thinking seems to be that if responsibility for wrongdoing can be traced to individuals, then the UN itself cannot possibly be to blame. Yet such an implicit externalization of responsibility conveniently avoids the fact that in most (if not all) cases, abuses are also attributable, at least in part, to failures in recruitment, training, or oversight by the UN. Hence, there is a strong case to be made in favor of the UN shouldering responsibility commensurate with its role.

Peace operations are complicated by the presence of an intervening variable-the troop-contributing state. The UN's typical response when specific problems arise has been to hide behind standard status-of-forces agreements (SOFAs), which specify that contributing states retain exclusive jurisdiction over their military. As UN spokesman Fred Eckhard put it in relation to the problems experienced during the Somalia mission, "Ultimately, when something goes wrong, the United Nations, under its arrangement with troop contributing countries, does not have the authority to discipline troops."

There are several problems with this state of affairs, the most notorious being that, although the secretary-general has recommended that the Security Council ask states to follow up on relevant investigations, under the present conditions the UN basically forfeits any leverage to ensure that these investigations are conducted. Most importantly, however, the problem with this approach is that even if the investigations launched by states were always adequate which they are not-it misses the point that state responsibility does not and should not exclude a residual UN accountability for the acts of those serving in its name, above and independent from the accountability of states. After all, it is not as if the UN does not have the power to minimally monitor the human rights compliance of its military deployments. Moreover, peacekeepers are serving under the UN flag and, for most purposes, will be perceived as representing the UN.

On the face of it, there are signs that some things may be changing. On learning of the accusations in Somalia, Kofi Annan, in a move that seemed designed to take at least partial responsibility for the acts of UN troops, insisted that "every possible effort will be made on the part of the United Nations to ensure that such incidents do not recur." After realizing that "avenues of recourse for beneficiaries are practically nonexistent," both the Office of Internal Oversight Services and the Inter-Agency Standing Committee have recommended that an "independent reporting procedure to reach into the refugee camps and communities" be established.

At times, the UN has even endorsed what looks like a more ambitious approach to the accountability problematique. For example, in the case of Rwanda and Srebrenica, the

Security Council created two commissions, which issued landmark reports examining the UN's role in allowing these tragedies to occur. These were clearly important and innovative steps to foster a culture of accountability throughout the UN. Yet there remain significant shortcomings with such initiatives: they are often very general exercises that usually stop short of naming people: they often conspicuously lack a framework to allow for direct victim involvement, thus minimizing the benefits of accountability as a fundamentally inclusionary concept; and the existence of formal mechanisms in some cases but not others begs the question of arbitrariness-if these, why not others?

Indeed, there seem to be significant disadvantages to the ad hoc nature implicit in the UN's response to date. First, there is a risk that accountability problems will be politically minimized by being reduced to isolated instances when, as argued here, they may be part of a more general trend. Second, potential institutional synergies are not exploited, and the effectiveness of any ad hoc measures is usually not monitored centrally across the system, so that few general "lessons" are actually learned. Third, less obvious abuses will easily fall through such an ad hoc accountability net, even though they may be, in aggregate, no less damaging than the more obvious scandals that attract the media's attention. Overall, therefore, the UN's accountability policy is vulnerable to the double criticism that it has been both insufficiently hard-headed and excessively haphazard when what is really needed is a more systematic and sustained effort to close the accountability gap.

THE CASE FOR SYSTEM-WIDE UN ACCOUNTABILITY

In view of the UN's relatively weak response, we reiterate that the case for accountability is an extremely strong one. Accountability is an essential feature of good governance, frequently promoted as such by the UN itself in various contexts. As one observer put it in the context of peace maintenance operations, "Nothing can be more contradictory than a United Nations force transgressing humanitarian law standards." A similar impulse seems to have led the secretary-general to note that abusive behavior toward refugees "violates everything the United Nations stands for." It will clearly become increasingly important for the UN, by its actions, to avoid being accused of unaccountability.

Aside from sheer concern for coherence, there are more pragmatic considerations involved. If accountability has become such a prominent issue, it is also because it has come to be seen as the indispensable corollary of the legitimate exercise of authority. This is why the Lessons Learned Unit, after having explored the successes and failures of several UN peace operations, felt confident enough to insist that "the United Nations must... demonstrate a commitment to the principles of transparency and accountability in its activities. It must not be perceived as being 'above the law.'"

Conversely, it is difficult to underestimate the impact that a perception of the UN as not measuring up to its own standards may have on those under its care. When it comes to peacekeeping generally, "legal unaccountability will definitely lose for a mission the support of the local population," so that being accountable is not only a moral imperative but also an operational one if the UN is to maintain the kind of credibility on which it relies. There is another, more subtle, reason why the UN should uphold the highest standards of accountability.

In many areas of the world, especially where the UN is taking over from weak or collapsed states-whether by keeping the peace, administering territory, managing refugee camps, or holding international trials-the UN will generate considerable local expectations. If the international community manages to rise to the highest standards of governance, it will not only facilitate its own work but, in leading by example, may also foster or consolidate a local culture of accountability. As Amnesty International put it in the context of Kosovo, "The conduct of UNMIK and KFOR will set the standard in Kosovo and the Federal Republic of Yugoslavia as a whole for the manner in which law enforcement officials and security forces responsible for maintaining public safety and order exercise their duties."

Finally, there is an emerging awareness that because of the complex nature of the problem, "accountability needs to be addressed at the individual agency and collectively." Fostering a culture of accountability throughout the UN would more generally signal a shift from an organization that was and probably still is to a large extent dependent on states, to one that is increasingly legitimate in the eyes of its ultimate beneficiaries. As such, it would be an enormous step toward winning the hearts and minds of those who, through a variety of routes, are becoming crucial partners.

Accountability has been described as a "multifaceted phenomenon," which at a minimum involves sensitivity to the possible impact of one's actions and a willingness to answer for the consequences arising from them. Thus, accountability lies somewhere between political responsiveness and legal responsibility. At one end, accountability is said to entail notions of democratic decision-making and political participation. An institution is accountable if, by means of regular reporting and monitoring procedures, its executive is made to answer for its conduct before some kind of legislative body.

In that sense, the UN has always been accountable to the General Assembly, for example. Whether it should improve its political accountability by reforming the Security Council or by opening the doors to international civil society is an important debate in its own right, but not one with which this chapter is primarily concerned. The fact that an institution is accountable in its decision-making should not obviate the fact that, under contemporary understandings of the term, institutions should also be accountable for their decision-making-that is, for the adverse substantive impact that their decisions may have regardless of their democratic legitimacy. This legal kind of accountability, in turn, needs to be distinguished from the traditional concept of international responsibility.

It is a long-recognized rule of international law that international institutions may be made responsible for the prejudice caused to others, along lines very similar to those of state responsibility. However, this concept is both too narrow and too heavy for the UN's more subtle accountability needs: too narrow because of its focus on a strictly defined, generally material, prejudice; too heavy because of its all-or-nothing approach to liability and the limited range of remedies it offers. The point is that international institutions such as the UN may want to be made politically accountable for certain decisions even though they are not strictly internationally responsible for them.

In that sense, the accountability problematique begs the larger question of accountability to whom? Both political accountability and legal responsibility have traditionally although not exclusively been geared toward states. The point of legal accountability is that it inaugurates a move away from a "shareholders" approach (in the context of political accountability) or "victims of prejudice" approach (in the context of international responsibility) to a larger concept of stakeholders, defined as all those who are directly or indirectly affected by the UN's policies and who have a distinct interest in ensuring that the UN is answerable for such policies.

Hence, if political accountability and legal responsibility occupy fairly fixed points in the UN's legal constellation, the concept of UN accountability promoted here aims to fill the gaps left by the former by providing a more fluid regime that is above all geared to ensuring the UN's responsiveness to some of the negative side effects of its activities.

THE INADEQUACY OF EXISTING MECHANISMS

One might think that the UN's intricate network of organs and mechanisms might be sufficient to safeguard and to promote human rights accountability, but a closer look reveals that none of these mechanisms, individually or as an aggregate, have been able to systematically bring the UN's otherwise prevalent human rights focus to bear on its own activities. The main reason for this inadequacy may lie not so much in a genuine lack of institutional values as in their structural separation: the promotion of good internal governance, on the one hand, and of human rights, on the other.

While the former is seen as essentially unrelated to human rights, the latter is treated as non-self-reflexive and hence unrelated to the UN itself, leaving a huge accountability gap at the heart of the UN's institutional setup. As for the existing internal governance mechanisms, these are all geared toward auditing and management control with none of them appearing to be seriously concerned with overseeing the human rights impact of the UN. Nominally, the most likely candidate, the Office of Internal Oversight Services (OIOS), looks prima facie as if it could be a real accountability watchdog. Its mandate is to "ensure compliance with the resolutions of the General Assembly, and with regulations, rules, and policies of the United Nations." The inspector-general, who heads it, is sometimes referred to as an "ombudsman."

Yet, in practice, the OIOS has always understood its mandate as essentially one of internal management control, which is almost exclusively geared toward "enhanc[ing] the way the United Nations does business." Indeed, its single-minded focus on "accountability for the stewardship of resources," "efficiency and productivity," or "cost-effective controls to ensure compliance with authority, minimize waste and deter fraud and dishonesty" has de facto prevented it from conceiving of its accountability role in human rights terms and from carrying out any form of systematic investigation in that respect.

Whenever the OIOS has exercised its oversight services over potentially human rights-sensitive areas it has done so in a human rights-neutral way. The only case where the OIOS came close to investigating issues of accountability as understood in this chapter was in the West African sex-for-aid scandal, in which it officially based its role on the Convention on the Rights of the Child. The investigation led to the interview of more than 1,500 refugees and to an important report that, though finding that some of the accusations leveled against the UN were unverifiable, clearly acknowledged that the problem was widespread.

The fact that the investigation was an isolated instance, that it was undertaken specifically at UNHCR's request rather than as part of any autonomous initiative, and that the OIOS at times seemed to be overwhelmed by the magnitude of the task demonstrates that even this case cannot be taken as an example of thoroughgoing human rights scrutiny. Those organs that are specifically geared toward human rights promotion have in turn tended to be largely oblivious to the UN's own occasionally less-than-positive role. The quintessential human rights body, the UN High Commissioner for Human Rights (UNHCHR), has mostly kept silent on the larger, more recent human rights blunders of the UN, speaking out usually only in relation to the conduct of the states involved and not explicitly in relation to the UN's behavior.

The treatment of the Somalia scandal by the UN's human rights apparatus is revealing. Both the Sub-Commission on Human Rights and the Commission on Human Rights have shown a distinct reluctance to thematize UN accountability. The then special rapporteur on Somalia for the commission seemed to base her report on the assumption that the UN was not in command and control of the mission's ground operations, which effectively ensured that the UN's accountability fell outside the scope of her study.

Because the UN is not technically a party to the major human rights treaties promoted under its auspices, none of the treaty bodies was ever called on to examine its behavior from a human rights perspective. However, when both the Human Rights Committee (HRC) and the Committee Against Torture (CAT) had the opportunity to examine the UN's role in Somalia indirectly through the reports of states whose troops had been accused of wrongdoing while serving under the UN, they failed to even allude to the UN's potential co-responsibility. This pattern of failing to see the UN as "part of the picture" only seems to have gotten worse in the context of international administrations. For example, when the Special Rapporteurs on extrajudicial summary or arbitrary executions, on torture, and on violence against women conducted on-site visits in East

Timor, their report did not allude to the possibility that UNTAET staff might have committed human rights violations.

It would seem that there are essentially two lessons to be learned from the inadequacy of the mechanisms currently in place: first, a self-reflexive human rights focus should become as much part of the UN's internal accountability approach as good administrative practices already are; second, the existing mechanisms need to be modified, or a new mechanism created, so that the UN will have at its disposal an internal human rights watchdog that would be truly independent, capable of receiving complaints about the human rights dimension of UN activities, and empowered to conduct thorough investigations and to provide effective remedies. In short, the UN needs an office whose characteristics resemble very much those of a human rights ombudsperson.

THE OMBUDSPERSON IDEA

The idea of an ombudsperson goes back to the beginning of the nineteenth century, notably to the Swedish Justitie ombudsman, which has served since its creation in 1809 as the general model for ombudsperson-type institutions to the present day. The idea has been remarkably successful, with currently over ninety countries having some kind of public sector ombudsperson. Although in many of these countries the ombudsperson has originally and essentially been conceived as a supervisory instrument for public administration, a broader association of an ombudsperson with accountability and the protection of human rights have developed over the years. So much so that ombudspersons have come to be identified as a hallmark of good governance in a wide variety of institutions, be they public or private, national or indeed, international.

As would be expected, ombudspersons differ widely in their institutional status, powers, jurisdiction, and mode of functioning. However, all ombudspersons share a number of basic features that strike a balance between the needs of accountability and institutional accommodation. At the minimum, ombudspersons are meant to be independent from both the body that created them and the agencies they oversee; they should be competent to receive complaints from the general public; they need to be empowered to carry out some form of independent investigation on those complaints; and they need to be able to take some form of remedial action.

Beyond these defining features, because the flexibility of ombudspersons is largely due to the fact that they are not full-blown judicial bodies, their remedial powers are usually recommendatory rather than binding, and their ability to effect compliance rests primarily on the publicity of their reports rather than on formal prosecutorial competences. Several international organizations have successfully established ombudspersons. Notably, the ombudsperson of the European Union (EU) has over the years established the office as an indispensable feature of EU governance.

According to one author, the EU ombudsperson has provided EU citizens with "a cheap, flexible and accessible form of redress for individual grievances... has reinforced the rule of law in the Community... has complemented the role of the courts... and thus enhanced public confidence in EU institutions." Moreover, ombudspersons are seen as particularly useful in the early stages of developing an accountability framework in institutional environments initially unfamiliar with or inhospitable to the idea of accountability. For example, there have been various projects coordinated by nongovernmental organizations (NGOs) to create ombudspersons in the context of humanitarian emergencies. Overall, the concept of ombudspersons would seem to provide an ideally flexible formula to address the UN's accountability needs.

THE UN'S EXPERIENCE WITH OMBUDSPERSONS

The UN and its agencies are no strangers to the ombudsperson idea. In fact, under the catch-all heading "national human rights institutions," the UN has considered (national) ombudspersons as a priority element of its "implementation and monitoring" methods as set out in the

Vienna Declaration. Through UN Development Programme (UNDP) or the UNHCR, the UN has supported many a nascent national ombudsperson institution. One interesting development is that the ombudsperson idea has been regarded as particularly relevant in post-conflict scenarios, where it is seen to serve as "a viable forum for the investigation and resolution of human rights complaints... [in situations] where the judicial system is weak, politicized, slow or otherwise incapacitated."

In this context, the international community has been increasingly solicited not only to advise states on the creation of ombudspersons institutions, but also to step in to actually manage some national ombudsperson institutions. For example, in the case of Bosnia, the human rights ombudsperson, created by the Dayton agreement, is appointed by the OSCE and has become an international civil servant. The main responsibility of ombudspersons created by the international community has been to deal with complaints against various emerging national authorities and, in that respect, to serve as a model for future domestic ombudspersons. But, for our purposes, the significance of the ombudsperson in peace building contexts where UN staff or troops with a UN mandate are deployed is that, for the first time and unlike in purely domestic settings, it also potentially brings the UN itself under the supervision of such institutions.

However, the UN's reaction has been typical of the institution's ambivalent attitude toward such developments, showing both the promise and the limits of its accountability. On the one hand, there are signs that the UN may slowly be picking up on the need to give its accountability-promotion approach a self-reflexive turn. As early as 1995, for example, the Secretariat's Department of Peacekeeping Operations (DPKO) suggested the creation of an ombudsperson for each peacekeeping mission, a suggestion that was then taken up officially by the secretary-general and several UN bodies.

It has also been suggested that a unit be set up within the UN's Department of Humanitarian Assistance that could "serve as ombudsman to which any party can express a concern related to provision of assistance or security." In a similar vein, there are discussions to establish special-issue ombudspersons for the most vulnerable groups-notably refugees, internally displaced persons (IDPs), women, and children. However, if one considers that some of the worst abuses occurred as early as 1994, it is noteworthy that it took a relentless campaign of sensitization before the secretary-general's proposal was taken up by an informal working group of the Security Council in 2000, where it seemed destined to further bureaucratic meandering.

The issue has nonetheless assumed a new dimension in the last generation of peace operations, where the UN exercises state like functions or, as with fully international administrations, is the main sovereign in a particular territory. In Bosnia, even though the Office of the High Representative exercises some state like functions and the human rights ombudsperson's jurisdictional clauses were drafted in broad and seemingly all-embracing terms, the immunity granted to the Office of the High Representative and the International Police Task Force has meant that in effect UN behavior has been considered off-limits-although interestingly this has not prevented the ombudsperson from at least a measure of informal bons offices and even the occasional public communication to settle issues of accountability.

However, a major symbolic turning point seemed, for a while at least, to have occurred in Kosovo where an ombudsperson is specifically asked to "investigate complaints from any person or entity in Kosovo concerning human rights violations and actions constituting an abuse of authority by the interim civil administration or any emerging central or local institution." The ombudsperson is managed by the OSCE and not by the UN, but it has clearly understood its mandate as covering both UNMIK and Kosovo Force (KFOR).

The Kosovo ombudsperson has emerged as a key institution in the reconstruction of Kosovo, handling dozens of complaints covering the whole range of human rights, the great majority of which had either UNMIK or KFOR as respondents. The ombudsperson's main input has been to monitor the conformity of several UNMIK regulations with international standards, but in some cases he has gone so far as to recommend that criminal proceedings be initiated against certain members of UNMIK. Specific deadlines have been set for UNMIK to modify certain regulations or to investigate certain cases of wrongdoing.

Despite these successes, this image of emerging accountability has been substantially blurred. The ombudsperson is essentially an OSCE institution, tolerated rather than supported by the UN. The UN's cooperation and responsiveness record vis-a-vis the ombudsperson has been dismal. The ombudsperson has been denied access to prisons under UN administration contrary to the UN's own regulations. Several if not most of his queries to UNMIK have not elicited any form of response from the international presence, even though they concern potentially grave violations of human rights.

Of the few responses obtained from the special representative of the secretary-general (SRSG), many were either to the effect that UNMIK authorities basically "did not agree" with the ombudsperson's viewpoint (implying that UNMIK's own assessment of the issues at stake was more authoritative than that of the ombudsperson, who was set up for that purpose); that the violations were justified on the grounds of the existence of a "threat to international peace and security" (implying that a state of emergency was present even though the ombudsperson had clearly argued that it was not); or that UNMIK had "the full support... of key members of the international community" (implying that political support could be a substitute for adherence to the rule of law).

Most problematically, UNMIK has promulgated a regulation that grants immunity to both its staff and KFOR's staff. In his "Special Report No. 1," Marek Antoni Nowicki, the ombudsperson, decided that immunity for UNMIK and KFOR staff was "not consistent with international conventions for human rights and fail[ed] to protect individuals in [Kosovo] from arbitrary behaviour by UNMIK and KFOR or by their personnel." Just before UNMIK's deadline to repeal the legislation expired, the SRSG answered with a letter announcing "further consultations with UNHQ and others." This is the last that has been heard of the UN's intent to deal with this embarrassing question.

The UN's mixed experience with ombudspersons in the specific context of peace operations would seem to have a variety of lessons to yield. The first is that when the political will is there, ombudspersons seem ideally suited to the UN's accountability needs and provide a much-needed channel for civil society to voice specific complaints. The second lesson is that institutional resistance remains high, and encouraging the creation of a public-oriented ombudsperson is likely to be an uphill struggle. The third, and perhaps most important, lesson is that, despite the difficulties, there seems to be nothing impossible in theory about having ombudspersons exercise vigorous scrutiny over the UN itself.

However, peace operations ombudspersons, even if they function satisfactorily, meet only a fraction-albeit an important and highly visible one-of the UN's accountability needs, which, as we have argued above, extend beyond the confines of such contexts. Moreover, there may be something about the ad hoc way in which they were created, not to mention their hybrid half-international/half-national status that may have made them particularly unsuited to take on the UN. Therefore, the kind of general and truly comprehensive UN accountability envisioned here seems to point clearly toward the need for a truly system-wide ombudsperson.

Three reasons would appear to militate in the direction of creating an ombudsperson for the UN. First, the existence of an ombudsperson office would entrench the idea of accountability in the UN's structure, where the current forays in this direction are hampered by administrative inertia and political procrastination. The permanent availability of an ombudsperson would improve the system's reactivity, a key feature in ensuring that accountability is not simply an after-the-fact corrective but a continuous process. Second, a system-wide ombudsperson with a suitable mandate would give accountability the holistic perspective that it has so far lacked, sending the clearest signal to date that the UN will consider itself accountable not only in certain specific contexts but in all its activities.

Third, a permanent ombudsperson would have a continuity that would both safeguard its independence and allow it to develop the requisite know-how and authority. If nothing else, a UN ombudsperson office could contribute to the coordination and streamlining of the current sprinkling of accountability initiatives in diverse sectors of UN activity. A system-wide ombudsperson institution would not replace existing ombudspersons institutions in peace operation contexts that have a reconstruction role and often provide the impetus for subsequent national institutions.

But a system-wide institution could usefully take on all the issues within the ombudspersons' mandates in peace operations that are related directly to issues of UN accountability. Contrary to peace operations ombudspersons, a system-wide institution would do so from the standpoint and with the authority and confidence of a centralized organ integrated into the UN machinery, rather than from one of the UN's scattered outposts. It would also release some of the pressure on ombudspersons operating in reconstruction contexts by limiting their mandate to complaints against local authorities.

Such an ombudsperson could have several functions. Above all, the office could serve as a focal point within the organization for all issues related to accountability. It should be authorized to receive and follow up on complaints not only from "victims," but possibly also from any third-party individual or group or any UN staff member. However, like the EU ombudsperson, it should also be competent to act on its own initiative. It should have the broadest possible investigatory powers, including access to all relevant documents and possibly the competence to summon UN staff for hearings. On the basis of such comprehensive investigations, it would then make recommendations to the relevant UN authorities regarding appropriate remedies. The ombudsperson should be able to recommend transfer or dismissal of personnel, structural or organic reforms, and appropriate compensation to victims.

Ultimately, recommendations would probably be of an advisory nature, but they should be public and thus lend the ombudsperson some informal sanctioning power. In the case of outright noncompliance by UN agencies, the ombudsperson might be able to refer a matter directly to the General Assembly-as the EU ombudsperson can do in relation to the European Parliament- or, where applicable, to relevant domestic authorities, including national ombudspersons. With regard to the ombudsperson's jurisdiction, the receivable complaints would have to be in relation to allegations concerning the adverse human rights impact of UN activities. The question of which types of human rights violations would fall within the ombudsperson's jurisdiction is multifaceted and difficult to answer briefly. However, in principle, it would be hypocritical to exclude from his or her jurisdiction any of those human rights that are protected within a UN framework, notably those contained in the International Bill of Rights.

The UN should endorse accountability for all its organs, programs, and agencies-and for its immediate agents, within the exercise of their functions. Clearly the UN cannot be accountable for all behavior that is even remotely attributable to it. A test of proximity, of causality, and of the significance of the prejudice caused would be necessary. The UN is not accountable in the same way for its failure to prevent genocide in Rwanda, the routine shortcomings of its international administrations, and the sporadic outbursts of violence by a group of peacekeepers. But it is important to understand that, rather than an all-or-nothing approach, what may be called for is a capacity to find different types of responses tailored to the harm done.

In mixed jurisdiction contexts, such as peacekeeping operations, the ombudsperson should have jurisdiction over any conduct that is attributable to the UN, regardless of whether it may also be attributable to state actors. Even if primary jurisdiction is with state authorities, the ombudsperson should be able to seize the matter and-like the different Special Rapporteurs of the commission and Sub-Commission regularly be informed of the domestic investigation process and, where necessary, put pressure on domestic authorities to comply with international human rights standards. In emergency cases, the ombudsperson should be allowed to order interim measures before a complaint is formally investigated, to safeguard individuals from potentially irreversible violations of their rights.

With regard to the core characteristics of the ombudsperson office, the experience with the OSCE-sponsored ombudsperson in Kosovo clearly shows that a UN ombudsperson cannot really be contracted out and that a system-wide ombudsperson, to be taken seriously, needs to have an institutionally enshrined position. Yet, at the same time, an ombudsperson must be able to act independently, so that purely in-house attempts to ensure accountability risk reproducing some of the travails that gave rise to the accountability problematique in the first place. Thus, to guarantee independence, the holders of the office should be chosen from outside the UN system-for example, from among national ombudspersons with a highly rated record of impartiality. In addition, the ombudsperson should enjoy security of tenure and full recruitment and budgetary competence.

In terms of an institutional arrangement, the ombudsperson could in theory be "niched" within an existing department or unit. One possibility is for the inspector-general's mandate in the OIOS to be expanded to include a clear human rights focus. Another possibility is for the UNHCHR to be asked to take on the role of ombudsperson, given that the office is well equipped to oversee the UN's own human rights record. However, it is probably not coincidental that neither of these organs has taken up anything remotely resembling an ombudsperson-type role in the past, even though a creative interpretation of their mandate could have led them to do so.

Also, it is inherently difficult to add a human rights brief to an organ like the OIOS, whose institutional culture is rooted in financial and management accountability. Another possibility is that there is a deeper contradiction involved between the UNHCHR's need for institutional support when carrying out general human rights activities and the risk of alienating key institutional partners as a result of internal scrutiny. Hence, if the UN wanted to send a strong signal to the world community that it was serious about accountability; the best solution would point in the direction of a new, *sui generis* organ along the lines of the EU ombudsperson.

The decision to create such an organ would most likely fall within the General Assembly's mandate, with the assembly possessing the power to elect the ombudsperson. In turn, and by analogy with the EU ombudsperson, the UN ombudsperson would report directly to the General Assembly, ensuring the ombudsperson's accountability. Although legitimate concerns about costs are bound to arise, centralizing the tasks of the ombudsperson in one organ would probably be a much more cost-effective measure than the multiplication of theater- or agency-specific mechanisms.

Clearly, much more research needs to be carried out on the precise institutional and jurisdictional configuration of a UN ombudsperson. But it should already be clear that a strong and authoritative institution with UN accountability as its primary goal could greatly help the UN approach the vision Secretary-General Annan expressed during his Nobel Prize acceptance speech-that is, to "place human beings at the centre of everything we do."

5

New Era in UN Human Rights Work

Kofi Annan did more than any UN Secretary-General before him to stress the close link between human rights and peace and security. In his inaugural address to the newly created Human Rights Council in Geneva on June 19, 2006, he said: "... lack of respect for human rights and dignity is the fundamental reason why the peace of the world today is so precarious, and why prosperity is so unequally shared." With the creation of the Human Rights Council, "a new era in the human rights work of the United Nations has been proclaimed."

The previous year, at the September 2005 World Summit in New York, Annan persuaded all of the world's leaders to agree that human rights constitute one of the three pillars-along with peace and security and economic and social development that form the base of all the UN's work. The summit's Outcome Document captured the results of the highly ambitious if not wholly successful UN reform agenda that Annan had initiated in his second term. Landmark outcomes from the vantage point of human rights include recognition by all states that the international community has a "responsibility to protect should peaceful means be inadequate and national authorities manifestly fail to protect their populations" from genocide, war crimes, and crimes against humanity; "that the regular budget resources of the Office of the High Commissioner for Human Rights must be doubled; and that a new Peacebuilding Commission will be created to "advise on and propose integrated strategies for post-conflict peace building and recovery."

Most important, world leaders decided that a new, more authoritative human rights body-a Human Rights Council-should be created to replace the fifty-nine-year-old Commission on Human Rights. After intense and at times highly divisive negotiations, "which were eventually resolved by General Assembly President Jan Eliasson of Sweden, the assembly adopted Resolution 60/251 by an overwhelming majority on March 15, 2006, resolving to create a Human Rights Council. In the 170-4 vote, only the United States, Israel, the Marshall Islands, and Palau voted against (with Iran, Venezuela, and Belarus abstaining). Nevertheless, U.S. Representative John Bolton graciously promised that "the United States will work cooperatively to make the Council as strong and effective as it can be," and added: "We remain committed to support the UN's historic mission to promote and protect the basic human rights of all the world's citizens."

The council's predecessor, the Commission on Human Rights, created in 1946, achieved a more substantive body of human rights work than is often recognized. The commission drafted major international human rights standards, including the two international human rights covenants, which, together with the earlier adopted Universal Declaration of Human Rights (1948), form what, is known as the International Bill of Human Rights. The commission advanced human rights protection globally through increasingly substantive thematic and country-specific work, inventing a unique system of Special Procedures-that is, a body of independent and objective human rights experts and working groups that includes, and is sometimes generally referred to as, Special Rapporteurs.

As the commission's-and now the council's eyes and ears," these Special Rapporteurs monitor and rapidly respond to reported human rights violations anywhere in the world, visiting countries, carrying out studies, intervening on behalf of individuals, and reporting back with recommendations for action. Now numbering forty-one, this body of country-specific and thematic experts began to grow in the 1980s, when they were first established to address enforced disappearances and other gross human rights violations in Chile and Argentina.

Their current mandates include torture, violence against women, issues of health and housing, and specific country situations, such as Myanmar, Sudan, and North Korea. They perform the crucial function of providing objective information to underpin the UN's human rights work. They have provided early warning of human rights crises and have pressured states to turn their human rights commitments into reality. Nongovernmental organizations (NGOs) concerned with human rights, whether big or small, national or international, have gained access to the commission in a manner unequaled elsewhere in the UN system.

Nonetheless, the commission suffered increasing criticism from NGOs for failing to address important issues on their merits. States complained of double standards, especially in the selection of countries for public scrutiny. Some states from the South rightly wondered why the Commission on Human Rights-on which the "Permanent Five" members of the Security Council (China, France, the Russian Federation, the United Kingdom, and the United States) were virtually guaranteed a permanent seat-never adopted a resolution condemning well-known and gross abuses in, for instance, Tibet, Chechnya (the commission did so exceptionally in 2000 and 2001 but subsequent draft resolutions were rejected), or in Guantanamo Bay.

Of particular annoyance to the United States was its unexpected failure to win a seat on the commission in 2002 and the election of the Libyan ambassador to chair the commission in 2003 (in which capacity she served rather well). Even the High Commissioner for Human Rights and the UN Secretary-General himself, in his landmark March 2005 report "In Larger Freedom," spoke of the commission suffering a "credibility deficit." In outlining his reform agenda, Annan severely criticized the commission:

Yet the Commission's capacity to perform its tasks has been increasingly undermined by its declining credibility and professionalism. In particular, States have sought membership of the Commission not to strengthen human rights but to protect themselves against criticism or to criticize others. As a result, a credibility deficit has developed, which casts a shadow on the reputation of the United Nations system as a whole.

In that report the Secretary-General proposed to replace the commission with a smaller Human Rights Council, a decision that appears to have been taken rather hastily. The idea was no more than an afterthought in the December 2004 report of the High-Level Panel on Threats, Challenges, and Change, which Annan had specifically commissioned to lay the groundwork for the recommendations in his own report.

In fact, the High-Level Panel's chief recommendation had gone in the opposite direction: it advocated that the fifty-three-member Commission on Human Rights be turned into a body with universal membership, adding at the very end that "in the longer term, Member States should consider upgrading the Commission to become a 'Human Rights Council' that is no longer subsidiary to the Economic and Social Council [ECOSOC] but a Charter body standing alongside it and the Security Council...."

Making this far-reaching human rights proposal immediately his own was certainly a bold initiative, and bold is what NGOs had asked Annan to be. The Secretary-General's decision was, however, made at a time of profound suspicion and distrust between North and South, sharpened by the U.S.-led invasion of Iraq and its aftermath. Certainly, this was not an easy time, as experience shows, to build an entirely new human rights body that must be better than its predecessor.

KEY FEATURES

Annan conceived the council as having "a more authoritative position corresponding to the primacy of human rights in the Charter." He expressed the hope that the Human

Rights Council, like the Security Council, the General Assembly, and ECOSOC, could be elevated to the status of a "principal organ" of the United Nations. Human rights would thus logically, in institutional terms, get their proper place next to peace and security and development as one of the three pillars of the UN. Although many countries wished the Human Rights Council to have that principal organ status, putting it on an equal footing with the Security Council was not a particularly welcome idea to some key developing countries.

They did not look favorably upon linking the UN's main human rights body to the all-powerful Security Council, which can take binding decisions. Rather, the Human Rights Council was eventually created as a subsidiary organ of the General Assembly, but the assembly agreed to review the council's status within five years of its formation. Meanwhile, the council was given a firm mandate "to address situations of violations of human rights, including gross and systematic violations," and to "respond promptly to human rights emergencies."

Arrangements and practices observed by the commission for NGO participation, based on ECOSOC Resolution 1996/31, were retained. General Assembly Resolution 60/251 places much emphasis on the principles of cooperation and genuine dialogue in the council's work; recognizes the need for "objectivity and non-selectivity" in considering human rights issues; and proclaims that "double standards and politicization" must be eliminated.

Although there had been growing support for the High-Level Panel's proposal to make the Commission on Human Rights a universal membership body-which would help enhance its authority by the sheer force of its members-the Secretary-General, probably with an eye on the United States, proposed to create a "smaller standing Human Rights Council." The United States had consistently advocated a smaller, leaner human rights body, arguing that a membership of twenty states would be ideal. Eventually, a compromise was reached and a body of forty-seven members (just under the commission's fifty-three) was decided upon.

What many diplomats did not realize until late in the negotiations was that any new UN body would have to be created along customary UN lines of equitable geographical distribution. In the case of the council, this comes down to thirteen for the African Group (which had fifteen in the commission), thirteen for the Asian Group (which had twelve), six for Eastern Europe (which had five), eight for the Latin American and Caribbean Group (which had eleven), and seven for the Western European and Others Group (known as WEOG, which previously had ten seats).

In the commission, African and Asian states had about the same number of votes as the Latin American and WEOG groups combined, but the lineup is very different in the council. The African and Asian members now have a comfortable majority (at least twenty-six out of forty-seven votes) in the UN's main political human rights body; and they are definitely using it to set the agenda, as is clear on a range of issues, including the selection of countries for immediate attention by "special session" and the reluctance of many African and Asian members to act on country situations apart from Israel.

WEOG and the Latin American Group have lost their power to win a vote on these and other issues unless their proposals attract the support of at least three African and Asian states. The changed political dynamics point to the need for European and Latin American countries to adopt a cross-regional approach to address human rights issues of common concern. Membership is for three years and shall end after a country has served two consecutive terms. Thus, the principle of rotation has been established, so that even the permanent members of the Security Council have lost their de facto claim to perpetual membership.

All council members are obliged to "uphold the highest standards in the promotion and protection of human rights" and "shall fully cooperate with the Council"-obligations unfortunately not taken seriously by some of its current elected members. Elections are held in secret and the votes of an absolute majority of the General Assembly's members-that is, at least 97 out of 192-are needed for election regardless of how many UN member states are present and voting.

Candidates' contributions to human rights as well as their pledges and commitments shall be taken into account in the vote. Interestingly, all regions except Africa put up more candidates than there were seats for the region, and countries with highly problematic human rights records-such as Sudan and Zimbabwe-did not stand for the first elections, held in May 2006. Iran and Venezuela two of the three countries that abstained in the vote to establish the council were not elected. The election outcome shows that the results would hardly have been different had the United States won its campaign for a two-thirds majority voting requirement for council membership. (Disregarding the vote in the highly competitive Eastern European Group, only Saudi Arabia and Sri Lanka would not have been elected under a two-thirds majority requirement.)

Although not obliged to do so, all candidates made written pledges outlining their human rights agendas, a major advance even though the quality of the pledges varies greatly from country to country. Louise Arbour, the High Commissioner for Human Rights, argued that a system of Universal Periodic Review (UPR)-put forward by Annan as Universal Peer Review-was the only logical answer to the criticism (largely considered justified) that the commission's old practice of selecting specific countries for scrutiny was marked by "selectivity and double standards."

Under this novel system of UPR, unique in the UN's human rights regime, the human rights record of all UN member states, including such powerful countries as China, the Russian Federation, and the United States, shall henceforth be examined by the council. Just how effective the UPR will be in holding all states to account, however, is yet to be seen. A major drawback of the former commission was that it only sat once a year, for six weeks in spring, and was ill placed to react in a timely manner to human rights crisis situations. The new council sits for ten weeks per year, and shall meet at least three times a year, including for a main session. Moreover, it can easily convene in special session: it is sufficient that only a third of its members make the request, and the council has shown a great appetite for it.

The council has had a difficult start. The simultaneous outbreak of renewed hostilities in the Middle East-traditionally the most sensitive issue on the former commission's agenda-complicated its early steps. As expected from a political body, strong political divisions among countries and groups are reflected in the council's debate, and its proceedings to date cannot be characterized as exemplifying the spirit of "constructive international dialogue and cooperation" that Resolution 60/251 so proudly proclaims. Nonetheless, there are also some definite signs of hope.

The council's first session, June 19-30, 2006, marked a substantive beginning, with two major new human rights instruments adopted. The International Convention for the Protection of All Persons from Enforced Disappearances was adopted by acclamation. (Fifty-seven states have already signed the convention after the General Assembly adopted the text by consensus at its sixty-first session.) The draft Declaration on the Rights of Indigenous Peoples, negotiated for more than eleven years, was adopted by vote with thirty for, two against, and twelve abstentions. (Unfortunately, the text is now running into difficulties in the current, sixty-first, General Assembly). In addition, a working group was established to draft a protocol to the Covenant on Economic, Social, and Cultural Rights to create an individual complaints procedure.

The council also took the first steps in the massive operation to build its entirely new human rights architecture. It decided to let all of its twenty-eight thematic and thirteen country-specific Special Rapporteurs continue their crucial work for one year, pending review. It created two working groups: one to review the system of these Special Rapporteurs, the other to establish the new UPR system to monitor all states' human rights performance, as required by Resolution 60/251. Both groups have started their daunting task and must deliver results within one year, by June 2007.

While the council is engaged in tense negotiations to establish the UPR and review the system of Special Procedures before the June 2007 deadline, its thematic and country work is taking a back seat. The first regular session discussed five "substantive issues" and adopted a resolution on Palestine. Given the rapidly deteriorating situation in the Occupied Palestinian Territories, the council voted for the first time in its young history to hold a special session on that situation. For whatever reason, the European Union thought it necessary to call for a vote and then proceeded to vote against the proposal, which was easily passed with twenty-nine for, twelve against, and five abstentions.

The Special Session on the Occupied Palestinian Territories was held on July 6, 2006, and was the first in a series of three special sessions all called for by the Group of Arab States, who were twice joined by the Organization of the Islamic Conference (OIC), to deal with actions by Israel. As a result, the council decided, by vote, to send the Special Rapporteur on the Palestinian Territories on a fact-finding mission. The second special session held on August 11, 2006, responded to the worsening human rights crisis in Lebanon and established, also by vote, a high-level commission of inquiry. The third, on November 15, 2006, adopted a resolution (by a vote of thirty-two for, eight against, and six abstentions) expressing the council's shock at Israeli killings of Palestinian civilians at Beit Hanoun and calling for a high-level fact-finding mission.

On their merits, all three situations were urgent and grave and deserved the special attention of the council. But their outcome was in some respects unworthy of a council expected to act in a "fair and equal manner," as Resolution 60/251 requires. Particularly regrettable was the one-sided resolution that the council adopted by a vote of twenty-seven for, eleven against, and four abstentions-on Lebanon (A/HRC/S-2/1).

The highly politicized resolution strongly condemned "grave Israeli violations of Human Rights and breaches of International Humanitarian Law in Lebanon," but entirely ignored the massive human rights abuses committed by

Hezbollah in using indiscriminate rocket attacks against Israeli civilians. This was a clear example of the "selectivity" and "double standards and politicization" that Resolution 60/251 seeks to eliminate. Moreover, the nearly exclusive focus of these special sessions on Israel, at the cost of disregarding equally if not more egregious human rights situations elsewhere in the world, started to raise serious questions regarding the council's credibility.

More recently, however, the council has begun to steer a more balanced course. Prompted by exceptionally strong statements by Secretary-General Annan as well as the High Commissioner for Human Rights, the council eventually convened a long overdue Special Session on Darfur on December 12-13, 2006, resulting in a decision calling for action in Darfur. Particularly encouraging is that no fewer than thirty-three members, representing all regions of the council, cosponsored the call for the Darfur special session a higher number than the three previous calls for a special session, which were twenty-one, sixteen, and twenty-four, respectively.

Moreover, the thirty-three included a significant number of African countries: Algeria; Gabon, Ghana, Mauritius, Nigeria, South Africa, and Zambia. Although the decision adopted (S-4/101) was not as strong as many observes felt it should have been (it failed to identify the Sudanese government and the Janjaweed as responsible for the serious human rights abuses), it is nevertheless the only resolution or decision adopted unanimously by the council in any special session to date. (In a move of defiance of the council's will, the Sudanese government in February 2007 refused to grant visas to the high-level fact-finding mission that the council dispatched to Darfur. Equally regrettable, in December, Israel refused access to the fact-finding mission created to investigate the Beit Hanoun killings.)

In all four special sessions the council decided to send inquiry commissions to investigate the situations and report back, suggesting that the council is serious about looking at new ways to address pressing human rights situations rather than simply sitting in Geneva and adopting condemnatory resolutions. Meanwhile, the council also continued its work in regular sessions, holding no fewer than three regular sessions in 2006 (June, September/October, and November/ December). These sessions concentrated on procedural decisions, institution building, and some thematic issues. Generally, these regular sessions have not yet resulted in concrete outcomes to protect human rights in specific countries, even in such pressing situations as Sri Lanka.

The resumed second regular session addressed Israeli actions in the occupied Syrian Golan and the Palestinian Territories. It took two consensus decisions, on Nepal and Afghanistan, urging these countries to cooperate with the High Commissioner for Human Rights and asking her to report on these countries to future sessions. At the end of that session, on November 28, the council also took a decision (2/115) on Sudan (Darfur), which was pushed through by Algeria as chair of the African Group, notwithstanding attempts by one African and many other countries to strengthen the text.

The decision was unacceptably weak, failing to identify the Sudanese government's responsibility for the gross violations committed; and it lacked any operational mechanism-such as an immediate call for action by the High Commissioner or follow-up by the council itself to address the particularly grave situation in Darfur. Dissatisfaction with the bland decision prompted an immediate and successful call for a Special Session on Darfur, as described above.

A human rights threat of symbolic proportions, as posed by Guantanamo Bay, has not yet surfaced in the council. Chronic and widespread human rights violations, such as in North Korea, Iraq, and Myanmar (Burma), also stand out to be addressed. The case of Myanmar will be an immediate test for the Human Rights Council's resolve to address such serious situations. Two of its members, Indonesia and Russia, which are also members of the Security Council, told the Security Council on January 12, 2007, that they favored action on Myanmar in the Human Rights Council after both countries failed to vote for a Security Council resolution that would have called for the release of all political prisoners in Myanmar. (In the Security Council vote, Russia vetoed the resolution and Indonesia abstained.)

This once more illustrates that the Human Rights Council cannot postpone acting on these and other serious country situations any longer. If it fails to do so, the Third Committee of the General Assembly, which also deals with human rights, will increasingly become the focus for country-specific human rights resolutions, detracting from the council's primacy as the UN's foremost human rights body. This brief overview shows that calling for a special session is now the de facto way to generate council action to protect human rights in specific countries.

Many other human rights situations have been discussed in the council in the context of the reports presented by the Special Rapporteurs, however, and these have generated many more proposed country visits-illustrating how essential the Special Rapporteurs are to the council's work. One of the most positive developments so far is the substantive "interactive dialogue" with Special Rapporteurs that the council held at its second regular session in September 2006. As these UN debates go, they were unprecedented in their vitality, the depth of interaction with the Special Rapporteurs, and the level and nature of participation.

Many missions participated at the ambassadorial level, and national human rights institutions and NGOs took part in the debate. This is unprecedented in Geneva, and NGOs remain unable to speak in similar dialogues with the Special Rapporteurs in the General Assembly's Third Committee in New York. Unfortunately, these debates have so far failed to lead to concrete outcomes to promote and protect human rights in the countries discussed and thus give effect to the recommendations made by the council's own thematic and country-specific Special Rapporteurs. This will be a key challenge for the council in the future.

Another remarkable development is that the council is in fact becoming the "standing" body to address human rights situations whenever necessary, as Annan had in mind. The result of the flurry of calls for special sessions whatever one may think of the highly politicized selection criteria-combined with the ongoing substantive regular sessions is that the council was in session every single month of 2006 since it opened its doors on June 19, 2006. The much greater frequency of sessions (compared to the once-yearly session of the commission) has created a range of options to swiftly react to human rights situations in countries that need urgent attention, including keeping the situations under review for the next session, depending on whether the governments concerned take steps to improve their human rights performance.

Another interesting development is the recent proposal made by the president of the council, Luis Alfonso de Alba of Mexico, to use the presence of ministers at the high-level debate to start roundtable discussions on topical human rights issues, and to schedule thematic debates throughout the year to allow more in-depth attention to a specific theme related to the council's work. Regrettably, these proposals for innovation have, so far, broadly met with skepticism. Nevertheless, the council now has different tools at its disposal that will be developed over time, and some members are thinking about how to use them creatively.

It is generally agreed that institution building has to be the council's highest priority. There must be an understanding of the time and effort that council members need to spend on this highly complex task, in which non-council members and NGOs are also playing a substantive role. Two imperatives stand out for the council's new human rights architecture. The first is to build an effective system of Universal Periodic Review to assess human rights performance in all countries. The second is to preserve and strengthen the system of Special Rapporteurs and to defeat attempts by some members to weaken their independence.

Concentrating on institution building alone, however, is not the way to create a better human rights body. As was the case with the commission, many members of the council have shown a tendency to put politics, and sometimes regional politics, above human rights. Many council discussions have been marked by suspicion and distrust, and the voices of some members have been stifled by regional or other group positions, leading Annan to caution the council last November that "States that are truly determined to uphold human rights must be prepared to take action even when that means, as it sometimes will, giving offense to other States within their own region."

The former UN Deputy Secretary-General, Louise Frechette, precisely identified the current predicament in an interview of January 17, 2007:

> To a certain extent we have sought institutional responses, institutional fixes, through reform to problems that are more fundamental and more political.... The Human Rights Commission was deemed to be ineffective by a lot of countries. The answer was to transform it into a new institution called the Human Rights Council. But it's not performing all that much better than the Human Rights Commission because the world is composed of countries that have very different views on human rights. And unless there's real political action to really strengthen the solidarity of all the countries that do believe in human rights across the North-South divide, you shouldn't be surprised that you have the exact same results. I think there's not enough attention paid to building this political consensus among countries that share the same views, and too much on the machinery.

As Frechette makes clear, the Human Rights Council must find new ways to work across regions. It must identify common human rights concerns and adopt confidence-building measures to address them on their merits, such as creating ad hoc cross-regional groups. A future challenge also is to link the work of the Human Rights Council to that of the Security Council. Once well established, the Human Rights Council should also hold one of its sessions in New York.

For the new council, this is a crucial period of construction and exploring new ways of operating. At the same time, those suffering human rights violations in all regions of the world need protection now. They and human rights defenders cannot wait. The council needs informed and critical support to help it to be impartial and effective. Civil society and opinion makers worldwide can do much to remind all forty-seven council members that they have been elected, individually, to promote and protect the highest human rights standards, not to play power politics.

THE UNITED NATIONS AND THE WCC

We the people of the United Nations, determined:

i. To save succeeding generations from the scourge of war which twice in our lifetime has brought untold sorrow to mankind,

ii. To reaffirm faith in fundamental human rights, in the dignity and worth of the human person, in the equal rights of men and women and of nations large and small,

iii. To establish conditions under which justice and respect for the obligations arising from treaties and other sources of international law can be maintained,

iv. To promote social progress and better standards of life in larger freedom, and for these ends

v. To practice tolerance and live together in peace with one another as good neighbours,

vi. To unite our strength to maintain international peace and security,

vii. To ensure by the acceptance of principles and the institution of methods, that armed force shall not be used, save in the common interest, and to employ international machinery for the promotion of economic and social advancement of all peoples, have resolved to combine our efforts to accomplish these aims.

This preamble to the Charter of the United Nations, adopted at San Francisco in 1945, remains one of the most compelling public documents of human history. It is also one of the least known to citizens of the nearly two hundred nations which have been accepted as sovereign states into membership of the United Nations organization. Few schoolchildren are required to memorize it alongside the timeless excerpts from the writings of the ancient Greek philosophers, the works of Schiller, Goethe or Shakespeare or such compelling public utterances as Abraham Lincoln's Gettysburg address. The lofty expectations expressed fifty years ago when the UN was erected on the ash heap of world war, if not completely forgotten, have been obscured by the thick haze of contemporary reality.

Public discussion about the UN today tends to concentrate not on these high humanitarian goals, but about the capacity of the world body to mobilize effective peacekeeping forces or to enforce the will of the Security Council by military means in accordance with the long-ignored provisions of Chapter VII of the Charter. Seen in this light, the UN appears impotent, lacking in imagination and incapable of holding in check the demonic forces moving in the post-Cold War world.

The spectacle of Blue Helmets withdrawing from Kigali, leaving behind anarchy, chaos and tens of thousands of bodies strewn in the streets of the Rwandan capital; international peacekeeping forces incapable of preventing the massive bombardments of Sarajevo; widely publicized charges of cowardice, corruption and criminal acts committed by members of UN forces - all these have sown doubt in the public mind about the UN's efficacy and contributed to a growing mood of global despair about the prospect of establishing a just world order based on compassion and respect for the rule of law.

The seventh assembly of the World Council of Churches met in Canberra in February 1991, as the Gulf war was raging. In its sweeping statement on this crisis, the assembly said:

The question of how major international decisions are made has become one of pressing urgency in the world today. The lessons learned from the way this first major world crisis in the post-Cold War era has been handled by the international community demand a critical examination of the emerging new world order. No one government or group of governments should either take or be allowed to take primary responsibility for the resolution of major conflicts beyond their own borders.

A study document provided to the WCC central committee in 1992 sharpened the critique of the new shape being given to the UN after the collapse of communism and the emergence of what President George Bush proclaimed as a "new world order". That paper questioned the growing concentration of decision-making power in the hands of a Security Council which was dominated by permanent members with the right of veto. It lamented the degree to which less powerful states were being marginalized from participation in global governance. It raised doubts about the political balance of the decisions taken, expressing concern that fundamental principles of the Charter, designed to protect the weak nations against the domination of the powerful, were being eroded.

THE CHURCHES' EARLY ROLE

For the ecumenical movement these were not new concerns. It is appropriate to recall how very influential was the contribution of international Christian social thought to promoting the idea of a United Nations organization and stating what the world could expect from such a universal body. Already thinking, in the midst of world war, about the shape of a new world order capable of managing a just peace and of protecting "future generations from the scourge of war", a Commission to Study the Bases of a Just and Durable Peace was created in 1940 in the US to implement the spirit of the 1937 conference of the Life and Work movement in Oxford on Church, Community and State.

Drawing on international ecumenical reflection on social principles, that commission issued in 1943 a "Statement of Political Propositions", which came to be known as the "Six Pillars of Peace":

The peace must provide the political framework for a continuing collaboration of the United Nations and, in due course, of neutral and enemy nations.

The peace must make provision for bringing within the scope of international agreement those economic and financial acts of national governments which have widespread international repercussions.

The peace must make provision for an organization to adapt the treaty structure of the world to changing underlying conditions.

The peace must proclaim the goal of autonomy for subject peoples, and it must establish international organization to assure and to supervise the realization of that end.

The peace must establish procedures for controlling military establishments everywhere.

The peace must establish in principle, and seek to achieve in practice, the right of individuals everywhere to religious and intellectual liberty.

Almost all these ideas found their way into the proposals developed in late summer 1944 at Dumbarton Oaks in Washington, DC, where the US, Great Britain, China and the USSR met to lay the groundwork for a UN Charter. Remembering the failure of the US to support the League of Nations after the First World War, the Commission on a Just and Durable Peace convened a national study conference in Cleveland in January 1945. Its message to the churches further elaborated on the "Six Pillars" and called for:

i. Addition of a preamble to the Charter to "reaffirm those present and long-range purposes of justice and human welfare which reflect the aspirations of people everywhere";

ii. Further development and codification of international law, "to the end that there shall be a progressive subordination of force to law";

iii. Establishment of a commission to further the "progress of colonial and dependent peoples to autonomy";

iv. Establishment of a special commission on human rights and fundamental freedoms which would, among other things, develop and implement guarantees for religious freedom;

v. Universal membership of the new organization;

vi. Specific provision for the limitation and reduction of armaments;

vii. Provisions to protect smaller nations from the exercise of arbitrary power by the great;

viii. Provision for amendments to the Charter which would not require the concurrence of the permanent members of the Security Council.

Church representatives present at the 1945 San Francisco founding conference pressed - with enormous success - for these points to be accepted. A preamble, cited above, was added along the recommended lines.

Most of the other ideas also commended themselves, though at times only after very vigorous debate. More than one observer in San Francisco credited the international Christian influence in particular with a determining role in achieving the more extensive provisions for human rights and fundamental freedoms which ultimately found their way into the Charter.

John Foster Dulles, a Presbyterian layman and later US secretary of state, said at the time:

> It was the religious people who took the lead in seeking that the organization should be dedicated not merely to a peaceful but to a just order. It was they who sought that reliance should be placed upon the moral forces which could be reflected in the General Assembly, the Social and Economic Council and the Trusteeship Council rather than upon the power of a few militarily strong nations operating in the Security Council without commitment to any standards of law and justice.

Church representatives also contributed significantly to the debate that resulted in the inclusion of Article 71, which provides for a permanent mechanism of consultation between the UN and non-governmental organizations (NGOs).

THE COMMISSION OF THE CHURCHES ON INTERNATIONAL AFFAIRS

In light of this new opportunity for continuing work within the framework of the new world body, the International Missionary Council and the Provisional Committee of the WCC organized a conference in Cambridge, England, in 1946, which formed a joint permanent Commission of the Churches on International Affairs (CCIA), which was one of the first international NGOs to be granted consultative status with the UN Economic and Social Council. The tasks of this new ecumenical body were set forth in terms of witness - to the lordship of Christ over man and history, by serving mankind in the field of international relations and promoting reconciliation and world community in accordance with the biblical testimony to the oneness of mankind by creation; to God's gracious and redemptive action in history; and to the assurance of the coming kingdom of God in Jesus Christ. This service is demanded by the church's participation in the continuing ministry of Christ in the world of priestly intercession, prophetic judgment, the arousing of hope and conscience and pastoral care for mankind.

In serving the churches as a source of information and guidance and a forum for discussion of international issues and common speaking and effective action on world problems, CCIA would encourage:

i. The promotion of peace with justice and freedom:
ii. The development of international law and of effective international institutions;
iii. The respect for and observance of human rights and fundamental freedoms, special attention being given to the problem of religious liberty;
iv. The international control and reduction of armaments;
v. The furtherance of economic justice through international economic cooperation;
vi. Acceptance by all nations of the obligation to promote to the utmost the welfare of all peoples and the development of free political institutions;

vii. The advance towards self-government of still-dependent territories:

viii. The international promotion of social, cultural, educational and humanitarian enterprises.

These remain the aims of the CCIA, which was early on incorporated into the World Council of Churches and continues today to be the instrument through which the WCC maintains very broad relationships with the UN and its specialized agencies, among them UNICEF, the UN High Commissioner for Refugees, the World Health Organization and other bodies.

NGO, CITIZENS' GROUPS, CHURCHES: THE CHALLENGE

Much of the UN system has come to rely heavily on its relationships with international NGOs. They provide agencies with information, analysis and ideas essential to the functioning of the international system. Often, they are the operative arm of the UN in such fields as delivery of humanitarian assistance, protection and sheltering of refugees and the delivery of basic health care. Increasingly, NGOs have become instrumental in elaborating national legislation for the protection of human rights and implementing these standards. Local, national and international NGOs have given the impetus for the creation of major UN programmes in the fields of improving the status of women, protection of the human environment and human settlements and on issues related to population and development.

In addition, more and more NGOs have become catalysts and actors in processes of mediation of conflicts, and are making indispensable contributions as the parties closest to peoples' movements for justice. Governments have always been somewhat uncomfortable with NGOs, and periodically threaten to restrict their role in relation to the UN. This has especially been the case in the field of human rights, where governments often feel that NGOs overstep their bounds in criticizing the behaviour of states. The 1993 World Conference on Human Rights, held in Vienna, brought many of these tensions to the surface very sharply, with some governments, particularly from the South, charging that NGOs, most of whom they regard as Northern, refuse to understand or to accept the special circumstances of developing nations and their non-Western cultures.

In fact, NGOs are proliferating all over the world, including especially in the South. This proliferation of expressions of "civil society" poses new challenges to the UN, which has increasing difficulty seeing how to manage the growing number of groups wishing to have a say in world forums. Independent citizens groups will almost certainly become an increasingly important factor in the process of global governance, and this reality demands more intensive study by those considering reform of the international system. Under the leadership of Secretary-General Boutros Boutros-Ghali, the UN promised a new dynamic. His oft-quoted "Agenda for Peace" has laid out a sweeping new perspective on this long-restricted dimension of the organization's responsibilities under the Charter. But in the perspective of many observers, this agenda has become bogged down in the peacekeeping and peacemaking phases.

The all-important peace building dimension has yet to be explored in depth, leading many to wonder whether the UN agenda has been led seriously off course - financially, politically and conceptually - by its increasing involvement with the application of military and economic sanctions as a means of restoring the peace and resolving conflict. Can there be peace anywhere in the world so long as the majority of the world's people are consigned to what seems to be a permanent crisis of poverty? Is it possible to proceed further without strengthening the role of the Economic and Social Council in its mandate to root out fundamental inequities and injustice among the nations and within particular societies?

The Vienna conference showed perhaps more clearly than any other recent world meeting that the present crisis in "world order" thinking has a clear spiritual dimension and pressing new religious overtones. There is a challenge here to the churches, in cooperation with peoples of other faiths. Having invested so much over the decades in promoting the international rule of law and effective instruments to protect human rights, what can we now contribute to recovering a universal vision of human rights, of peace with justice and the international promotion of social, cultural, educational and humanitarian enterprises?

What can we do to infuse a new awareness of and enthusiasm for the aims stated in the preamble to the UN Charter? What can we contribute concretely to the further development of international law in terms of implementation of the norms and standards which have been developed over this fifty years of impressive UN work in a range of fields? How can we contribute to a process of reform of the UN which makes it a fully participatory world body, where even the weakest and smallest nation has a respected role in decision-making and standard-setting? How can we contribute to a new spirit of tolerance where the powerful respect the weak, where every people is respected in its own right, and where the citizens of the world - "We the people of the United Nations" - can affect the course of history through an instrument they can respect as their own?

THE RATIFICATION OF HUMAN RIGHTS TREATIES

The ratification of international human rights treaties is critical to the worldwide observance of human rights and fundamental freedoms. The United Nations General Assembly and Commission on Human Rights have repeatedly emphasized the importance of ratification and have frequently encouraged states to ratify the relevant international instruments. Despite these efforts, acceptance of human rights treaties has been uneven; a considerable number of states have failed to ratify.

Recognizing that a regular mechanism for encouraging ratification would be more effective than general exhortations, the Sub-Commission on Prevention of Discrimination and

Protection of Minorities, a subsidiary body of the Commission on Human Rights, established in 1979 a sessional working group to consider ways and means of encouraging acceptance of human rights treaties. The procedures of the Working Group on the Encouragement of Universal Acceptance of Human Rights Instruments were modeled on the highly successful methods used by the International Labor Organization to encourage its members to accede to labor standards.

In 1980 and 1981, the working group began by systematically considering the written explanations of governments as to impediments they had encountered in ratifying human rights treaties and by receiving representatives from several countries to discuss these difficulties. This Note will discuss the rationale for the establishment of the working group, the group's accomplishments thus far, and recent debate concerning its authority. Finally, suggestions will be made for future objectives on which the group may profitably focus.

IMPORTANCE AND APPROPRIATENESS OF ENCOURAGING RATIFICATION

In keeping with its mandate to promote universal respect for human rights, the General Assembly has promulgated over 35 standard-setting treaties, which set forth obligations to be undertaken by ratifying countries for ensuring the observance of human rights. The General Assembly acknowledged in its often cited Resolution 32/130 that [i]t is of paramount importance for the promotion of human rights and fundamental freedoms that member States undertake specific obligations through accession to or ratification of international instruments in this field; consequently the standard setting work within the United Nations system in the field of human rights and the universal acceptance and implementation of the relevant international instruments should be encouraged.

Recognition of the importance of encouraging ratification of international human rights treaties is not new to the United Nations. The General Assembly and the Commission on Human

Rights have urged member states to accept these instruments on numerous occasions. But despite the frequency and eloquence of the general exhortations to ratify, ratifications continue to be made at only a moderate pace. Clearly, the goals of widespread ratification and implementation of human rights treaties cannot be met by relying on general resolutions requesting ratification.

ESTABLISHMENT OF THE WORKING GROUP

At its 32d session in 1979, the Sub-Commission on Prevention of Discrimination and Protection of Minorities adopted Resolution IB (XXXII), which established the Working Group on the Encouragement of Universal Acceptance of Human Rights Instruments. The Sub-Commission gave the working group a threefold mandate: 1. to make requests, through the Secretary-General, to governments that had not yet ratified the principal instruments that they inform the Sub-Commission of circumstances or difficulties preventing ratification or adherence; 2. to examine replies and, if necessary for further clarification, to invite representatives from such governments for discussions with the working group; and 3. to consider what assistance the United Nations might offer to enable them to ratify as soon as possible.

The working group was to accomplish its purposes during regular Sub-Commission sessions, which would avoid the expense of pre-sessional meetings. It was to direct its attention to certain human rights instruments enumerated in the resolution and to such other instruments as might be designated by the Sub-Commission. Pursuant to Resolution 1B (XXXII) of the Sub-Commission, the Secretary General in December 1979 asked governments that had not ratified the treaties to forward the specified explanatory information. Through the report on its 32d session, the Sub-Commission in the spring of 1980 informed the Commission on Human Rights of the creation of the sessional working group. The Commission offered no objection, taking note of the Sub-Commission's report without a vote.

The Working Group on the Encouragement of Universal Acceptance of Human Rights Instruments held its first meetings during the 33d session of the Sub-Commission in the fall of 1980. During the interim, 20 countries had responded to the Secretary-General's initial request for information. The group examined the replies and representatives of Australia, France, and the Netherlands appeared before it with oral clarifications of their countries' positions.

These representatives explained the remaining obstacles to ratification in their respective countries. A common difficulty was the question of extraterritorial criminal responsibility arising from the Convention against Apartheid. The group ended the session with plans to discuss the designation of additional instruments for attention at the next session. The Sub-Commission took note of the working group's report without resolution, decided to allot more time to future sessions, and requested that the Secretary-General make a study of the issue of extraterritorial criminal responsibility.

SCOPE OF AUTHORITY QUESTIONED AT THE 1981 HUMAN RIGHTS COMMISSION

In February and March 1981, the Commission on Human Rights held its 37th session in Geneva; the report of the Sub-Commission received close attention and was the subject of considerable debate. The representative from Brazil, Jardim Gagliardi, criticized the Sub-Commission's work in some instances as beyond its terms of reference. In particular, he assailed the Sub Commission for communicating directly with member states and for adopting resolutions and recommendations with budgetary effects that had not first been submitted for authorization by the Commission and ECOSOC.

After some debate, the Commission finally adopted a resolution reaffirming the Sub-Commission's significant role. Although the Commission referred to the debate surrounding the issue of competence, it only invited the Sub-Commission to take note and to bear in mind its tasks. Thus, the Commission did not take steps to delimit or redefine the Sub-Commission's terms of reference.

The working group on treaty ratification was not even mentioned in the resolution. Also at the 37th session, the Commission considered the Draft Medium Term Plan for the Human Rights Programme for the Period 1984-1989, which was submitted for comment by the Secretary-General. In setting out the general orientation of the program, the drafters "expected that useful contributions to the further ratification of international instruments will be made by the Sub-Commission's Working Group on the ratification of international standards in the field of human rights."

THE WORKING GROUP MEETS AGAIN

In August and September 1981, the working group and the Sub-Commission considered the questions raised in February and March by several Commission members. Members of the Sub-Commission supported its right to communicate directly with member states on human rights issues, as it had done for many years without objection. At the same time, the working group met for six sessions, carefully continued its country-by-country review of governmental replies, discussed the adequacy of the replies from the point of view of completeness and substance, and reconfirmed its authority to discuss replies directly with governments by inviting Sweden and Syria to participate in its deliberations. Neither Sweden nor Syria interposed any objections.

Based upon the recommendations of the working group, the Sub-Commission adopted a resolution by a vote of 20 in favor, none against, and only the Soviet expert abstaining, that continued the efforts of the working group by asking the Secretary-General to renew in 1981 the requests of 1979 and 1980 for governments to explain their difficulties in ratifying the principal human rights treaties.

The Sub-Commission sought to make the Secretary-General's inquiry even more pointed by individualizing the notes verbales to governments, that is, by drawing attention to those specific treaties each government had not yet ratified. The United States, for example, has signed but not ratified many of the principal human rights treaties. The Sub-Commission's resolution also requested that the Secretary-General invite the Governments of the Philippines, Rwanda, Iran, the Solomon Islands, and Suriname to supply additional information because the working group was not satisfied with the previous responses from those countries. The Sub-Commission resisted efforts to expand the mandate of the working group to include other human rights treaties, but decided to reconsider this issue at its next session.

All in all, the working group continued its work with the support of the Sub-Commission. Several states, including Australia which had appeared before the working group in 1980, had ratified the human rights instruments by 1981. While the working group has not yet generated substantive discussion of the general problems raised by ratification, which one might expect in the future, it has begun to establish itself as a relatively innovative institution for achieving the ratification, and thus ultimately the implementation, of human rights standards.

LEGITIMACY OF THE WORKING GROUP

The Brazilian delegate to the 1981 Human Rights Commission called into question the very heart of the working group's mandate: the mechanism of soliciting information from non ratifying states. This challenge to the Sub-Commission's competence presents two issues. First, does the Sub-Commission specifically have the authority, within its terms of reference, to encourage ratification by requesting information directly from governments regarding reasons for failure to ratify? The second, broader question is: should an international organization involve itself in encouraging ratification of its treaties, once adopted, and if so, to what extent?

As to the first issue, Mr. Gagliardi of Brazil asserted that direct communication with states is outside the Sub-Commission's competence. However, its terms of reference of 1948, which were expanded in 1949, seem to contemplate the receipt of information from governments by mandating that the Sub-Commission is to "undertake studies" in regard to human rights and to perform other functions delegated by ECOSOC and the Human Rights Commission.

The Sub-Commission's request for information from member states follows a very common practice of the Sub-Commission in particular and of the United Nations in general. The Sub-Commission has long studied human rights issues by means of inquiries to governments. For example, in preparing his Study of Discrimination in Education, Charles D. Ammoun, who was special rapporteur of the Sub-Commission, was supported by a note verbale of April 13, 1954, from the Secretary-General to member governments requesting assistance. Such inquiries to governments have become a standard practice.

The working group's invitation to several states for oral presentations, however, provides a greater opportunity for encouraging ratification and is a substantial innovation in the Sub-Commission's practice. Within the human rights field, only the Human Rights Committee organized under the UN Covenant on Civil and Political Rights and the Racial Committee under the International Convention on the Elimination of All Forms of Racial Discrimination have regularly pursued this approach.

Nevertheless, the Sub-Commission's working group does not violate the Sub-Commission's rules or terms of reference by inviting state representatives to discuss treaty ratification. Rule 69 of the Rules of Procedure of the Functional Commissions of the Economic and Social Council specifically provides authority for the Sub-Commission to "invite any State to participate in its deliberations on any matter of particular concern to that State." Hence, the Economic and Social Council has long authorized the Sub-Commission to pursue the approach it adopted for the working group on discussions of treaty ratification.

As to the second, broader question: on the one hand, Gagliardi argued that once an international organization has adopted a treaty and opened it for acceptance, the organization has no authority to take steps to encourage its entry into force. On the other hand, international organizations exist to promote certain goals that in principle all members share. In pursuit of those goals, organizations adopt conventions and treaties in accordance with Charter authority. Encouraging the acceptance of those instruments is simply further promotion of the goals of the organization. As noted above, United Nations bodies have often encouraged states to ratify instruments. The effect of such encouragement is not to interfere with a government's sovereign determination to ratify or not to ratify, but to urge governments to exercise that discretion.

Responding to the criticisms of the Sub-Commission, the Director of the UN Human Rights Division noted that the 1962 advisory opinion of the International Court of Justice in regard to Certain Expenses of the United Nations provides some guidance about the authority of the Sub-Commission to encourage ratification of human rights treaties and to communicate directly with governments. In determining whether peacekeeping expenses were improperly incurred by the United Nations, the Court was asked first to consider whether the peacekeeping activity was improper or unauthorized by the Charter.

The Court responded that "each organ [of the United Nations] must, in the first place at least, determine its own jurisdiction." This reasoning could support the Sub-Commission, as it determines its own jurisdiction to promote human rights. The establishment of the working group represents the Sub-Commission's effort to organize its work as efficiently as possible. Such an internal procedural affair has always been within the competence of the Sub-Commission.

The experience of other international organizations confirms the propriety and efficacy of these techniques. Since 1919, the International Labor Organization has operated a successful reporting mechanism to encourage ratification of its conventions. The working group's approach follows the ILO model in which member states report on their ratification of ILO conventions and recommendations. The reports, or the failure of members to report, are examined by a group of independent experts, the International Labor Committee of Experts on the Application of Conventions and Recommendations. Supplementing the formal reporting procedures, informal discussions between ILO staff and government representatives during sessions of the International Labor Conference have been perhaps the most effective means of resolving technical difficulties that impede ratification.

In 1930 the League of Nations adopted a similar procedure for encouraging ratification of League conventions. The League's reporting procedure and the attention it focused on the importance of ratification resulted in a large increase in ratifications. Historical records do not explain why the League's system of reporting on the status of ratifications was not immediately incorporated into UN practice, if not the Charter. The Economic and Social Council was given the authority to "make arrangements with the members of the United Nations and with the specialized agencies to obtain reports on the steps taken to give effect to its own recommendations and to recommendations on matters falling within its competence made by the General Assembly." In practice, ECOSOC has frequently obtained reports from governments regarding actions taken on individual resolutions and on groups of recommendations.

A 1971 study by the United Nations Institute for Training and Research entitled Toward Wider Acceptance of U.N. Treaties found that it would be within the competence of the United Nations to institute procedures similar to those of the ILO. The UNITAR study suggested the establishment of a committee of experts that would systematically review states' positions on treaty ratification. In the field of human rights, the Sub-Commission's Working Group on Universal Acceptance of Human Rights Instruments is just such a body.

The sessional Working Group on Universal Acceptance of Human Rights Instruments has just begun its efforts and it may be too soon to assess what contribution it may ultimately make to encouraging treaty ratification. Nevertheless, based upon the initial governmental replies to the working group's inquiries about impediments to ratification and the working group's early sessions, several observations and suggestions may be offered with a view toward maximizing the success of the group.

First, following the example of the ILO, the group should focus its attention on certain particularly important treaties. Even the nine treaties that were identified in its authorizing resolution may be too many for the group to consider efficiently during the few days available for meetings. The working group might address one or two treaties at a time to achieve the greatest effect upon ratifications, for example, by beginning with the two Covenants, which are the central human rights instruments, and then proceeding to the other instruments.

Second, the working group might delineate or concentrate on one or two issues that frequently delay or prevent ratification. It could explore those issues in detail and identify measures the United Nations might take to assist states in overcoming their problems. Such an issue was the question of extraterritorial criminal responsibility raised by the Apartheid Convention, which, as mentioned above, troubled many governments and prompted the working group at its first sessions to request a study of that issue.

Several other problems deserve study and attention by the working group. For example, Australia's reply mentioned the problem of federalism, and the Senate hearings that discuss this impediment to ratification of the Covenants were incorporated by reference in the U.S. response. The working group could determine the extent of this problem and could consult with federal states like Australia and Canada, which have apparently overcome such difficulties in ratifying some of the principal treaties. Indeed, the group might convene a discussion at which those countries could offer advice to others encountering similar impediments to ratification, and thus foster a valuable dialogue among countries.

Specifically, Canada could explain how it has been able to overcome provincial objections to ratification of the

Covenants and the Optional Protocol to the Civil and Political Covenant. Such a presentation might prove useful to Australia, which has ratified the Covenants and is still considering the Optional Protocol, and to the United States. While the U.S. Departments of Justice and State have attempted to protect state prerogatives regarding the human rights treaties, they have not generally consulted state officials, as apparently have Australia and Canada. Perhaps such consultation will clarify which objections states actually have and which might be overcome.

The working group at its 1981 session found many other problems of ratification in the governmental replies, but it has not yet fully considered them. For example, governments gave the following reasons for not ratifying the Optional Protocol to the International Covenant and Civil and Political Rights: 1. that the title included the word "optional"; 2. that individuals would be entitled to file complaints against states; and 3. that the procedure in the Protocol overlapped with regional human rights structures. With regard to the Slavery Convention, one government expressed concern over the compulsory jurisdiction of the International Court of Justice. In addition, the working group's 1981 report had this to say about the International Convention on the Suppression and Punishment of the Crime of Apartheid:

> [I]t was noted that the reasons often given by States for not having become parties to it were that:
>
> a. Such States had already become parties to the International Convention on Elimination of All Forms of Racial Discrimination;
> b. In their view, the definition of the crime of apartheid itself was rather vague;
> c. The Convention established extra-territorial criminal jurisdiction for the crime of apartheid; and
> d. There was incompatibility between the obligations imposed by the Convention and domestic legislation. Incompatibility with domestic legislation was evoked by States as a reason for not adhering to several other instruments as well.

A third possible approach that the working group might consider is suggested by the UNITAR study of 1971, which demonstrated that some impediments to treaty ratification are not substantive. An extreme example emerged in the replies to the working group of Rwanda and the United Republic of Cameroon, who explained that they lacked the texts of several human rights instruments. The Secretary-General promptly supplied the texts.

A number of states, including Belgium, the Dominican Republic, Ethiopia, Iran, Italy, Luxembourg, Mexico, Morocco, Rwanda, Spain, Suriname, the United States, and Venezuela, indicated that various treaties had been under consideration by administrative or legislative bodies for some period. The UNITAR study found that treaty ratifications were often delayed by such non substantive matters as inefficient bureaucratic coordination, administrative lethargy, the drafting of implementing legislation, and a lack of trained personnel to consider ratification issues. The working group might ask these countries whether technical assistance or some of UNITAR's ideas for coordinated administrative consideration of treaties might be helpful to them.

Moreover, some of the governments that were considering the treaties assured the working group that they would complete the ratification process "in the near future" or in a short time. Hence, after an appropriate interval, the group might inquire of Ethiopia, Iran, Mexico, and the Solomon Islands, for example, whether they had made any progress or might need assistance. A fourth approach that the working group might consider derives from the experience of the ILO. Certain UN staff members could be assigned responsibility for offering technical assistance identified by the working group as necessary for speedy ratification. Papua New Guinea indicated in its reply that the Covenants may conflict with customs and laws of that country. Perhaps technical assistance and knowledge of the way the Covenants have been applied in countries with similar problems might aid the Government of Papua New Guinea in achieving ratification.

Finally, the Director of the Human Rights Division and his staff could follow the example of the ILO by holding informal meetings with governmental representatives on the difficulties of obtaining acceptance of human rights treaties, using the working group's material as a basis for discussion. In addition, in the course of receiving governmental delegations during the sessions of the General Assembly, the Secretary-General could initiate discussions about ratification of the principal human rights instruments.

The new Working Group on Universal Acceptance of Human Rights Instruments has the potential of encouraging greater ratification of human rights treaties, if questions about its competence raised at the 37th session of the Human Rights Commission do not impede its efforts. A specific grant of authority to solicit governmental reports and appearances would be clearly preferable to the current implied authority. If doubt remains about the competence of the Sub-Commission to assign such tasks to its sessional working group, ECOSOC and/or the General Assembly should give the necessary authorization.

Indeed, a resolution by one of those bodies would endow the working group with an incontestable mandate, higher visibility, and consequent increased effectiveness. Without such a resolution, however, the working group would still be able to pursue significant United Nations objectives while remaining within its mandate. It can continue to encourage the communication of difficulties encountered by states in the ratification process and to determine what assistance can be given. The group's approach combines previously tested reporting techniques with an innovative method for open discussion of human rights treaty ratifications. The present mandate of the Sub-Commission certainly encompasses such efforts.

The working group's efforts to study and communicate problems commonly encountered in the ratification of human rights instruments, and to provide states with assistance, should make it possible to increase the number of states parties to human rights treaties. Other organizations such as the International Committee of the Red Cross and the UN High

Commissioner for Refugees might also consider such methods for encouraging ratification of their respective treaties. The ILO and now the Working Group on Encouragement of Universal Acceptance of Human Rights Instruments could provide valuable models for other international organizations concerned with the implementation of a variety of important standards.

THE EVOLUTION

The 50th Anniversary of the adoption the Universal Declaration of Human Rights by the United Nations General Assembly occurred on 10 December 1998. During 1998 there were a series of commemorative events in New Zealand and elsewhere. Included were books and articles. Thus this journal, late last year, published an article by Paul Lauren, Regents Professor in the University of Montana's Department of History, on New Zealand's role in the evolution of international human rights. Professor Lauren had just published his major contribution to the history of human rights, The Evolution of International Human Rights. This is a text which should be on the desk of every practitioner in the field of human rights.

At a function on 10 December the Don McKinnon launched the New Zealand Handbook on International Human Rights, published by the Ministry of Foreign Affairs and Trade and intended as 'an entrance point for New Zealanders who would like to know more about the international human rights system and how it works'. A reader of this Handbook or of Lauren's Evolution cannot but be impressed, and probably surprised, at the ramifications and achievements of the international human rights movement as it has developed since the adoption of the UN Charter in 1945.

However, as the name suggests, Evolution also provides an account of the development of international recognition of and responsibility for the rights of the individual person from its religious and philosophical beginnings. Lauren follows three themes. He recalls the visionaries - prophets, philosophers, religious and political leaders - who at different times and in diverse locations have challenged traditional patterns of authority, privilege, and vested interest. They have envisaged a world in which all people enjoyed certain basic and fundamental rights simply by virtue of being human. He examines the part that the doctrine of national sovereignty, or domestic jurisdiction, has played in frustrating these visions. And he has recognised the significance of political, economic, social, and intellectual upheavals, in particular wars and revolutions, in their realisation.

EVOLUTIONARY PROCESS

Early religious doctrine and philosophical theories of natural law focused on universal responsibilities and duties rather than on rights, but the Renaissance and Reformation helped to pave the way for the spiritual emancipation of the individual. Political upheaval played its part. The barons in England imposed the Magna Carta on King John and so helped to establish the principle that liberties could be guaranteed by law. Political unrest in England led to three further constitutional milestones - the Petition of Right 1628, the Habeas Corpus Act 1679 and the Bill of Rights 1689. These became landmarks in the history of civil and political rights, often referred to as first degree rights. Then it was revolution that provided the impetus for the Declaration of Independence, the Constitution, and the Bill of Rights in the United States and the Declaration of the Rights of Man and Citizen in France.

Lauren points out that these human rights landmarks reflected more vision than reality. Thus actual practice in the United States denied equal rights to at least four categories of Americans: slaves, women, the unpropertied and indigenous peoples. The principle of national sovereignty placed issues of human rights firmly in the domain of the national state - there could be no interference from without. Nevertheless, national recognition of individual rights, along with the works of visionaries like Hugo Grotius, John Locke and Thomas Paine, contributed to the building up of widely recognised standards that would be essential elements of an international human rights regime.

Lauren provides an absorbing account of the development of particular human rights issues: the campaign to abolish the international slave trade; missionary, humanitarian, and international efforts to ameliorate the impact of imperial expansion in Africa, Asia, and the Pacific; the crusade for women's fights; care for the victims of armed combat with the work of the Red Cross; relief for victims of class distinction, whether left over from feudalism or created by modern capitalism and the Industrial Revolution. The class issue saw the emergence of a second generation of human rights - social and economic rights. Another issue - one that clearly raised the question of limits on national sovereignty - was that of humanitarian intervention to deal with cases of religious and ethnic persecution that generated international outrage, as in the case of the Ottoman Empire's treatment of its minorities.

ACCELERATED VISION

The First World War accelerated both the vision and practice of international human rights. There was an extended role for the Red Cross movement and for humanitarian assistance to civilians affected by the war. The extensive use of non-whites and non-Westerners in the armed forces led to claims by blacks in the United States to full citizenship rights, while Africans and Asians from dependent territories began to have visions of self-determination. The responsibilities that women were called upon to assume meant that they were released from traditional restraints.

The peace treaties reorganised the map of Europe in the name of self-determination, but there continued to be religious and ethnic minorities to protect. This protection was to be provided by the Minorities Treaties, under which new and vanquished states assured protection of life and liberty to their inhabitants, 'without distinction of birth, nationality, language, race, or religion'. The League of Nations assumed responsibility for guaranteeing the new national borders and for enforcing the provisions of the Minorities Treaties. Recognition of the rights of labour saw the establishment of the International Labor Office.

Signatories to the Covenant of the League assumed human rights responsibilities: fair and humane conditions of labour for men, women and children; control of traffic in women and children and in opium and other drugs; international prevention and control of disease; freedom of communication and transit; and encouragement and promotion of the work of the Red Cross.

IMPASSIONED DEBATE

The issue of racial discrimination provoked the most impassioned debate. The Japanese delegation proposed that there should be a clause in the Covenant supporting the principle of the right of all to racial equality. Intransigent opposition came from President Woodrow Wilson, although his Fourteen Points had been the focal point of Allied war aims. When the issue came to a vote the Japanese prevailed by 11 out of 17. There was no unanimity rule, but Wilson, in the chair, insisted that the proposal had failed because it had not received unanimous support. The reluctance of the imperial powers to give up their colonial territories and their resort to the Mandate System also led to criticism that the Peace Settlement established a regime under which self-determination was for whites alone.

The fact that the League of Nations was made up of nation-states jealous of their national sovereignty led to its failure and the handling of the issue of minorities illustrated its powerlessness. The jurisdiction of Minorities Committees was confined to minorities in Europe. The League was inundated with approaches from minorities outside Europe, but all were told that it was not possible to help them. This was the response given to Maori leader T.W. Ratana when he went to Geneva. Indeed, a League majority declared in 1928 their determination 'to insure that states with a minority within their borders should be protected from the danger of interference by other powers in their internal affairs'.

PEOPLE'S WAR

The Second World War, as a war against Fascism, was to be a people's war, a war which could not be won unless the fundamental rights of the peoples of the Earth were secured. President Roosevelt responded with his Four Freedoms: freedom of speech and expression; freedom of worship; freedom from want; and freedom from fear. Then Roosevelt and Churchill issued their Atlantic Charter, followed in 1942 by the Declaration of the United Nations, signed initially by 26 nations, one of which was New Zealand.

It is at this point that the New Zealand contribution to the evolution of international human rights became significant. In 1994 Paul Lauren was teaching at Massey University, having come to New Zealand as a Senior Fulbright Scholar. He lectured at most university campuses throughout New Zealand and conducted research in the Ministry of Foreign Affairs and Trade's archives in Wellington. He also held significant interviews. As a result, his book is particularly valuable to a New Zealand reader, because of the attention he gives to the New Zealand contribution to the development of international human rights. Indeed, the critical non-New Zealander might suggest that the compliments that Lauren has paid in his book and his published articles might be over-generous!

In his article in this journal, Lauren filled out material in Evolution relating to this New Zealand contribution. In the League New Zealand had adopted a negative approach to human rights issues, but this changed with the advent of the Labour government in 1935. Then, Peter Fraser and Walter Nash ' [t]hroughout the course of the war... spoke frequently, eloquently, and with conviction' about the goal of human rights set out in the Declaration of the United Nations.

DRAFT CHARTER

Nevertheless, war and peace aims that emphasised human rights had little impact on the four great powers (the United States, Britain, Soviet Union and China) when they came together at Dumbarton Oaks to draft a Charter for a new international organisation to be known as the United Nations. They designed a powerful Security Council, which the great powers would dominate through permanent membership and a power of veto.

All nations would be represented on a weak General Assembly and a subordinate Economic and Social Council.

One of the purposes of the United Nations would be to 'achieve international co-operation in the solution of international economic, social, and other humanitarian problems'. The General Assembly was given some responsibilities in this area, and the Economic and Social Council was 'to facilitate solutions of international economic, social, and other humanitarian problems and promote respect for human rights and fundamental freedoms'. This was the only reference to human rights. Furthermore, the draft contained no provision for the future of colonial possessions.

It is ironical that the Chinese were not satisfied with this limited recognition of human rights. No doubt aware of the difficulties the Japanese had faced after the First World War; they proposed that the new organisation should support the self-determination of peoples and uphold the principle of equality of all states and all races. The Chinese were no more successful than the Japanese.

AMENDMENT PROPOSALS

Peter Fraser and other middle and small state leaders were critical of the Dumbarton Oaks draft. The host of amendments submitted at the United Nations Conference at San Francisco included those relating to human rights. New Zealand and Australia submitted their own proposals and they joined the majority that was successful in having a range of human rights provisions included in the Charter of the United Nations.

The Charter preamble begins 'We the Peoples of the United Nations determined to reaffirm faith in fundamental human rights, in the dignity and worth of the human person, in the equal rights of men and women of nations large and small' The same theme appears as a purpose of the United Nations with an important addition: promotion and encouragement of respect for human rights and fundamental freedoms for all is to be 'without distinction as to race, sex, language, or religion'.

A General Assembly with enlarged authority was given human rights responsibilities, while the Security Council would be able to determine that a serious human rights violation constituted a 'threat to the peace', thus justifying United Nations action, including humanitarian intervention. In the Charter chapter on 'International Economic and Social Co-operation', the United Nations is required to promote 'Universal respect for, and observance of, human rights and fundamental freedoms for all without distinction as to race, sex, language, or religion.' Then, all members pledge themselves to take joint and separate action in cooperation with the organisation to achieve this purpose. An Economic and Social Council, promoted to the status of Principal Organ of the United Nations, could 'make recommendations for the purpose of promoting respect for, and observance of human rights and fundamental freedoms for all' and was required to set up a Commission for the promotion of human rights.

The Charter provisions were a huge step forward in the recognition of international human rights, but the language used did not suggest that vision had yet become reality: statements of principle about human rights and provision for their promotion and observance did not amount to effective enforcement. Did the signatory states appreciate that enforcement would involve limitations on national sovereignty? Their answer was given in Article 2(7) of the Charter:

Nothing contained in the present Charter shall authorise the United Nations to intervene in matters which are essentially within the domestic jurisdiction of any State or shall require the members to submit such matters to settlement under the present Charter; but this principle shall not prejudice the application of enforcement measures under Chapter VII.

Clearly the pressure of arriving at a consensus on a Charter text led to the acceptance of contradictory provisions. The discussion of Article 2(7) in the New Zealand report on the San Francisco Conference would suggest that the New Zealand delegation was one of those which in Lauren's words 'either did not completely understand the full implications of their decisions or somewhat naively believed that they might just be able to have their cake and eat it too'. The report explained that the text had been introduced by the sponsoring powers and amended in accordance with proposals by Australia, with whom 'New Zealand had closely collaborated on this issue.'

Lauren describes how the adoption of the United Nations Charter precipitated claims for self-determination and racial equality from colonial territories, while non-governmental organisations and individuals became much more active in criticising abuses of human rights both at home and abroad. When the United Nations Commission on Human Rights was established, it received a veritable flood of petitions. 'Literally thousands of people from all over the world sent written appeals to the commission begging for help against the abuses of their own governments and pleading for the United Nations to apply the principles delineated in the Charter to them.' The Commission had no authority to deal with these appeals and had to declare its impotence.

TRANSFORMING VISIONS

Lauren goes on to discuss the progress that has been made in 'Transforming Visions into Reality'. The first important step was to decide more clearly what the vision was. Other than its emphasis on non-discrimination, some description of social and economic rights and provisions relating to non-self-governing territories and trusteeship, the Charter does not set out the human rights that are to be promoted and observed hence the significance of the adoption of the Universal Declaration of Human Rights in 1948. The General Assembly proclaimed the Declaration 'as a common standard of achievement for all peoples and all nations'. Lauren recognises that the New Zealand delegation made an important contribution in the drafting of the Declaration, particularly in its support for the inclusion of social, economic, and cultural rights.

Henceforth the vision centered on the Universal Declaration, but it still had to be implemented. This phase of the transformation - vision into reality - can be discussed under two headings:

The adoption of international conventions establishing legal obligations:

The Universal Declaration was envisaged as part of an International Bill of Rights which would also contain an International Covenant on Human Rights and measures of implementation. This would mean that states could voluntarily accept the rights set out in the Covenant as legal obligations and agree on procedures for their enforcement. In the event, two International Covenants, one on Civil and Political Rights and the other on Economic, Social, and Cultural Rights, each incorporating its own measures of implementation, were not adopted until 1966. At the same time, the Assembly adopted an Optional Protocol to the Covenant on Civil and Political Rights, under which individuals who have exhausted their domestic remedies would have the right to complain to a United Nations Human Rights Committee that their rights under the Covenant had been violated.

There are other Conventions in the human rights area which create legally binding obligations for those states which become parties. The International Convention on the Elimination of All Forms of Racial Discrimination had preceded the Covenant. Other core conventions deal with discrimination against women, the rights of the child, and torture. New Zealand is party to these conventions as well as to the International Covenants and the Optional Protocol. All are conveniently published as appendices to the Handbook.

Action by United Nations organs operating under the provisions of the Charter:

Controversial human rights issues were introduced at the first session of the General Assembly. Encouraged by an Assembly resolution condemning persecution and racial discrimination, India attacked South Africa for its policies of racial discrimination. There was a violent reaction from Jan Smuts of South Africa, asserting domestic jurisdiction. Without support from Britain, Canada, the United States, Australia, and New Zealand, the Assembly passed, with the necessary two-thirds majority, a resolution recognising that the treatment of

Indians in South Africa was not in conformity with international obligations under the Charter. The two governments were called on to discuss their problem and report back to the General Assembly.

The succession of resolutions dealing with South Africa's racial policies, which became more radical as the membership of the United Nations expanded to include former colonial territories, marked the decline of the effectiveness of Article 2(7). This is illustrated by the dilemma faced by New Zealand governments and their advisers as New Zealand moved from opposing, to abstaining on, and then to supporting resolutions criticising South Africa. Support came for the first time in 1958.

Violations of human rights can seriously jeopardise international peace; indeed it is difficult to envisage an international incident that does not have a human rights ingredient. It has, therefore, become accepted that the Security Council can consider humanitarian intervention, including the imposition of sanctions if necessary. Thus the deployment of United Nations peacekeeping forces, such as those in Bosnia-Herzegovina and Croatia, has included human rights components as part of their mission.

Given increasing international acceptance of human rights issues as legitimate matters for international scrutiny, the United Nations has established a significant number of non treaty mechanisms and procedures. For instance, the Commission on Human Rights, as the main United Nations body dealing specifically with human rights issues, has been transformed from a standard-setting body to one which can respond to human rights violations and pursue a wide range of measures to handle human rights.

In 1993 the General Assembly established the post of United Nations High Commissioner for Human Rights as the UN official principally responsible for UN human rights activities. Mary Robinson, the present High Commissioner, has a wide mandate. She is to be guided by the recognition that 'all human rights - civil, cultural, economic, political, and social - are universal, indivisible, and interdependent and interrelated'.

Paul Lauren concludes his survey: the international community now accepts that any serious disregard for the vision of human rights proclaimed by the Universal Declaration and elaborated in other standard-setting documents and conventions is a matter of legitimate concern requiring the community to take appropriate action.

There are, without a doubt, universal human rights. The 1948 Universal Declaration of Human Rights represents a broad consensus on this. There is no doubt that philosophy and philosophers have contributed deeply to the content and nature of human rights. At the same time, however, my studies of the practice of human rights law indicate that rights involve much more than just theory; they entail a process involving grievances, the articulation of claims based on those grievances, followed by political negotiations, the recognition of rights, and the battle for the implementation of those rights.

There are those who say that economic, social, and cultural rights are not human rights because they are not philosophically grounded. It is critical to bear in mind that past codification of rights-including the Magna Carta, the English Declaration of Rights, the French and US declarations, and the Universal Declaration of Human Rights were all results of political processes. In this sense, while philosophers are relevant, they are not decisive. From what international actors and intellectual circles do the most serious challenges to human rights come?

At a formal level, there is no real challenge to human rights today. The United Nations Commission on Human Rights, while mired in many problems, has successfully held a one-week high-level summit at the beginning of its session for the last two years. During this conference, high-level personalities from about 80 to 100 countries come to explain their actions with reference to human rights. In this sense, whatever other faults the commission has, it provides a forum for leaders of countries who come to the United Nations to be held accountable in terms of human rights.

The more powerful challenges to human rights come first from global poverty and second from internal conflicts. Currently, we are seeing religious or cultural challenges to human rights, but rather challenges that are economically or politically rooted. It is these challenges, in turn, that sometimes produce cultural and religious tensions. Under what circumstances a government might be justified in violating human rights? The general answer is that, especially in today's world, we must be very careful when we make for such allowances.

As the Acting High Commissioner of Human Rights issued a statement asserting that, "ours is a world in which human rights are affected by poverty, conflicts, equality, and gender discrimination, and state violence against its own citizens." Because we are dealing in a world plagued with such problems, I think it is important as a matter of principle to hold fast to the human rights norms when possible. In all other cases, however, we must look to the answers given in international human rights law. International human rights law says that there are, in fact, a few limited situations in which states may derogate from human rights. Article 4 of the International Covenant of Civil and Political Rights states that human rights norms may be curtailed if the life of a nation is threatened or if there is a public emergency affecting the life of a nation.

Moreover, there are grounds of limitation specified for the definitions of the rights themselves. In this regard, therefore, many conditions must be met before a human rights violation is deemed acceptable: there must be an emergency that affects the life of a nation, the existence of the emergency must be officially proclaimed, and the measures taken must be proportional to the emergency. In the last decade, what have been the most important developments in the law and practice of international human rights?

The biggest developments in the international human rights field have been the establishment first of the High Commissioner of Human Rights in 1993 and second of the International Criminal Court (ICC) in 1998. Whatever debates there are about the ICC, its establishment and existence sends a powerful message to those who have committed or are tempted to commit criminal violations of human rights that they could have gotten away with before the ICC. One element that is important to the development of international human rights law is an increasing effort within the United Nations to enhance national protection systems.

A national protection system takes into account six questions. First, is your constitution in conformity with international human rights law? Second, are your laws in conformity with international human rights law? Third, can your courts draw on human rights standards? Fourth, are you teaching human rights in schools? Fifth, do you have institutions like national human rights commissions? And sixth, are you monitoring the state of human rights in your country?

The power of the concept is that it is based on international norms. We must now seek to build stronger national protection at home in every country. On that note, are human rights better preserved and promoted through the legal doctrine of institutions like the ICC and the International Court of Justice (ICJ), or through legislative processes like those of the United Nations and domestic governments?

The fact that former Chilean President Augusto Pinochet had to go through the legal procedures in the United Kingdom and Chile, the fact that former Yugoslav President Slobodan Milosevic has to go through the legal procedures elsewhere, and the fact that people in the Democratic Republic of Congo have cases brought against them in Belgium are all very strong ways of enforcing human rights. Therefore, legal mechanisms have to exist as well as political and social action. To what extent has non-compliance with international human rights law been a problem? Why do countries like Libya follow international legal rulings even though there is no formal mechanism by which to enforce those rulings?

In the international arena, there is a high level of implementation because it is in the self-interest of governments to abide by the basic rules of international law. Of course, when it comes to the vital national interest of the state, there is a pronounced preference for negotiation over judicial arbitration. The stakes in a judicial ruling are just too high.

That applies to big countries as well. For example, there was a case concerning fishing rights in the Gulf of Maine that involved the United States and Canada, and it took a lot of negotiation before the two countries would agree to go before a chamber of the ICJ. To gauge their chances in court, each country wanted to be sure about how the case was going to be handled and who was going to handle it. So there is a fair measure of compliance when it comes to vital national interests, and states usually prefer to negotiate.

Moreover, we are still living in a decentralized international community in which we depend largely on the cooperation of states for compliance. For example, while the UN Security Council can instill some degree of order in situations of war and peace, it can very rarely enforce that order unless the major powers of the world help and even this level of enforcement has complications of its own. In the past months, I have researched three things: first, what is it that the United Nations contributes to international security? Second, I have asked questions about the United Nations and the future of international law. I think the future culture of the United Nations should further accentuate the role of international law-not in a preachy manner towards the powerful, but over a period of time to help build up a culture of understanding and loyalty to international law. Finally, I have looked at what I consider to be the key principles of international human rights law.

In the 1970s, one still saw movements such as the World Peace Through Law movement, backed by institutions of international law and professors of international law. Nowadays, however, we have left these movements aside because we have to work at the business of extending and strengthening international law. It comes back to what I said about human rights education: we all believe that we must live in a world under the rule of law, but even the United States in some situations cannot impose and enforce it. So we are still working at what I would call a "culture of legality."

You had a role in drafting the UN Secretary-General's 1992 Agenda for Peace. Was the Agenda-which was bold but nonetheless did not stop, for example, the Rwandan genocide from occurring-successful? If you could go back and rewrite the document, what would it look like? It was a visionary and important document. In arguing for peace enforcement, the United Nations made claims on which it could not deliver.

Also, for one of those years, the UN mediator was simultaneously the Special Representative of the Secretary General in charge of the peace operations. If the mediators are pushing for peace but the major powers think that they should support one side or the other, it becomes difficult to achieve a peace agreement.

The second thing that learned from the Yugoslav peace process is that there comes a time when the United Nations must take a stance of principle. The treatment of the people in the safe areas is a case in point. In retrospect come to think that the United Nations should have taken a firmer stance of principle. The UN Security Council declared a safe area, but let us say the general public did not understand or accept that the United Nations could not fully protect the people stationed there.

The third thing that learned is that the United Nations and the Secretary General must explain to the general public what it is that he can and cannot deliver. If the public has such high expectations that the United Nations cannot possibly live up to them, then it is bound to lead to disillusionment. The United Nations has strength in contributing to the prevention of conflicts, but there are other things the United Nations just simply cannot do and in the Yugoslav process, we the Secretariat may have given the impression that we could do things we could not.

Today, international law is confronted with changing circumstances including the perpetually imminent threat of terrorism. What tradeoffs do contemporary nations face between stopping terrorism and upholding human rights? The international human rights movement and national human rights organizations are complaining that the war on terrorism has been abused by some to violate human rights.

The subcommittee produced a digest of jurisprudence on international and regional human rights protection. What came out of this work is that both international and domestic courts insist that respect for the law is not only possible but is vital in the fight against terrorism. There is significant jurisprudence that provides guidance in this regard. An emergency must be officially proclaimed and the measures taken must follow the principle of proportionality.

If you look at this issue more closely, you find cases going back to the 1970s in the United Nations Commission on Human Rights and in regional courts like the European court of human rights that articulate that one must be wary of this route to the largest extent possible. One must maintain use of civilian tribunals. In other words, international human rights law and the recent resolutions of the UN Security Council all emphasize that the fight against terrorism must be based on respect for human rights.

UN SPECIAL RAPPORTEUR

The United Nations Commission on Human Rights (CHR) appointed its first special rapporteur in 1979 to report on abuses in Chile under the Augusto Pinochet dictatorship. This initiative established an important precedent for the institution of special procedures to examine serious human rights violations in any country. In 1982, for the first time, a thematic rapporteurship was set up to examine summary and arbitrary executions. Consequently, the fifty-three member states of the CHR have taken steps toward a worldwide system for monitoring human rights. In mid-2002, there were forty-one Special Rapporteurs: thirty on thematic issues, eleven working in specific countries.

The selection process for Special Rapporteurs is somewhat inscrutable, perhaps even byzantine. It is entirely controlled by the chair of the CHR. Through direct consultations with the members of the bureau, the chair appoints specialists. The overall quality of appointees thus depends largely on the courage, insight, and negotiating skills of the chair. It does not suffice to want to be a special rapporteur, much less to nominate oneself, nor does having a particular interest in a given country or theme carry much weight. Vacancies arise when the CHR, which authorizes and renews mandates, proposes new missions or when someone resigns.

Country-specific and thematic mandates are reviewed annually. In April 1999, the commission instituted a term limit of six years for experts. It is extremely unlikely to assign Special Rapporteurs who do not have at least the acquiescence of their own governments, although some candidates may not enjoy enthusiastic support from their home countries. Many civil society organizations, at higher decibel levels since the CHR's fifty-eighth session in spring 2002, have criticized the growing politicization of the appointment process, in which the expertise of candidates sometimes appears to be secondary to their political acceptability.

Criticisms have also arisen related to the advisability of appointing Special Rapporteurs who originate from the same region in which their mandate is located. During the fifty-eighth session, for example, the African group insisted on appointing a mandate holder by name in the resolution on racism, clearly contrary to established procedures. Whatever the merits of the candidate, this initiative was criticized vociferously and appropriately by civil society organizations because of the precedent-setting implications and the perceived threat to the autonomy of appointments.

A common complaint raised by the Special Rapporteurs themselves is the lack of availability and poor quality of support they receive from the Office of the High Commissioner for Human Rights (OHCHR). Threats to international human rights norms require the creation of new mandates each year; as a result, services quickly become overloaded, especially because they were inadequate in the first place. Quite simply, mandates proliferate without a corresponding increase in the resources to support them. To perform their duties, Special Rapporteurs must secure invitations from member states. Too many governments do not reply or delay responding to requests for a mission.

A small but growing group, consisting of thirty-eight forthcoming countries, has issued "standing invitations."

Brazil, Costa Rica, Georgia, Peru, and Switzerland have just joined this select group. Donor governments should provide incentives for others to join the club. Special Rapporteurs take pains to maintain their independence, impartiality, and objectivity; to weigh the information on human rights provided by governments and civil society groups; and to report fully on the progress made and obstacles faced. Special Rapporteurs perform a delicate balancing act.

They must discharge their duties with thoroughness and sobriety, bearing in mind their essential role of protecting the interests of victims. At the same time, they must avoid high-profile appearances that draw excessive attention to their office. However, discretion sometimes has its advantages. For instance, which I would label "principled engagements." with authorities in Rangoon, whereas neither Human Rights Watch nor Amnesty International has been, unfortunately, able to conduct research in Myanmar for over a decade.

For many of us, the role model remains Tadeuz Mazowiescki, former prime minister of Poland. He pushed the limits with his outspoken condemnation of gross human rights violations and with his accessibility to the media. He struggled with his conscience and resigned as Special Rapporteur for the former Yugoslavia when he judged that his influence was being overshadowed by events on the ground, especially ethnic cleansing. His own integrity and forthright manner, along with his willingness to resign when his own actions proved futile, provide an exemplar.

Media exposure between missions is decisive for building awareness about each mandate. Under the right conditions, it helps Special Rapporteurs foster contacts between countries concerned with the human rights situation or thematic mandate of a country, and it helps inform public debate. During what would be my last mission to Burundi in August 1999 (it was followed by a serious auto crash, which left me unable to perform my duties during the last year of the mandate), I authorized Arte a French-German television network to cover my mission.

Very little is known around the world about the standard operating procedures for Special Rapporteurs. Governments and civil society organizations tend to attribute greater powers to Special Rapporteurs than we actually have and, at the same time, underestimate the moral authority conferred by the job. We are often regarded as yet another type of UN official in that we have the status of "experts on an official mission" and enjoy a series of privileges and immunities while in the field. In fact, Special Rapporteurs receive no compensation, only reimbursement for travel-related expenses. The logic behind pro bono service is to ensure that Special Rapporteurs are more autonomous and are less constrained than UN officials. We are, however, expected to comply with the terms of a UN code of conduct.

Owing to their close working relations with member states, Special Rapporteurs often encounter highly ambiguous reactions from observers and feel certain ambivalence. They serve as voices for the voiceless and as spokespersons for the victims, but our effectiveness depend on maintaining a dialogue with host countries and concerned capitals around the world, and most especially with the permanent members of the Security Council. An essential aspect of the job description is to foster contacts with other countries concerned with a particular human rights crisis. To this end, it is essential to maintain dialogue within the extended diplomatic community.

Their work essentially entails gathering facts and recording serious violations-indeed, it is not so very different from the function performed by many nongovernmental organizations (NGOs) working on human rights. Hence, they cannot merely assign blame but must be capable of acknowledging genuine advances made by governments. We must seek not only to make known personal views but also to express the official UN position with respect to universal norms.

They should not merely point fingers. Though fact-finding is the essence of our duties, we should avoid heaping shame upon hosts or leveling the power of embarrassment at them as human rights organizations do to such great effect when calling attention to gross violations in a given country. The role of a special rapporteur goes well beyond that of NGOs because we work closely with all parties interested in improving the status of human rights, especially the state. As suggested earlier, there is room for both styles of engagementindeed, vocal and visible criticism and behind-the-scenes negotiating are complementary and often mutually reinforcing.

There is an inescapable tension between impartial fact-finding and clear and sound public assessments. Objective fact-finding does not mean neutrality; Special Rapporteurs will sometimes be required to denounce abuses for which there is evidence. We may conclude that the principle of impartiality contradicts a personal assessment of the problem during a mission. If Special Rapporteurs witness a consistent pattern of allegations of gross human rights violations, summary executions, torture, or acts of genocide, we must denounce them and not be limited to discreet documenting. However, this is an important tactical decision. The situation must be conscience-shocking enough to risk setting aside the leverage resulting from privileged access. We must always bear in mind, though, that the nature of our mandates involves fact-finding and not political advocacy, even if, for instance, some overlap between the two approaches may occur in countries undergoing processes of political transition.

Our duties encompass the analysis of problems and efforts to find solutions, as well as the transmission of support and encouragement from the international community of states. Constructive criticism is more easily accepted than tongue lashings, especially when such criticism is accompanied by concrete gestures of cooperation. If a special rapporteur seeks to achieve progress in a particular human rights situation, responsibility must be shared with the government, opposition forces, and civil society a kind of a "joint venture" among these different actors. Special Rapporteurs expect reciprocal cooperation, openness, and evidence of a serious commitment demonstrated by deeds and not merely words. We can only report progress backed by hard evidence.

If we fall short-by maintaining momentum with encouraging words when they are not justified-our role is devoid of significance. It is clearly infeasible for a Special Rapporteur to tackle simultaneously all the human rights problems of a given country. Accordingly, we should be selective and pursue critical issues that have the highest likelihood of an immediate payoff and that can most easily be addressed during the course of brief fact-finding missions, generally lasting no more than fifteen days. It is thus crucial during such missions to maintain dialogue with the government while building confidence, developing a process of consultation, and fostering partnerships with other relevant players.

Without cowering or pandering, we must also be mindful of governmental priorities and areas of concern while seeking to address them honestly. At the same time, we should be careful to address those issues that are of greatest concern for the majority of the population and that may constitute long-term structural hardships. We should thus concentrate on establishing a set of operating principles and a framework for cooperation. Visiting prisons and labor camps and conducting confidential interviews with political prisoners and other detainees are certainly prerequisites for a modicum of credibility. Also essential are an overall appraisal of basic security conditions, an assessment of fundamental civil and political rights, and an investigation of the degree of compliance with basic rights to health and education.

As country mandates are renewed annually, they usually lack anything like a long-term vision; they tend to focus on attaining immediate goals. Thus, Special Rapporteurs may be obliged to emphasize small steps rather than more ambitious strategies. In selecting goals and priorities for a given mission, we typically isolate a set of issues for which data can be readily gathered or for which confidence building with representatives from both government and civil society seems plausible in the foreseeable future. Sometimes it is desirable to tackle issues on which the government is already taking an initiative. Incremental progress is thus far more likely than any dramatic breakthroughs.

What difference do Special Rapporteurs make for the promotion and protection of human rights? How effective are their actions? At the CHR's 2002 session, certain member states continued to undermine the ability of the special procedures mechanisms to function effectively. The speaking time for many Special Rapporteurs was cut to five minutes, too short a time even to introduce their reports let alone debate their substance in the plenary. These facts merely reinforce many of the lamentable shortcomings listed above.

The work of Special Rapporteurs remains a powerful tool for the powerless. Reports ask member states for clarifications about allegations, request responses to specific problems, expose perpetrators, develop analyses, and propose recommendations. They may not produce immediate changes, but they do contribute to the struggle for human rights; they increase transparency and accountability. This is not a minor accomplishment. And the victims appreciate the effort.

6

Inter-governmentalism and Transnationalism

There is a tension within the United Nations between inter-governmentalism and transnationalism, two forces that encompass different sets of interests and reflect distinct constituencies. As an intergovernmental institution, the UN reflects the overlapping interests of its member states, particularly those on the Security Council. Major initiatives and policies are promoted by accredited delegations, all of whom represent their governments. As a transnational organization, however, the UN also often represents a common good that transcends the sum of individual state interests. Such concerns are promoted by nongovernmental organizations (NGOs) and by the UN's specialized agencies, affiliated organizations, bureaucracy, and office of the Secretary-General. In many cases, transnational concerns such as human rights or humanitarian relief conflict with the more traditional intergovernmental ones such as security. When this occurs, the UN is unable to function effectively.

This conflict between inter-governmentalism and transnationalism reflects a similar tension within the international system itself. Inter-governmentalism is certainly the dominant force in world politics, but transnational actors have also achieved increased visibility and influence within the global organization. From this perspective, the UN not only provides a forum for states to resolve their disputes, it also serves as a medium through which state and non state actors promote their often competing interests. Thus, the conflict between these forces within the UN can help to illustrate their respective roles in international politics.

Those activities that require the active cooperation and participation of the states are intergovernmental. Those that rely primarily on UN agencies, NGOs, specialized agencies, or the Secretariat are considered transnational. Third, through what process are state interests defined in a particular issue: domestically, through consultation with representatives from other countries, through interaction among specialists or representatives of NGOs, or by initiation of the secretary-general? Interests that develop through diplomatic or domestic political channels are intergovernmental, while those that evolve from within the UN structure are transnational.

THE UNITED NATIONS AS AN INTERNATIONAL ORGANIZATION

From an analytical perspective, the UN is an enigma. It does not fit neatly into the traditional category of an international organization, nor does it embody the characteristics of a budding world government. It was originally conceived primarily as a collective security organization, yet its goals, practices, and institutional structure suggest a far broader and more ambitious social agenda. It is an organization of, by, and for independent sovereign states, yet it is also a semi-independent actor staffed with a semiautonomous civil service. Its constituency is the states, yet it also serves a wide range of non state actors, regional organizations, and even individuals regardless of nationality or boundaries.

On the one hand, the UN reflects the basic principles of inter-governmentalism. It was created by member governments and is governed by representative consultative conference organs; it has a permanent secretariat. Delegates representing the interests of their governments largely develop its policies and programs through a process of bargaining and collaboration. And like all intergovernmental organizations

(IGOs), the UN is designed to equip the multi state system with an administrative mechanism that can do things for the states that they cannot do well by themselves.

Alan James describes this side of the United Nations as follows:

[The United Nations] fundamentally is nothing more than an association of sovereign states... each member will be trying to use the United Nations to further its own interests... States have not joined out of respect for the "U.N. idea" (but) for what they can get out of it.

Both neorealist and liberal institutionalist theories can account for this face of the United Nations. For neo-realists, the UN reflects the distribution of power and capabilities among its members. Created after World War II by the winning coalition, substantive authority rests with the great powers through the Security Council. During the Cold War, the organization's security policies largely reflected the dynamics of bipolarity and, subsequently, the interests of the only remaining superpower, the United States. In the area of political economy, the UN has reflected the structural conflict between North and South that comes from the skewed distribution of national material power capabilities in the international system.

As predicted by most realists, the outcome of this conflict has been generally determined by this same distribution of power. Finally, as realists would expect, the major powers have usually hesitated becoming involved in potentially violent situations where their vital interests were no t threatened; indeed, they have demonstrated a clear unwillingness to trust their security to the global organization. As a result, the organization has not fulfilled the promise of collective security as espoused by the founders.

Institutionalists, in both their strong and weak varieties, can also explain the intergovernmental side of the UN. The world organization brings together governments that support the fundamental goals of peace, security, and prosperity but recognize that in an interdependent world they can accomplish this only through interstate coordination and collaboration. Governments often find that by themselves they cannot achieve their objectives, since doing so depends upon exerting authority over actions within other states' jurisdictions. As a state's own vulnerability to others' actions increases, its willingness to trade some legal freedom for additional influence over others increases.

Thus, the United States sought to create an international order along broadly multilateral lines, but it did not seek to endow the UN with extensive independent powers. The creation of the UN did not challenge the basic assumptions government leaders held about the nature of interstate relations. The primary intergovernmental function of the organization the coercive control of state conduct-reflects the conventional wisdom of balance of power and collective security theory: order in a multi state system depends upon the ability of states to check and control each other's behavior. This can explain why states would create and participate in a multipurpose, universal membership organization that involves itself even in areas where no normative consensus exists.

THE UNITED NATIONS AS A TRANSNATIONAL ORGANIZATION

Despite this strong inter governmentalist orientation, there is also another face to the UN. More than simply a forum to facilitate interstate negotiation on issues of mutual concern, the "UN system" is also a complex network of specialized agencies, NGOs, and affiliated semiautonomous organizations that serve a variety of constituencies in a wide range of areas. Many of the organization's regional commissions, for example, have developed a high degree of autonomy that is based on deep political ties to local (non state) constituencies. Similarly, many of the specialized agencies and affiliated organizations were established by multilateral treaty independently of the UN structure.

UN member states and the Security Council have little control over these autonomously governed and financed bodies. The UN Conference on Trade and Development (UNCTAD), for example, has its own secretariat and secretary-general. It operates semi-autonomously from the UN Secretariat, although it is technically under the authority of the General Assembly. The various agencies and affiliated organizations often initiate projects and policies that are at odds with the most powerful states. Moreover, their constituencies go well beyond states and governments.

For example, the International Labor Organization's (ILO) tripartite structure places personnel from labor ministries, trade unions, and employee associations at the center of its work, and the World Bank maintains close ties to autonomous central banks and private financial institutions. Moreover, the UN itself has become an independent international actor in both a legal and political sense. As the International Court of Justice (ICJ) ruled in 1949, the UN has an international legal personality, is subject to international law, and is capable of possessing international rights and duties.

This is reinforced by the way member states treat the organization. While at times the states view the organization as simply a forum for negotiation and conflict management, at other times they act as if the UN has its own identity, negotiating with and often blaming "it" for outcomes produced by the organization's actions. This is particularly true within peacekeeping missions and programs initiated by the UN's specialized agencies. All of this helps to create a transnational identity for the organization, conferring upon it the status of "international actor."

Another indication of the UN's transnational nature is the multiple sources of power and authority within the organization. The United States and other great powers dominate the organization's security agenda, yet initiatives in other issue areas-for example development programs, technical and humanitarian assistance, and human rights activities-are led primarily by non state actors, semiautonomous agencies, and developing states. The Secretariat, which is composed of international civil servants headed by the secretary-general, is an autonomous organ, constitutionally independent from the Security Council and the General Assembly.

Although appointed by the intergovernmental organs, the secretary-general is technically responsible only to the UN Charter. As former Secretary-General Javier Perez de Cuellar argued, the framers of the UN saw the need for someone who could "speak for the wider international interest, an interest greater than the sum of the interests of the member states." Consistent with this, Perez de Cuellar added that his office had to serve two constituencies: the governments of the member states and the people for whom the governments act. Thus, the Secretariat's concerns must embrace the situation of the human community in general.

This means that sometimes he or she must act above and beyond the national positions of the membership. This side of the UN cannot be easily explained by either neorealist or institutionalist theories of international relations. This is because the UN is both an intergovernmental and a transnational organization. While inter-governmentalism can be captured within traditional theories of international relations, transnational relations cannot. In a generic sense, transnationalism refers to relations maintained by clearly identifiable actors linking at least two societies or subunits of national governments.

The term, however, does not encompass a single meaning, nor does it explain a single phenomenon. Rather, the literature on transnational relations discusses at least three related but distinct understandings. First, it refers to those activities conducted regularly by non state actors across juridical borders. This could include multinational corporations, social movements, transnational advocacy networks, or cultural groups. Second, it can refer to contacts between government bureaucracies charged with similar tasks who act on their own in the absence of national decisions. Such networks include state officials within subunits of national governments, international organizations, and regimes; these officials often pursue common agendas independent of their governments.

Finally, the literature on epistemic communities explains how transnational networks of knowledge-based experts develop, transmit, and legitimize a set of ideas and beliefs across national borders. These ideas help state officials to identify their interests, frame the issues for collective debate, and clarify salient points for negotiation. Ernst Haas, for example, demonstrates how communities of knowledge among independent actors can lead to policy consensus among state elites.

In one sense, the legitimation of certain ideas-such as the nonuse of force, decolonization, and human rights-is the most important role of the UN in global affairs. Many development programs are not aimed at resolving interstate disputes or providing for collective action among states. Rather, they are focused on disseminating ideas on economic policy and providing technical assistance and resources to facilitate these policies. In fact, the concept of sustainable development has spread largely because of the UN's action s. To the extent that these ideas are transmitted and legitimized independently of state interests or actions makes them transnational.

Each of these approaches explains how international organizations can develop policies and behaviors that transcend the sum of individual interests among their members. Trans-governmental networks, such as those that develop within the specialized agencies of the UN or within the Economic and Social Council (ECOSOC), can lead to transnational coalitions on particular policy questions. The UN system provides a forum for trans-governmental interactions that involves parts of governments dealing with their opposite numbers in other governments and with functionally identified parts of international organizations.

Moreover, the involvement of NGOs in the UN network through Article 71 and "subcontracting" services has helped to expand the organization's identity from a strictly intergovernmental to a transnational organization as well. This has practical consequences. Although governments remain the primary participants in the organization, NGOs have been deeply involved in norm and policy setting, policy execution, contracting, and inter level mediation. This influence is felt the greatest at international conferences where their specialized knowledge and professional leadership help to shape the outcomes.

For example, the UN Conference on the Human Environment in 1972 was heavily influenced and attended by NGOs. While it accomplished little in the way of changing state policy, it empowered a growing transnational environmental movement, making the environment an important issue within the UN. NGOs can also play an important role in influencing member states in voting and in creating new programs. Amnesty International, for example, was the primary force in influencing the UN to create and fund an independent High Commissioner for Human Rights.

This transnational aspect of the UN and within the global system in general has been developed and strengthened by several factors. First, some issues and missions do not specifically involve the actions of states and therefore do not easily lend themselves to intergovernmental cooperation. In some areas, states simply lack the competence to undertake the missions. In these areas, UN agencies and personnel are better positioned to initiate and oversee programs. Examples include the protection and relocation of refugees, humanitarian assistance, and community economic development and training.

Second, there are some tasks that the great powers would rather avoid or at least not expend their own resources in pursuing-for example, keeping the peace, monitoring elections, and exposing human rights violations. Third, in some issue areas, states individually or collectively lack the legitimacy to act-for example, in prosecuting war crimes or international criminal activity. Since states strongly resist being judged by other states, any involvement by governments is usually tainted by political interest. Fourth, many non state actors, such as NGOs and individual specialists, have developed close working relationships with UN agencies, creating a new constituency within the world organization.

Finally, as the UN developed its own independent identity, it has come to represent an "international community" that goes beyond the sum of its membership. Individuals and domestic groups often look to the UN to provide services and assistance. In cases where transnational relations play a significant role within the organization, the distribution of power among states is not the most important factor in determining outcomes. The interests of NGOs, officials in specialized agencies, and even the Secretariat may not be the same as those of the most powerful member states.

To the degree that these actors initiate programs and operations, the outcome may reflect organizational (bureaucratic) interests, consensual knowledge, or the perceived good of the populations they serve. In fact, this is one of the major complaints levied by the great powers against the organization.

THE UNITED NATIONS AND THE INTERNATIONAL COMMUNITY

To the extent that the politics of the UN reflects the political dynamics of the international system, inter-govemmentalism and transnationalism together can account for much of the UN's role in world affairs. Neorealist and institutionalist theories can explain the intergovernmental aspect of the UN, and theories of transnational relations can account for the participation of non state actors in the UN structure.

There is, however, one additional factor. Traditionally, transnational models have been positioned at the micro level of analysis: interactions among individuals or groups produce global or regional networks that transcend juridical borders. Yet, there is a deeper foundation for transnationalism, one that operates at the macro level the level of the international community. It is on this level that I wish to focus, because as I will argue, this provides a unique foundation for the UN as a transnational organization.

Whether an international community exists is central to understanding the tension between inter-governmentalism and transnationalism in the UN. Kenneth Waltz's systems theory posits an international environment where autonomous, atomistic states interact on the basis of competition, rivalry, necessity, and mistrust. States build relationships and occasionally cooperate, but they do not develop deep social bonds between themselves. Under these conditions, it is difficult for cohesive institutional structures to develop, because the kinds of institutionalizing mechanisms that can work so powerfully in domestic polities are not available.

Others, however, have suggested that there is a broader community that transcends the individual actors. In particular, two bodies of literature posit, alternatively, an international community of states and a global community of humankind. The former builds on the "anarchical society" model developed by Hedley Bull, Martin Wight, and other members of the "English School." Robert Jackson, for example, argues for the existence of an international community of sovereign states that can be identified by generally accepted procedural norms and standards of conduct that are specified in the charters of international organizations and in public international law.

Underlying this is a more fundamental association that consists of the traditional community of diplomats and customary international law that would exist even in the absence of a formal, universal organization such as the UN. In essence, the international community is one of diplomats and national leaders. Within this context, the world organization is guided not only by the interests of its members and associates, but also by norms that transcend the state interests. For example, the norm of sovereign equality has significantly shaped the procedural and substantive policies of the UN. While power remains an important variable in determining how policies are made and negotiations are conducted, the exercise of power is greatly constrained by this principle. Moreover, the norm of self-determination constrains even powerful states by influencing the legitimation of statehood and the decisions as to who may become a state.

Some people view the international community as emanating not from states, but from the social condition of humankind. This community cuts across national boundaries and is governed by a set of fundamentally moral and ethical norms that even sovereign states are obliged to observe. According to Christian von Wolff, for example, individuals do not cease to be members of that great society which is made up of the whole human race, because several have formed together a certain particular society.... After the human race was divided into nations, that society which before was between individuals continues between nations.

This view was also articulated by Immanual Kant, who argued that "the peoples of the earth have thus entered in varying degrees into a universal community, and it has developed to the point where a violation of rights in one part of the world is felt everywhere." Thus, the essential nature of international politics lies in the transnational social bonds that link individuals around the world. This approach sees human interests as being more important than national interests.

Within the context of this community, the institution of sovereignty is strongly balanced against the interests of state populations. When state interests conflict with accepted cosmopolitan values, the latter outweighs the interests of the state. As the global organization representing the international community, the UN becomes responsible for protecting populations and promoting individual interests. I suggest an international community that falls somewhere in between these two models, and it is this community that is partly represented by the UN. States and their agents are certainly the primary actors in international politics, but there is growing evidence that a transnational civil society exists independent of states.

The practices of NGOs are an institutional manifestation of this phenomenon, yet some argue that it exists on a deeper level. In other words, civil society is created not only through specific intergroup contacts across borders, but also by the institutional structure of the nation-state system. Thus, the international community has both intergovernmental and cosmopolitan aspects. John Boli, John Meyer, and several other sociologists see the development of a world polity as a broad cultural order that has explicit origins in Western society.

Within a highly institutionalized world polity, contemporary constructed actors (including nation-states) organize and legitimize themselves in terms of universalistic models like citizenship, socioeconomic development, and rationalized justice. From this perspective, the UN is at least partly a reflection of this world polity. If we assume that there is both a community of states and some elements of a global civil society, then the institution of an "international community" should reflect both. Yet since the actors and institutions and the norms guiding their relations change over time, it would be misleading to talk of the international community in the abstract. The international (European) community that developed after the Napoleonic Wars was based on different sets of actors and norms than the one that evolved after World War II.

Therefore, I would define international communities as historically situated collectivities of recognized political actors who maintain formal, ongoing relationships with each other in international affairs on the basis of an integrated set of procedural and political norms. Such actors include government officials, diplomats and representatives from international and transnational organizations, and social movements. They can be identified through membership in intergovernmental and transnational institutions, but also through common practice. For example, transnational social movements and organizations, such as Greenpeace, become international actors when they are treated as such by state officials and officially sanctioned institutions.

From this perspective, international communities are historically specific and reflect the political organization and normative character of the international system as it develops during a particular era. Once the underlying principles become embedded within international institutions, they can help to shape both state practices and the attitudes of national leaders by defining types of acceptable behaviors.

Through these institutions, the international community can take on a life of its own independent of the individual states it comprises. That is, once norms become diffused, adapted, and implemented, they become a political force in international relations and the institutions embodying these norms become independent actors. In this sense, the international community becomes a unit of analysis. Adding the concept of international community to our analysis enhances our understanding of international relations and the UN in two ways.

First, the concept is more specific and thus more operational than either Bull's anarchical society or Waltz's international system. Both models are conceived as broad environmental conditions that allow for a limited set of generalizations about state behavior. Neither concept can account for what Robert Gilpin calls "systemic change," which can occur without changing the essential features of the international system (or society) itself (that is, the nature of the units and the constitutive rules underlying the structure). Second, it allows for a wider range of actors other than states without diminishing the influence of states. International communities reflect specific configurations of actors, each of whom may represent different constituencies.

The identities and relative influence of these actors are historically contingent. Thus, one does not have to settle the debate over the importance of transnational organizations or international institutions in global affairs. Rather, we can engage in empirical study about specific actors within a specific context during a specific historical era. How, then, do we know when an international community exists and how can we measure the level of cohesion? There is no simple formula for determining this, but I suggest three possibilities: First is the degree to which there is a consensus among the most influential states on the fundamental principles of global politics.

Recognizing that the great powers drive much of international politics, a stable international community requires a fair amount of cohesion among the leading states in the system. Since all political communities have dissidents and outsiders, absolute consensus is not required for an international community to form. At the same time, a strong organized opposition by powerful revisionist states can greatly disrupt its cohesion. Thus, the bifurcation of the world into two hostile great power blocs during the Cold War prevented the development of such a community.

Second is the degree to which these principles are supported by secondary states and domestic groups. A collectivity comprising a select group of states may constitute a type of community; however, if closed and exclusive, it cannot be called an international community. Similarly, principles shared by a collectivity of state elites but rejected by domestic social and cultural groups cannot form the basis of an international community either. Third is the extent to which there is a universal-membership organization with the legal and moral authority to create and enforce norms of behavior. Stability and cohesion require an institutional expression of the community as well as a means for facilitating group commitment.

INTER-GOVERNMENTALISM VS. TRANSNATIONALISM IN THE UN

The above discussion suggests that transnationalism and inter-governmentalism reflect distinct constituencies and therefore produce different behavioral incentives to the actors involved. The UN system comprises at least four different types of actors serving at least three distinct constituencies. The actors include the intergovernmental decision-making bodies (Security Council and General Assembly), the affiliated organizations and specialized agencies, the Secretariat, and the associated NGOs. Its constituencies are the member states, local populations who are the recipients of programs and services, and the broadly defined international community.

The fact that the UN assumes both intergovernmental and transnational tasks is not in and of itself a problem. Conflict arises when the organization fails to distinguish between its role as an intergovernmental organization coordinating the activities of its membership and its role as a transnational network promoting some type of common good. The cosmopolitan values that underlay the international community often conflict with the needs and interests of the member states. This poses a problem in cases where the UN assumes commitments that are not in the states' interest to fulfill.

Governments represent the interests of their states, interests they are expected to pursue. They are often unwilling to promote transnational goals on behalf of a foreign population or a broader "international community," particularly when these goals do not either directly benefit their domestic constituencies or fulfill a vital state interest. While the Security Council is technically empowered to act on behalf of the global organization, it usually represents the interests of the great powers. For this reason, it is not well suited to deal with the many transnational issues that fall within the UN's mandate, such as human rights, humanitarian assistance, and sustainable development.

The coercive control of state behavior is probably the most important intergovernmental function of the UN. It requires the use of military and economic sanctions, something that only states can apply effectively. In the case of interstate aggression, genocide, or war crimes, the intergovernmental bodies of the UN can legitimately evoke the "breach of the peace" clause and mobilize member governments to take action. Yet, since inter-governmentalism is primarily concerned with the relations between states, it is less effective in addressing other relationships within the international community. This is particularly true with issues in which coercion is not an effective means for resolution.

The issue of human rights offers a good illustration. The principle of sovereignty clearly prohibits states from either interfering in the internal affairs of other states or passing judgment on their legal or judicial systems." This is reflected in Article 2(7) of the UN Charter. Human rights violations are an affront to the affected population, but a violation against one party by another does not automatically vest a third party with the legitimacy to correct the infraction.

If, however, human rights abuses are understood to be violations of generally accepted cosmopolitan norms, the affront is an offense against the international community and therefore a transnational issue justifying collective intervention. This was the thinking behind the International Criminal Court. The intergovernmental bodies of the UN are not able to adequately represent the international community on these issues for several reasons. First, the great powers in the Security Council do not wish to accept the protection of human rights as an obligation.

This would require them to become involved whenever a situation was labeled as such, even if their vital interests were not at stake. The Council has demonstrated this attitude by the way it frames human rights issues. The few times they became directly involved in a humanitarian or human rights situation-for example, Haiti, Somalia, and Bosnia-the Council labeled them as "breaches of the peace" rather than as violations of human rights agreements. This allowed them to justify their involvement under Chapter VI, thereby considering it a matter of international security.

As a result, the actions of the Security Council tend to be highly inconsistent, a function of self-defined interest rather than international law or treaty obligations. When treated as an intergovernmental issue, human rights have been highly politicized, particularly during the Cold War. For that reason, it has been extremely difficult for the UN to act even in cases where there is a general agreement on the infraction. Second, since intergovernmental bodies tend to reflect the distribution of power among its members, weaker states hesitates to grant the organization substantive authority in any area that could potentially threaten their sovereignty. Tension and mistrust between North and South, for example, greatly hampers human rights work, since many developing countries view it as internal interference.

For these reasons, the most effective action on human rights has been conducted by NGOs and the UN's specialized agencies. While human rights enforcement has been weak to nonexistent, the UN has been successful in establishing widely accepted standards, investigating serious abuses, and promoting human rights activism at the domestic level. A similar conflict has arisen within the UN's peacekeeping function. Peacekeeping evolved as a form of non coercive conflict control when Cold War constraints prevented the Security Council from taking steps permitted in the charter. Thus, it was not a result of strategic interaction among states but an innovative program initiated by the secretary-general.

Under the direction of the Security Council, the role of the peacekeepers has been expanded from acting as a barrier between previously warring parties to include aiding in state-building efforts, creating civil administration, facilitating democratization, promoting human rights, disarming militias, protecting populations from attack, caring for displaced persons, and even enforcing Security Council resolutions.

Peacekeeping thus increasingly requires that civilian political officers, human rights officials, election monitors, and refugee and humanitarian aid specialists play as central a role as the military. Divorced from the UN's intergovernmental coercive function, it often requires more technical than military training. This necessarily brings in NGOs and experts from specialized agencies. The increase in involvement by different types of actors has made it difficult for those overseeing the missions to balance the humanitarian aspects of their missions that are promoted by the transnational bodies with the overtly military directives coming from the intergovernmental Security Council.

Part of the problem is the failure by states to distinguish between the intergovernmental and transnational activities of the UN. Boutros Boutros-Ghali categorizes at least four different operations that now fall under the single label of peacekeeping. They include preventative diplomacy (non coercive action to prevent disputes from arising); peacekeeping (the deployment of a UN presence in the field); peacemaking (action to bring hostile parties to an agreement, through Chapter VI); and peace building (action to identify and support structures that will ultimately strengthen peace). To this, one could add peace enforcing (imposing a peace settlement through Chapter VII). The first two could be considered to be UN organizational functions, but the latter three involve intergovernmental coercion.

Negotiations leading to a dispute settlement clearly fall within Chapter VI, an intergovernmental function; however, once the agreement is made, the states are supposed to turn the operation over to the UN Secretariat, an agency that claims to represent the collectivity. Yet the great powers often resist providing troops from their own militaries for peacekeeping, particularly if it does not fall within their definition of "vital interests." Such sacrifices tend to be unpopular domestically.

Moreover, state militaries are rarely trained for the highly technical task of peacekeeping. Finally, since the great powers often refuse to allow their soldiers to serve under a UN command, the UN presence is often paralleled with national ones. As a result, peacekeeping has often expanded into military operations.

The UN was created by and for states, and diplomats generally consider the organization to be a forum for interstate negotiation, cooperation, and conflict resolution. However, the UN's agenda also encompasses transnational concerns that do not directly involve state officials or state interests. Over the past several decades, the UN's missions and services have expanded far beyond their original conception to include humanitarian relief, democratization, the promotion of economic development, and the protection of human rights.

Accompanying this expansion has been an increase in the authority of the organization's specialized agencies and a growing involvement of transnational NGOs. As a result, international institutions, such as the UN, provide opportunities for nongovernmental actors to promote their agendas. This complicates international politics because traditional state concerns such as security and stability are balanced against cosmopolitan values.

This not only empowers new actors but also creates new constituencies. UN special agencies and NGOs have responded by expanding their functions and forging close relationships with many of these new groups and populations. Yet, since states tend to view their domestic populations as their primary constituents, they have been unable to effectively resolve many problems and issues that transcend state borders.

UN intergovernmental organs have their own problems that have little to do with transnational concerns. Collective security has been elusive, many state interests appear to be irreconcilable, and vast discrepancies in wealth and power clash with the democratic ideals of the organization. Yet even with issue areas and programs that do not involve interstate relations, the intergovernmental bodies are unable to represent the mythic international community.

This is largely because inter-governmentalism and transnationalism are often incompatible. The former promotes state interests, while the latter pursues cosmopolitan concerns. Although states often prefer to ignore the latter, it is becoming increasingly difficult to do so in an interdependent world. Yet states are not well disposed to act in these areas. Transnational issues not only often clash with issues of state, but governments lack the competence and capabilities to deal with them.

From the perspective of IR theory, this suggests a paradox in international relations. IGOs, such as the UN, increasingly assume a wide range of tasks that their member states lack the competence, will, and/or technical expertise to perform-for example, peacekeeping. As a result, the member states are forced to assign many of these responsibilities to NGOs and other non state actors, whose interests and constituencies are often at odds with those of the states.

The larger and more complex these IGOs become, the more tasks they assume and the more they are forced to "contract out" their services to specialized agencies and NGOs. The greater the involvement of NGOs within the IGOs, the more transnational concerns threatens to replace intergovernmental ones on the organizational agenda. Thus, states dominate the global agenda, but international organizations such as the UN provide opportunities for nongovernmental actors to exercise a level of influence in world politics that they would otherwise never be able to achieve.

7

Critique of the United Nations

For over 40 years, the Cold War conflict between the United States and the Soviet Union paralyzed the peacekeeping functions of the United Nations. With few exceptions, the United Nations and other multinational organizations were ineffective in resolving major conflicts because of the zero-sum nature of the Cold War. Now that the Cold War is over, many believe that the United Nations can play a greater role in resolving conflicts and maintaining order in the so-called new world.

Glowing in the success of the Persian Gulf War, the United Nations has renewed stature and expanding peacekeeping operations in Cambodia, the former Yugoslavia and elsewhere. At this point, some believe the time has come to further expand the peacekeeping responsibilities of the United Nations.

Advocates of this position call for the creation of a standby U.N. army; the expansion of the definitions of security threats to include environmental and humanitarian concerns; the increase of the United Nations' powers to intervene in the internal affairs of states; and the creation of what has been referred to as the New World Order, in which the United Nations (and perhaps other multinational organizations) will be the world's main body for not only keeping the peace, but enforcing it.

To be certain, the passing of the Cold War offers new opportunities to make the United Nations more effective. The success of the United Nations in the Gulf War demonstrates that the organization can be used as an effective vehicle of war making against an aggressor. In El Salvador, Angola, Namibia and other former Cold War crisis zones, the United Nations has proven to be effective to different degrees in facilitating the establishment of peace and order once a cease-fire has been established.

Yet the millennium for the United Nations and other multinational organizations has not arrived. In all cases of recent U.N. involvement in war making or peacekeeping operations, the underlying cause of success was neither the triumph of the multinational ideal in international politics nor was it the birth of a new belief in the ideals of global democracy. Rather, it was the natural and logical consequence of the end of the U.S.-Soviet rivalry, and the general collapse of Soviet support for client states and groups.

As policy makers ponder the wisdom of expanding the United Nations' role in peacekeeping, they should remember one fact: The United Nations remains a mere instrument of nation-states, and its success or failure depends, as always, not mainly on the United Nations itself, but on the degree to which sovereign nation-states believe that international cooperation suits their own national interests. This fact defines both the limitations of and the opportunities for the United Nations as a peacekeeping body.

In order to understand the new global context within which the United Nations must act, an analysis of the current state of the world will begin this chapter. Following that, a terminology will be developed to define expanded U.N. operations, and will be incorporated into a review of current U.N. peacekeeping efforts.

Through an analysis of U.N. successes and failures, the limitations of U.N. peacekeeping will then be explored. The article will conclude with a discussion of risks for both U.S. and international involvement, followed by suggested guidelines for the international community to follow in sustaining the United Nations.

EXPANDING THE U.N. ROLE IN CONFLICT RESOLUTION

NEW WORLD DISORDER

The success of the United Nations in the post-Cold War transition period depends on the organization's awareness of whether a New World Order - based on global democracy and the triumph of the international ideal - actually exists or whether a New World Disorder is arising in its place. History has shown that peace and harmony do not necessarily follow the collapse of old state systems.

Consider the historical parallels. Religious revolution and dynastic ambitions destroyed the state system of medieval Europe, giving rise to the Thirty Years War and countless other dynastic wars in seventeenth-century Europe. Political revolution in eighteenth-century France destroyed the state system of the ancient regime, leading to the Napoleonic wars. At the end of the nineteenth century, the collapse of Bismarck's balance-of-power system in Europe paved the way for the two world wars. And because Europe and the League of Nations could not create a new workable international system, chaos erupted after the First World War, leading eventually to the rise of Nazi Germany.

Now with the end of the Cold War, the international community, particularly the United Nations, is facing unfamiliar new dangers. Behind much of the new disorder today are three trends causing geopolitical upheavals around the world: 1. the collapse of large empires - the Soviet Union is a case in point, but China or India may be next; 2. the rise of post-modern nationalism, which is partly a consequence of the first trend; and of course, 3. the revival of religious fundamentalism as a potent political force.

Foremost within this turmoil is the danger of the proliferation of weapons of mass destruction and ballistic missiles. As many as 21 nations are likely to have ballistic missiles by the year 2000. Right now 10 countries have nuclear weapons, and 11 more are developing them. Another danger for the United Nations in this new world disorder is the threat of regional wars, particularly in the Persian Gulf and Europe.

REDEFINING STATE SOVEREIGNTY

As the peacekeeping role of the United Nations expands in the post-Cold War era, the definitions of international security and state sovereignty may need to evolve to accommodate the desired capacity of that organization. In the Security Council's 31 January 1992 Summit Declaration, definitions of new threats to international security included "non-military sources of instability in the economic, social, humanitarian and ecological fields." Here the United Nations is moving well beyond traditional definitions of international threats involving civil wars or the aggression of states. In fact, some at the United Nations go so far as to see that body as an international police force to protect the environment, avenge human rights abuses, stop humanitarian tragedies and even right perceived social and economic wrongs.

An apt example of this sentiment is contained in the words of former U.N. Under Secretary-General Sir Brian Urquhart, who stated, "It is no longer acceptable that international action is taken only when a situation threatens the interests of the most powerful nations." Believing that the days of state-specific national interests are over for good, Urquhart proposes establishing a U.N. police force deployed to end random violence and perform armed police actions. He concludes, "The unraveling of national sovereignty seems to be a feature of the post-Cold War period." Clearly he views the traditional concept of autonomous states as eroding somewhat with the end of the Cold War.

This disregard for national sovereignty has also surfaced in discussions of the now-expanded U.N. operations in Somalia. Private relief experts, including CARE President Philip Johnston and Bread for the World president David Beckmann, have proposed that the United Nations take over and rule Somalia, claiming the country is in chaos and has no government. Furthermore, the U.S.-led, U.N.-authorized

Operation Restore Hope has set the precedent for military intervention based on strictly humanitarian grounds. Further involvement and control, including increased military oversight, is being sought by the United Nations as the United States backs resolutions to enforce humanitarian assistance.

The United Nations has begun a new type of operation, unlike the peacekeeping or wars that the Security Council authorized in Korea and the Persian Gulf. This may become a model for similar crises in the future. Andrew Natsios, Assistant Administrator for the Bureau of Food and Humanitarian Assistance at the U.S. Agency for International Development, has said concerning Somalia, "We may have to redefine sovereignty." Others are saying that the United Nations should establish a trusteeship over the territory to establish law and order and control relief efforts.

During much of the Cold War, the United Nations championed the idea of state sovereignty, primarily because most less-developed countries (LDCs) were sensitive to outside interference in their internal affairs. Whether it is Mexico, Israel or Cuba, most non-Western countries raised the banner of state sovereignty to protect themselves from the unwanted interference of larger states, and the United Nations repeatedly upheld this principle in Security Council resolutions.

As the United Nations adopts the principles of global democracy and redefines the notion of state sovereignty, LDCs' ability to restrict international interference will be diminished. The new thinking is that if all U.N. member-states are equal voices in a global democratic order, then LDCs not only have a right to interfere in the internal affairs of other states through the United Nations, but can expect to have their independence restricted as well by that organization.

Restrictions of this type are already occurring with the U.N. peacekeeping operation in Cambodia, where the United Nations has taken control of major government ministries. The action in Somalia, though draped in humanitarian concern, points to further disregard and redefinition of state sovereignty by the United Nations.

U.N. MILITARY INDEPENDENCE

The idea of broadening the role of the United Nations in conflict resolution has an influential champion in the current U.N. Secretary-General, Boutros Boutros-Ghali. In An Agenda for Peace, Boutros-Ghali states:

United Nations operations in areas of crisis have generally been established after conflict has occurred. The time has come to plan for circumstances warranting preventive deployment. The Security Council has the authority to take military action to maintain or restore international peace and security. While such action should only be taken when all peaceful means have failed, the option of taking it is essential to the credibility of the United Nations as a guarantor of international security. This will require bringing into being, through negotiations, special agreements... whereby member states undertake to make armed forces, assistance and facilities available to the Security Council... not only on an ad hoc basis, but on a permanent basis.

Boutros-Ghali's recommendation is tantamount to creating a standing U.N. army. Member-states presumably would turn over troops to the U.N. Military Staff Committee (MSC), which is composed of the military chiefs of staff of the five permanent members of the Security Council - the United States, France, United Kingdom, China and Russia. Although dormant for many years, the MSC, according to the U.N. Charter, is "responsible under the Security Council for any armed forces placed at the disposal of the Security Council."

Boutros-Ghali's proposed U.N. standing army includes force contributions from 20 member-states, each providing 2,000 troops on 48-hour notice. To pay for the program, Boutros-Ghali has suggested an international sales tax on weapons and international air travel providing $50 million for emergency humanitarian purposes and a $1 billion peace endowment. The primary concern for any member-state contributing to the proposed U.N. force is an elusive command structure. The MSC's command of a U.N. force would likely alternate periodically between the five permanent members, meaning four-fifths of the time permanent members would not command their own forces.

This allows the use of force to be taken out of the hands of those nations that provide and support the forces. Furthermore, non-democratic nations would have the opportunity to participate with and even control democratic forces, thus undermining the will of the people in all democratic nations.

As the United Nations expands its role in resolving conflicts, it is necessary to clarify definitions of its various peacekeeping activities. The need for a new vocabulary of U.N. operations will be further illustrated by the review of cases that follows the terminology section.

PEACEKEEPING

Today the term peacekeeping applies when the United Nations sends lightly armed soldiers from neutral countries into an area, usually to preserve a cease-fire and provide a buffer zone between warring combatants. Peacekeepers are only allowed to use their weapons in self-defense, and arrive with the consent of all parties. Peacekeeping also involves monitoring elections and ensuring that warring factions adhere to demobilization agreements. A good example of this activity is the U.N. Interim Force in Lebanon (UNIFIL), which was established in 1978 and is still in existence today.

PEACE-ENFORCEMENT

The term peacekeeping has also been used to define what could be more appropriately termed peace-enforcement. Peace-enforcement occurs, essentially, when peacekeeping goes awry. If a cease-fire breaks down, a revolt breaks out or the peacekeepers lose the support of one side and become themselves the targets of a warring faction, U.N. peace-enforcers can pacify the aggressor army. U.N. peace-enforcement occurred during the 1960-64 United Nations Operation in the Congo (ONUC) in which 234 U.N. troops were killed as various factions turned against the United Nations.

There is the potential for this type of situation to develop in the conflict in the former Yugoslavia if the United Nations were to launch military operations against Serbian-backed forces in Bosnia and Herzegovina. U.N.-authorized Operation Restore Hope in Somalia can also be considered to be peace-enforcement, though it has taken on the additional unprecedented aspect of being strictly humanitarian in purpose and scope.

A third category might be called U.N. war making, illustrated by the United Nations' endorsement of the use of force in the Korean War and the Persian Gulf War. In obvious contrast to peacekeeping, war making exists when the use of force is employed without the consent of all parties. In both instances of this type of war making operation, the United States led a coalition against an aggressor nation, using the United Nations essentially to mobilize international support.

The nature of U.N. war making may change as the reasons for its undertaking broaden. In the past, aggression against nations was the only acceptable reason for war. Now, however, human rights abuses or humanitarian crises may be defined as sufficient cause for the United Nations to wage war against a country or guerrilla faction.

CASES

In the aftermath of the Cold War, the United Nations is currently involved in 13 peacekeeping operations around the world. U.N. peacekeepers are involved in Angola, Cyprus, Cambodia, El Salvador, Iraq, Israel, Kuwait, Lebanon, Pakistan, Syria, the former Yugoslavia and the Western Sahara. Peace-enforcement has only been used in the Congo and in Somalia. Among the most recent and politically important of these are the operations in Cambodia, Somalia and the former Yugoslavia. The largest peacekeeping operation is in Cambodia, where the U.N. Transitional Authority in Cambodia (UNTAC) has deployed some 16,000 troops. Rival guerrilla groups have been fighting the Vietnamese-installed puppet government of Cambodia since 1979, repeatedly violating cease-fire initiatives and peace agreements.

The United Nations plans to implement the United States-China-Soviet Union peace agreement by demobilizing 70 percent of military forces, repatriating Cambodian refugees now in Thailand, monitoring cease-fires and overseeing elections. This will cost the United Nations $1.9 billion, plus $900 million in additional voluntary contributions, of which the United States will pay $516 million. Meanwhile, the Khmer Rouge seems determined to continue the fight, making it necessary for more U.N. troops to halt the conflict. In Somalia, the U.N. peacekeeping operation (UNOSOM) was approved in April 1992, to monitor cease-fires and protect deliveries of humanitarian aid at a cost of $634 million.

Yet clan warfare and anarchy have prevented effective distribution, while millions continue to starve. After U.S. Senate approval and President Bush's endorsement, on 2 December 1992 the U.N. Security Council approved a draft resolution authorizing the United States to lead an international military force to Somalia to protect the delivery of food and medicine, thus making it a peace-enforcement mission. Operation Restore Hope is supported by 25,000 U.S. troops and 10,500 troops from 20 other countries.

The cost will be an additional $583 million - far exceeding original estimates - to be offset by canceled military programs. The U.S. will pay the majority of the costs, with other nations contributing $115 million so far. U.S. troops have already begun to withdraw, and the United Nations is ill-prepared to assume responsibility, hoping that the United States will stay as long and do as much as possible. U.S. commanders estimate a U.N. force of 15,000 is needed, but early indications by Boutros-Ghali have suggested much lower figures. In the former Yugoslavia, the United Nations has attempted to monitor the cease-fire set in January 1992 through the U.N. Protection Force in Yugoslavia (UNPROFOR).

The 14,000-member force costs $634 million per year and has been unable to maintain any cease-fires. The civilian situation, in the meantime, has deteriorated rapidly, causing shortages of food and medical supplies. The growing demand to halt human rights abuses and Serbian atrocities spurred by the Western media has put pressure on the United Nations, the United States and the European Community to increase intervention. There are presently 15,800 soldiers, police officers and civilian administrators deployed; by the end of November 1992, the number of U.N. personnel was expected to exceed 22,500, making it the largest U.N. force in recent history.

The no-fly ban has been repeatedly violated, and at least four U.N. soldiers have been killed and 48 injured. No end to the violence seems near at hand. The U.N. peacekeeping operations in Cambodia, Somalia and the former Yugoslavia are particularly significant because they are truly post-Cold War phenomena and involve new ideas about the character of U.N. peacekeeping operations.

These operations differ from earlier efforts in Angola, for example, where the United Nations was used to facilitate post-Cold War restructuring: U.S.-Soviet negotiations established the controls of the peace agreement which was then enforced by the United Nations. In Cambodia, the United Nations has moved beyond merely monitoring cease-fires and buffer zones, to the actual administration of the government. In Somalia, the Bush administration has opened the door to pressures for the United States to intervene in most of the world's hot spots now that humanitarian concerns alone are legitimate for armed intervention.

THE LIMITS OF U.N. PEACEKEEPING

The United Nations is now undoubtedly a more effective peacekeeper, and to some extent peace-maker, than during the Cold War. It served a useful purpose in the Persian Gulf War and in the many peace settlements associated with post-Cold War restructuring. Before expectations are unrealistically elevated, however, the limits of the United Nations in the areas of peacekeeping, peace-enforcement and war making should be examined given the organization's successes and failures in those areas.

Such an examination may temper the more utopian visions held by those who believe that the world has entered into a new age where state sovereignty, national interest and war are passe. The lessons to follow can be viewed as guiding principles to practical U.N. expansion. Most important to note is that U.N. peacekeeping has been most effective when its role involved only mediating and observing peace successfully brought about by other parties.

This was the case in U.N. operations in Angola, El Salvador and Nicaragua, for example. As the Cold War ended, the warring factions backed by the Soviet Union lost their patron and were forced to give up fighting and accept the democratic process. The United Nations was called in afterwards to help implement agreements already reached by individual states.

Furthermore, the United Nations cannot end conflicts unilaterally, but only when all warring parties call for peace.

Once again El Salvador serves as a useful example of this type of peacekeeping. Both the government and the Farabundo Marti National Liberation Front (FMLN) were exhausted by their civil war and so turned to the United Nations as a neutral, third party to negotiate a settlement. When the two parties signed a cease-fire in 1992, they called on the United Nations to verify the settlement and help demobilize the FMLN guerrillas. At no point did the United Nations actually force an agreement on the Salvadoran government or the FMLN. Both sides wanted an end to the war, and the United Nations worked effectively as an objective peace-broker to facilitate the process.

Finally, when warring factions have agreed to a cease-fire only for tactical reasons, the United Nations can guarantee a cease-fire or peace settlement only through the deployment of large numbers of ground troops. The best example of this lesson is Korea, where the United States sent tens of thousands of troops to guarantee the armistice. Since North Korea never completely accepted the terms of the armistice, the Communist North remained a threat to the South. Failing to achieve peace, the United Nations had to retreat from what became a permanent war zone and rely on U.S. troops to deter future attacks by North Korea.

Another example of a U.N. operation failing to enact peace and order due to a misguided peace-enforcement effort was in the Congo from 1960 to 1964. Originally supporting the U.N. operation there, the Soviet Union reversed its policy and opposed the authority of the United Nations. Eventually, the Congo's government dissolved and the warring factions turned on the United Nations.

The situation in the Congo proved that in volatile situations, the circumstances of U.N. involvement can change and shatter the consensus that originally led to the United Nations' involvement. When a government turns against the United Nations, as it did in the Congo, the United Nations itself becomes a military target. The United Nations could not create through peace-enforcement what did not already exist: a willingness on the part of the warring parties to negotiate for peace.

These examples demonstrate that the motivation of states or warring factions in any U.N. peacekeeping operation would be to maximize security and political gain or to reduce the possibility of political instability or loss. Whether a U.N. peacekeeping operation is successful will be determined by the outcome of this political calculus and will be little affected by the commitment of states to some preconceived international order, ideal or cooperative effort.

Indeed, the states comprising the international community as a whole will become involved in or support U.N. peacekeeping operations only so long as they do not conflict with state-specific interests. International stability and cooperation are welcomed by most states in the world; only because most states support the international status quo, but this does not mean that their commitment to some ideal of international cooperation supersedes or contradicts their attachment to their own state interests.

Notwithstanding the high expectations of the global democracy of the new world order concept, the fact remains that wars are still "politics by other means," as Carl von Clausewitz believed. People fight and die for a variety of reasons, but the organized violence of a military operation, whether sponsored by a state or a guerrilla movement, still aims for a state-specified political goal. If the political goals of the warring factions are ignored - if they are seen as a politically neutral, humanitarian tragedy, for example - then no peacekeeping operation sponsored by the United Nations or any multinational organization will succeed. Peacekeeping will meet resistance by local fighters who have more to lose than the U.N. forces, and more to gain if the United Nations fails.

Bearing these lessons in mind, U.S. policy makers will surely assess the risks associated with increased involvement in U.N. peacekeeping operations. The Bush administration was extremely cautious, for example, in making commitments to U.N. operations in Yugoslavia. In making this policy, Bush apparently believed that too little was at stake for the United States - and the likelihood of success too low - to take the military and political lead in this tragic conflict. President Clinton may be less cautious than Bush, but nevertheless limits will exist on U.S. policy no matter who is president.

Only America has the military power to be the world's policeman; this was once again proven in Somalia. The danger for the United States lies in the fact that, as the world's sole remaining military superpower; it may become militarily involved in U.N.-sanctioned conflicts that it would otherwise avoid. Additionally, with the Soviet Union out of the world scene, the barriers to U.N.-sanctioned military action have dropped. Suddenly anything is possible, and all sorts of problems seem solvable by U.N.-backed force. The United States will be asked repeatedly by its allies and friends to back U.N. operations. If it agrees, America will not only become involved in obscure international police maneuvers, but will do so in places where it may have no clear-cut national interests.

This is certainly the case in the former Yugoslavia. No U.S. interest in that troubled region is so critical as to require the deployment of U.S. forces there. However under the auspices of the United Nations, the United States has agreed to enforce a no-fly zone over Bosnia. Requests from the United Nations for further U.S. military action can undoubtedly be expected.

Thus the United States has made an open-ended military commitment to resolving a conflict in which it has no critical interest, without knowing the U.S. political objectives that the use of force is supposed to achieve. This is also a legitimate concern with Operation Restore Hope, though only time will tell.

While one danger of expanding U.N. peacekeeping operations is the entanglement of the United States in unwanted conflicts, preventing the United States from acting unilaterally to protect its own interests is equally problematic. The United States' involvement in the Gulf War, and the other post-Cold War peacekeeping operations, has established a precedent of increasing U.S. reliance on the United Nations for building military coalitions and negotiating peaceful settlements of regional conflicts.

This approach, however, is a double-edged sword for the United States: If Washington continually seeks U.N. support of the use of military force, there may be a time when that organization does not honor the request. The U.N. Security Council did not sanction the use of U.S. force in Grenada or Panama, and it would not do so today. Yet these military operations were deemed to be in the national interest of the United States, and were pursued on that basis. It is possible that Washington, after years of appealing to the United Nations for legitimacy, would not be willing to act against the wishes of its colleagues on the Security Council.

With expanding U.N. peacekeeping operations, another question arises for the United States if the United Nations expands its peacekeeping operations greatly: Who will pay for the growth? If it is assumed in the post-Cold War era that wars are no longer political exercises, but merely criminal activities requiring police action by the United Nations, then the United Nations - and the United States - will not only be involved in more conflicts, but will have to ask for more money and funding from its member states.

The Stockholm International Peace Research Institute estimates that there are 30 wars in the world today, while the United Nations currently has only 13 peacekeeping operations worldwide. Expanding to take care of the 17 other military conflicts would require a substantial increase in funding, particularly from the United States, which already funds 30 percent of the current peacekeeping costs for most U.N. missions. For fiscal year 1993, the United States has allocated $460 million for peacekeeping operations, up from $377 million spent of the total $900 million U.N. peacekeeping budget in 1992. Under a major U.N. expansion, this figure could easily double or even triple.

Of course, other countries besides the United States would face risks as well. Countries contributing financially to peacekeeping operations would be exposed to the same financial risks as the United States. If Japan and Germany were to join the Security Council, as they aspire to, they would be particularly affected by the expansion of U.N. peacekeeping operations. As they would wish to contribute primarily money and not troops, these economic powers would be called upon to make a disproportionately high financial contribution. This may be resisted by governments already strapped by economic troubles or high budget deficits.

There is yet another troubling trend for the international community: the United Nations' growing infringement on national sovereignty. Boutros-Ghali and others in the U.N. leadership have stated that the United Nations has a right to interfere in the internal affairs of nation-states to correct human rights abuses. According to Boutros-Ghali, the way a nation treats its own people is a threat to all. He is unclear about how the United Nations plans to right all these wrongs with its peacekeeping forces, but the point is unmistakable: The United Nations has the right to use force against a sovereign nation, not because it has invaded another, but because it mistreats its own people.

The practical implications of this idea are mind-boggling. Given the fact that many of the U.N. member-states are ruled by dictators, it is wildly optimistic to expect the United Nations to develop an effective consensus on human rights. It would be impossible to respond to each and every reported human rights abuse. Not taking such action, however, would only make a mockery of the United Nations' solemn declarations on the purported security threats of human rights abuses. Ultimately, every country attacked by the United Nations for human rights abuses would hide behind the hem of national sovereignty, and since there are so many violations, the more effective the U.N. policy is, the greater would be the outcry of member-states. Under these circumstances, the United Nations would undoubtedly rediscover the virtues of national sovereignty.

U.N. peacekeeping has its limits, but it can work under some circumstances. The challenge for U.S. policy makers is to identify these circumstances and to develop guidelines for ensuring that U.S. interests are protected. The United States should, in this regard, be sensitive to three variables: 1. how a peacekeeping operation affects American national security; 2. how much it costs; and 3. the degree to which it erodes American sovereignty. As a rule, the United States should not lend direct military support to a U.N. peacekeeping operation unless a valid U.S. security interest is at stake.

If American force is used, it is not enough to say that Washington has a vague interest in international stability, democracy or human rights. Some vital U.S. interest must be at stake if American soldiers are asked to risk their lives. Vital interests were at stake in the Korean War and the Persian Gulf War, so it was wise to work with the United Nations in these cases. This is not the case in Cambodia, the former Yugoslavia or Somalia, where no vital U.S. interests are involved. In these instances the United States should do all it can to resolve the conflicts, short of sending in military forces to back the United Nations.

Another goal for U.S. policy should be to avoid the creation of a standing U.N. army. A U.N. force commanded by a rejuvenated Security Council MSC would be impractical and ineffective. U.N. politics and bureaucratic red tape would guarantee that the organizational command and control of such a force would be a military commander's nightmare. Besides, it is highly implausible that the United States would turn over control of even a small part of its armed forces to the Security Council. Because of political and constitutional considerations, the White House and Congress would place many restrictions on the use of U.S. forces by the United Nations - so many, in fact, as to render the move meaningless.

For any major U.N.-sanctioned military operation to be successful, the United States must take the lead. This is what happened in the Persian Gulf War when Washington worked with the Security Council, and bilaterally with such regional powers as Egypt, Saudi Arabia and Syria, to forge a fighting coalition against Saddam Hussein. This approach is far more practical than creating a standby U.N. army as it not only allows smaller powers to have a greater voice, but gives the United States and its allies the flexibility to fight a war without interference from the United Nations.

In any event, the United States should be cautious about repeatedly seeking the United Nations' sanction for military operations. Washington should not automatically assume that every regional conflict affecting U.S. interests can and should be addressed by the Security Council. This is particularly true for Latin America, where the Organization of American States may be more appropriate than the United Nations for settling regional conflicts. Moreover, Washington should be very careful about raising Latin American security issues in the Security Council. U.S. security interests can best be protected by such existing agreements as the Rio Treaty and the Panama Canal Treaty. When it comes to securing the Americas, Washington should work primarily with its neighbors and not with the United Nations.

As for other countries, they too should be skeptical of a rash expansion of the United Nations' peacekeeping powers. Most LDCs should find it troubling that through its current policy goals, the United Nations is challenging the legitimacy of national sovereignty and developing non-traditional definitions of international security. While most countries in Africa, Asia and Latin America have little to fear from an intrusive United Nations, some of them could nonetheless find themselves on the wrong side of U.N. sanctions. An LDC government facing an armed insurrection, for example, could easily find the United Nations demanding negotiations with a domestic political enemy.

At the very worst, a U.N. peacekeeping force could actually side with that enemy. While it is true that many of the groups opposing U.N. forces today are international pariahs - Serbia and the Khmer Rouge, for example - this may not always be the case. As history has shown, a U.N. peacekeeping force can easily end up in the middle of a civil war where no one side is the clear villain.

Aside from the United States, other members of the Security Council and other powerful nation-states in the world, such as Japan and Germany, should also be leery of too great a peacekeeping role for the United Nations. Assuming that the United States will demand that other countries participate significantly in peacekeeping ventures, the most likely candidates are members of the Security Council and, especially when it comes to financing the operation, Japan and Germany. An out-of-control peacekeeping apparatus would quickly prove to be expensive and burdensome to those countries because they would be called upon to keep the apparatus functioning.

The end of major wars often leads to high expectations for international cooperation. After the First World War, the League of Nations was born. After the Second World War, the United Nations was to succeed where the League had failed, including creating a new international order of peace and democracy. Now that the Cold War is over, the belief is widespread that the world has entered a new age in which the United Nations can fulfill its original mandate and help establish a new world order. Yet just as the League of Nations and the United Nations failed to meet expectations after the two world wars, the United Nations today will disappoint those who expect too much from it.

The ebb and flow of utopian internationalism in this century, following in the wake of great and costly conflicts, have left a mixed legacy. The United Nations cannot be any more successful than international politics and powerful international players allow. The United Nations can never be an independent political force on the world scene; at best, it will be an accurate reflection of the competing interest of sovereign nations. For all the current talk about the purported anachronism of states and national sovereignty, it is instructive to remember that the United Nations is indeed a body of states dedicated to the notion that the sovereign unit of international politics is still the nation-state.

If expectations are realistic, the United Nations can be a useful player in settling international conflicts. However, if it attempts to overreach its powers, and pretends to be an independent force in international politics, the United Nations will surely fail in maintaining any kind of world peace and stability. Only a United Nations anchored in the reality of the international state system can hope to grapple with the political realities of war and peace in the post-Cold War era, and accomplish its mandate as the most powerful multilateral peacekeeping body.

HOPE FOR THE FUTURE

Hopes for the future, for peace, prosperity and a fairer and more just world led to the establishment of the United Nations following the second war to devastate the world in the first half of the twentieth century. Today, we discuss the topic of hope amidst the despair of the death and destruction of a war in Iraq, and the questioning of the relevance of the United Nations. The Iraq War represents the failure of international consensus and efforts to achieve the agreed goal of Iraqi disarmament by peaceful means. It represents a failure to resolve an international problem through multilateral channels. For the critics of the United Nations, it represents a failure of that organisation. They have accused the United Nations of lacking credibility and relevance.

As views over how to deal with Iraq polarized within the international community, the United Nations was increasingly thrust into a no-win situation. The Security Council, in passing

Resolution 1441, had agreed unanimously on the goal of the disarmament of Iraq. Deep divisions subsequently emerged over the timing and methods to achieve that goal.

The United States and other members of the 'Coalition of the Willing' were determined that Iraq should be disarmed by force if after a short period of time it failed to comply with the resolution.

It was a no-win situation because if the Security Council had passed the second resolution proposed by the Britain, the United States and Spain, many around the world would have dismissed that outcome as representing the enormous influence and pressure that the United States, as the world's sole superpower, is able to exert on other countries. It would not, therefore, have been regarded by some within the international community as properly legitimising the use of force or of being a genuine exercise in multilateral decision-making.

UNILATERAL ACTION

On the other hand, the failure to pass a second resolution-in the end not put because it appeared unlikely to be able to muster majority support-simply led to coalition countries bypassing the UN process and unilaterally taking military action. President Bush criticised the United Nations as not being a responsible body. With the United States opting out of the multilateral process, the United Nations was seen as failing to constrain its most powerful member within its decision-making processes.

Parallels have inevitably been drawn with the League of Nations in the 1930s when that body proved unable to prevent the rise of fascism, to curb the aggression of major powers and to prevent the Second World War. While the war in Iraq does graphically represent the constraints on the power of the United Nations to control its members' actions or failure thereof, the analogy with League of Nations has limited value. The League was regarded as having such irrelevancy that two of the three most powerful countries in the world at that time did not bother to join it.

The United Nations today represents nearly every country in the world, some 191 nations. The decision by President Bush last October to take the Iraq issue to the United Nations indicated that his administration recognised the value and desirability of having a UN mandate. The difference in the readiness of the public in countries such as Britain and Australia to support military action against Iraq depending on whether or not it was UN-mandated also reflects a popular view of the importance of having that mandate.

MANY FAILURES

The United Nations has, of course, failed on many occasions to resolve issues and to avoid conflict over the 57 years of its existence. It has been written off many times for not being able to achieve what was beyond its power. As Shashi Tharoor, UN Under-Secretary for Communications and Public Information has aptly put it, 'the United Nations at its best is a mirror of the world. It reflects our divisions and disagreements as well as our hopes and convictions.'

The United Nations has been buried many times by critics, but it has survived. It has done so because the world does need a multilateral forum and a framework of international rules to create order and assist security. Whatever difficulty the United Nations has had in trying to manage divided international opinion over the use of force against Iraq, I believe it will be found once more to be essential in managing the post-conflict situation in Iraq. It will be essential firstly in addressing Iraq's humanitarian needs.

Already the Security Council has adopted a draft resolution on continuing the Oil for Food programme. The Office for the Coordination of Humanitarian Assistance will have responsibility for raising money and ensuring assistance is delivered to those in needs. A range of UN agencies-the World Food Programme, UNICEF, the UN High Commission for Refugees, the UNDP and the Mine Action Service-will spring into action to alleviate hardship and suffering in the civilian population.

KEY ROLE

There will also be the need for UN action to re-establish post-conflict governance and civil functions in Iraq. I read with interest a statement by Clare Short, the British Secretary for Development, who had just returned from discussions with UN officials. She emphasised the key role which the United Nations will need to play, noting that without a UN mandate for the reconstruction of Iraq, coalition countries would have the status of occupying powers under international law following military action.

This would severely hinder Iraq's longer-term development prospects, as steps to reform Iraqi government institutions would be illegal under international law.

While it is not yet clear what role the United Nations will perform after the conflict, a close analogy to the current situation is Kosovo in 1999. In that situation, NATO had waged war against Yugoslav forces without an explicit UN mandate. The Security Council subsequently authorised the Secretary-General to establish 'an international civil presence'. That mandate included promoting self-government, carrying out basic civilian administration functions, overseeing the development of democratic institutions, supporting reconstruction and humanitarian aid and maintaining civil law and order. The United Nations' role in that instance also included the holding of elections to create legitimate government. While countries opting for unilateral action against Iraq may have sidelined the United Nations, it is somewhat ironic that the world body may be called upon to pick up the pieces after the conflict.

Those challenging the relevance of the United Nations also, of course, ignore the critical role it plays in wider areas of development, human rights, refugees and the environment. No other organisation is able to confront the plethora of cross-border challenges: global diseases including HIV/ AIDS, malaria and tuberculosis, climate change, environmental degradation, refugee issues, people smuggling, human rights, poverty and hunger. If anything stands as a test to the United Nations, it is how it responds to these cross-border challenges.

Against the backdrop of the war in Iraq, the United Nations carries on: for example, in March it concluded this year's session of the Special Committee on Peacekeeping Issues, the Commission on the Status of Women met and the annual Commission on Human Rights commenced.

INTERNATIONAL NORMS

The UN system continues to set the international norms by which every member state should abide. In today's globalizing world, no member state, no matter how powerful it is, can disengage from multilateralism entirely. The United Nations remains a relevant organisation and will continue to have a central role to play in the twenty-first century.

Notwithstanding media criticism of the United Nations, what seems to be forgotten is that the organisation is only as strong as the will of its member states. The United Nations system relies on the collective will of all its members. It is these member states that set its priorities. The United Nations cannot act without their consent. It falls, therefore, upon us all to make the United Nations relevant in today's world. In this regard, the United Nations and its members are very aware of the shortcomings of the organisation. For the United Nations to meet its potential it needs to reform. It needs to better prioritize its work to meet the needs of member states.

REFORM INITIATIVE

This was the essence of the Secretary-General's second-term reform initiative, presented last September, which seeks to strengthen the organisation better to respond to the priorities established in the Millennium Declaration and to meet the needs of member states. The General Assembly adopted by consensus a resolution that supported efforts to reform the organisation. New Zealand has been actively involved in supporting the proposed reform initiatives. We will continue to speak out in favour of strengthening the organisation and reforming its organs, including the Security Council and the use of the veto.

New Zealand remains a firm believer in the multilateral system. The United Nations is not a perfect organisation, but it remains true that New Zealand and any state can achieve far less in isolation than it can by working collectively with other states under UN auspices.

CUSTOMARY INTERNATIONAL LAW

Consider the above quote from a federal district court judge in light of the following: In the early 1990s, members of an Algerian fundamentalist group brutally raped and tortured several Algerian women in Algeria. In addition, the group butchered and summarily executed friends and family members of the women in Algeria. When the Algerian military government banned the fundamentalist group, one of the group's members fled to the United States, sought political asylum, and conducted business on behalf of the group from Washington, D.C. The Algerian women then brought suit against the group in the United States District Court for the District of Columbia, alleging that the actions taken against them, their friends, and their family members in Algeria constituted violations of international law.

Despite the fact that the alleged events described above took place in Algeria, concerned only Algerian citizens, and involved a claim of a violation of international law, a United States district court had jurisdiction over the case under the Alien Tort Claims Act (ATCA) provides: "The district courts shall have original jurisdiction of any civil [tort] action by an alien... committed in violation of the law of nations or a treaty of the United States." Rather than claiming a violation of a treaty to which the United States was a party, the Algerian women based their ATCA claim on a violation of the "law of nations.

Ascertaining whether a violation of the "law of nations" has occurred involves delving into the territory of "customary international law," a growing body of law that includes norms that emerge when "conduct, or the conscious abstention from certain conduct, of states... becomes in some measure a part of [the] international legal order."

Determining the scope of customary international law is often difficult. Although the Restatement (Third) of the Foreign Relations Law of the United States ("Restatement") and a few federal court cases provide clarification and reinforce the authority of customary international law in U.S. courts, ambiguities remain. The Restatement itself acknowledges some of this uncertainty: "No definition of customary law has received universal agreement.... Each element in attempted definitions has raised difficulties. There have been philosophical debates about the very basis of the definition: how can practice build law?"

The ambiguities inherent in defining and using customary international law have sparked heated debates regarding its use, particularly in international human rights claims in domestic courts. On one side of the debate are those who maintain that U.S. courts have a responsibility to enforce and uphold international law, and should continue to do so even when deciding a claim requires the courts to make difficult customary international law findings.

On the other side are critics who argue that the ambiguities of customary international law are too great, that U.S. courts lack the authority to "find" customary international law, and that letting them do so offends federalism and separation of powers principles. For example, some critics assert that customary international law is unenforceable in U.S. courts without an explicit congressional authorization. An increase in the number of international human rights cases reaching federal courts, and the recent trend toward loosening the requirements of and decreasing the time necessary for establishing customary norms, have intensified the customary international law debate and imposed urgency on the need to resolve it.

Almost a century ago, in The Paquete Habana, the Supreme Court acknowledged that "international law is part of our law, and must be ascertained and administered by the courts of justice of appropriate jurisdiction." The Court, in The

Paquete Habana, upheld the idea that U.S. courts should not ignore cases with international law elements; rather, they should engage in a legal analysis that incorporates recognition of international law principles.

The Paquete Habana also specifically acknowledged the validity of customary international law by further clarifying that international law could be binding even when no treaty or legislation codified that law:

> Where there is no treaty, and no controlling executive or legislative act or judicial decision, resort must be had to the customs and usages of civilized nations; and, as evidence of these, to the works of jurists and commentators, who by years of labor, research and experience, have made themselves peculiarly well acquainted with the subjects of which they treat.

Since Justice Gray wrote the Court's opinion in The Paquete Habana, major world events have expanded the scope of international law and increased the significance of its definition, interpretation, and enforcement. As international law has grown in importance in the United States, domestic judicial decisions on international law issues, particularly those involving human rights, have cited The Paquete Habana in support of the use of customary international law as authority in U.S. courts.

A court's decision to find and adhere to a customary international norm thus has important implications for the legacy of respect for international law fostered by The Paquete Habana. Finding and adhering to customary international norms reinforces the legacy of The Paquete Habana and conveys the United States's commitment to ensuring that it serves as a cooperative member of an increasingly globalized world; refusing to find and adhere to customary international norms unravels the legacy and suggests a rebellion against international constraints.

This Note contends that U.S. courts should reinforce-not unravel-The Paquete Habana's legacy by recognizing and upholding norms of customary international law in international human rights cases, in spite of the growing criticism of that practice. As this Note argues, the ambiguity inherent in the nature of customary international law is not a justification for ignoring the authority of customary international law.

That ambiguity is in fact quite similar to uncertainties in other areas of law in which courts routinely make decisions. Foreclosing or severely limiting the viability of international human rights claims based on customary international law in U.S. courts not only eliminates the possibility of relief for many injured plaintiffs, it also sends a disturbing message to the world community that justice in the United States does not encompass challenges of internationally recognized abuses of human rights.

The first section of this Note discusses attempts made to define customary international law, including those in the Restatement. The second section discusses successful, albeit controversial, uses of customary international law in ATCA claims in U.S. courts, including the Second Circuit's decisions in Filartiga v. Pena-Irala and Kadic v. Karadzic, and the recent federal district court decision in Doe v. Islamic Salvation Front (FIS).

The third section addresses some of the criticisms regarding the use of customary international law in U.S. courts and discusses an unsuccessful attempt to use customary international law, without ATCA, that is consistent with those criticisms. The fourth section proposes reasons why, in spite of those criticisms, U.S. courts should continue to reinforce the legacy of respect for customary international law as the new century approaches.

ATTEMPTS TO DEFINE CUSTOMARY INTERNATIONAL LAW

Although a full discussion of the history of customary international law is beyond the scope of this Note, some background on past attempts to define and identify it is necessary. In The Paquete Habana, the Supreme Court noted that ascertaining customary international law entails "resort...

to the customs and usages of civilized nations; and, as evidence of these, to the works of jurists and commentators, who by years of labor, research and experience, have made themselves peculiarly well acquainted with the subjects of which they treat."

These words may not provide an explicit definition of what customary international law is, but they do provide a guide as to how to find it. In accordance with the words of The Paquete Habana, courts seeking to identify international legal norms have looked to experts in the field of international law for guidance on the extent to which certain practices have become so widespread as to be considered part of international law. These experts have been instrumental in determining the status of various practices; however, their role is not to steer the law in a specific direction. Rather, they work with existing definitions and examples of practices that already have become customary international law in making their assessments.

In their analysis, experts and judges may look to the Restatement. The Restatement acknowledges that a precise definition of customary international law remains elusive; nevertheless it attempts to provide a workable definition. In its section on sources of international law, the Restatement describes customary international law as "result[ing] from a general and consistent practice of states followed by them from a sense of legal obligation." Clarification in the comments and reporters' notes to section 102 indicates that the determination as to when a practice actually becomes law through custom is "often difficult" and that today a practice can achieve customary international law status in a short period of time.

The Restatement's "Human Rights" section is more precise, explicitly listing practices that have achieved the status of customary international law. According to section 702:

A state violates international law if, as a matter of state policy, it practices, encourages, or condones:

i. Genocide,

ii. Slavery or slave trade,

iii. The murder or causing the disappearance of individuals,

iv. Torture or other cruel, inhuman, or degrading treatment or punishment,

v. Prolonged arbitrary detention,

vi. Systematic racial discrimination, or

vii. A consistent pattern of gross violations of internationally recognized human rights.

This list is not meant to be exhaustive. Comment a. of section 702 offers a caveat: "The list is not necessarily complete, and is not closed: human rights not listed in this section may have achieved the status of customary law, and some rights might achieve that status in the future." The comments also note that systematic religious discrimination, the right to own and not be arbitrarily deprived of property, and gender discrimination were either already principles of customary international law at the time the American Law Institute (ALI) adopted the Restatement in 1987, or were on the verge of achieving that status.

According to the Restatement, therefore, a plaintiff seeking to prove a violation of customary international law can offer evidence that the practice at issue constitutes one of those stated in a. through (f) of section 702 of the Restatement, is part of a consistent pattern of gross violations within section (g), or is not on the list, but has achieved the status of customary law since the ALI's adoption of the Restatement. A court then weighs the evidence offered in support of the alleged violation to determine whether customary international law should apply to the action in question.

In Forti v. Suarez-Mason, a federal district court offered three additional criteria for ascertaining whether an act or practice falls within the scope of ATCA as part of customary international law. According to Forti, in order to establish a violation of customary international law, the act or practice at issue has to be "universal, definable, and obligatory." Several experts have adopted these categories as a means of demonstrating whether a customary international norm exists.

Even with these criteria, however, it remains difficult for courts to discern identifiable norms of international law. The fact that the list of customary norms constantly increases only compounds the problem. One expert has noted that "developments affecting human rights in the past decade indicate that the list of customary law rights may have significantly increased."

The right to basic sustenance; the right to public assistance in matters of health, welfare, and basic education; and the rights of women to full equality and protection against discrimination has all gained such acceptance in international legal thought that courts may begin to acknowledge them as customary international law. On the other hand, just because the list of customary international norms continues to grow and the standards remain somewhat ambiguous does not mean that every practice that apparently violates international standards inevitably will become part of customary international law.

Despite numerous attempts over the past few years to enlarge the list of customary international norms binding on the United States, the list remains quite small. For instance, courts have yet to find uniformly that cruel, inhuman, or degrading treatment of an individual violates customary international law. Similarly, courts have yet to rule that the right to education and the right to free speech are customary international law norms, despite strong arguments for their inclusion.

Perhaps the absence of a definitive explanation of what it takes to establish a customary international law norm contributes to the fact that the list of customary international law-norms remains small. The various attempts to define customary international law remain largely unsuccessful because this area does not lend itself to static definition. Most experts and judges agree that judges must assess whether a violation of the "law of nations" has occurred according to current rather than past definitions of international law? The definition of what constitutes a violation therefore will constantly evolve as individual international practices gradually develop into customary international law.

A brief illustration of successful uses of customary international law in U.S. courts helps provide a logical context for the above-mentioned attempts to define and identify customary international law. At least two important cases from the Second Circuit, Filartiga v. Pena-Irala and Kadic v. Karadzic, and one from the district court for the District of Columbia, Doe v. Islamic Salvation Front, illustrate judicial acceptance of the authority of customary international law in U.S. courts. In all three cases, the court relied on the "law of nations" and on customary international law to hold that individuals bringing claims under ATCA have a right to use U.S. courts to enforce norms of international law.

FILARTIGA V. PENA-IRALA

In Filartiga, a father and daughter from Paraguay brought a suit under ATCA against a fellow Paraguayan for acts of torture committed in Paraguay against a member of their family. The father and daughter alleged that a member of the Paraguayan police violated international law by kidnapping Joelito Filartiga, a local physician, and torturing him to death because of his father's opposition to the Paraguayan government. They based their claim on a violation of the "law of nations" rather than on any action arising directly under a treaty.

The court relied on the U.N. Charter and the Universal Declaration of Human Rights in holding that official torture "violates established norms of the international law of human rights, and hence the law of nations." The court cited The Paquete Habana as well as the U.N. Charter to support the proposition that "in this modern age a state's treatment of its own citizens is a matter of international concern." Filartiga also reaffirmed the existence of a binding international law that confers rights on individuals, and referenced U.S. foreign policy prohibiting security assistance to countries that violate human rights as support for the notion that the United States abides by international law on human rights issues.

The Filartiga decision helped verify the credibility of customary international law and the ability of U.S. courts to recognize and enforce such law. The Second Circuit noted that even the district court, which had dismissed the case on jurisdictional grounds, had "recognized the strength of appellants' argument that official torture violates an emerging norm of customary international law."

KADIC V. KARADZIC

In Kadic, Croat and Muslim victims of crimes committed in Bosnia sued the President of the unrecognized Bosnian-Serb State for rape, forced prostitution, torture, summary execution, genocide, and other atrocities. As in Filartiga, the plaintiffs based their suit on a violation of the "law of nations," under ATCA, rather than on any action arising under a treaty.

Although the district court had found that it did not have jurisdiction under ATCA to review acts of torture allegedly committed by private actors, the Second Circuit panel reviewing the decision disagreed. Chief Judge Newman acknowledged at the outset of the Second Circuit's opinion that "[m]ost Americans would probably be surprised to learn that victims of atrocities committed in Bosnia are suing the leader of the insurgent Bosnian-Serb forces in a United States District Court in Manhattan," yet the court found that the plaintiffs sufficiently alleged violations of customary international law for purposes of ATCA, and held that a U.S. court could hold Karadzic liable for the violations.

Kadic reiterated the validity of using customary international law to establish jurisdiction to litigate international human rights cases in U.S. courts. The decision, viewed as an expansion of Filartiga, relied heavily on that case and the idea that the "law of nations" and customary international law provide jurisdiction for a cause of action in U.S. courts. Karadzic had argued that ATCA, like the Torture Victim Protection Act of 1991 (TVPA), requires a "state actor," but the court rejected his argument.

Instead, the court declared:

We do not agree that the law of nations, as understood in the modern era, confines its reach to state action. Instead, we hold that certain forms of conduct violate the law of nations whether undertaken by those acting under the auspices of a state or only as private individuals.

The court also noted Congress's desire to sustain a separate cause of action that would "permit suits based on other norms [not specified in the TVPA] that... may ripen in the future into rules of customary international law." Finally, the court cautioned against judicial retreat from disputes that have foreign policy implications, quoting from the Supreme Court's opinion in Baker v. Carr that "it is `error to suppose that every case or controversy which touches foreign relations lies beyond judicial cognizance.'" Doe v. Islamic Salvation Front (FIS)

Islamic Salvation Front, the case described briefly at the beginning of this Note, involved eight anonymous Algerian and French women suing a high-ranking official in the Algerian Islamic Salvation Front. Like the plaintiffs in Filartiga and Kadic, the women in Islamic Salvation Front based their claim on ATCA, alleging that the defendant violated customary international law-and thus the "law of nations"-by participating in crimes such as summary execution, rape, mutilation, sexual slavery, and murder.

At the outset, the district court declined to follow a prior fragmented D.C. Circuit decision, Tel-Oren v. Libyan Arab Republic, which had found that the court lacked subject matter jurisdiction over Israeli citizens who had claimed relief under ATCA for acts of torture committed against them by armed members of the Palestine Liberation Organization (PLO).

Instead, in Islamic Salvation Front, the court adhered to the reasoning set forth in Kadic. Judge Sporkin stated: "The decision in [Kadic v.] Karadzic came after this Circuit's opinions in Tel-Oren.... Because of the clarity of the Second Circuit's decision and because the facts there are similar to those in the instant case, this Court finds that it is the appropriate precedent to apply in this case." Discussing the validity of the customary international law claims at issue, the court restated the same ATCA legislative history cited in Kadic that left open the possibility of ATCA being used to find remedies for undefined customary norms.

The court then denied the defendant's motion to dismiss, reiterating that U.S. courts could hold private actors responsible for claims under ATCA and that the alleged acts of the defendant violated international law. Filartiga, Kadic, and Islamic Salvation Front embraced the legacy of The Paquete Habana by supporting the validity of international human rights claims in U.S. courts based on customary international law. These decisions make clear that the United States has codified the "international law is our law" concept through ATCA, legislation that facilitates U.S. court resolution of claims with international elements. The legacy of respect for international law obtains further potency from the Restatement, cited in Islamic Salvation Front, Kadic, and Filartiga.

Although such evidence suggests that the legacy of support for the use of customary international law in U.S. courts is strong, counterevidence demonstrates a solid and growing resistance to the idea that "international law is our law." This counterevidence, which includes specific criticism of Filartiga and Kadic, general criticism of judicial encroachments into international law, a notable rejection of customary international law by the United States Court of Appeals for the Eleventh Circuit, and overall questions about the sincerity of the United States's commitment to human rights issues, exposes several weaknesses in The Paquete Habana's legacy.

Critics of the use of customary international law in U.S. courts have attacked the Filartiga and Kadic decisions for their flawed reasoning and "inappropriate leniency in allowing U.S. courts jurisdiction over international human rights cases." Some fault Kadic for broadening the scope of viable claims under ATCA, thereby "increas[ing] the number of potential defendants and consequently the amount of litigation pertaining to international human rights cases."

One complaint is that, in an already crowded judicial system, a flood of international human rights cases based on unidentified customary norms, to be decided by judges lacking expertise in international law, poses inherent dangers. Presumably, without clarity on how to assess the validity of customary international law claims adequately, stability and predictability of judicial review evaporate, injecting confusion into courtrooms and fostering arbitrary decision-making.

To avoid this problem, critics have called for a more narrow construction of ATCA. These critics argue that courts have interpreted the legislation facilitating international claims in U.S. courts too broadly.

Chief Justice Fuller's dissent in The Paquete Habana provides ammunition for these critics as well as for those who remain generally opposed to the use of customary international law in U.S. courts:

"I am unable to conclude that there is any such established international rule, or that this court can properly revise action which must be treated as having been taken in the ordinary exercise of discretion in the conduct of war. It cannot be maintained "that modern usage constitutes a rule which acts directly upon the thing itself by its own force, and not through the sovereign power."

Many arguments of those opposing the use of customary international law hinge on what Chief Justice Fuller alluded to-the lack of express domestic authorization for enforcing such law. Critics also can point to a lack of legislation on international human rights issues and ambiguities in the Restatement that make it challenging for the judiciary to rule on the authority of international human rights law in the United States. In addition, critics can highlight the fact that courts in other countries, such as Canada and Great Britain, almost never allow customary international law to be used in human rights litigation in their courts, indicating that the United States should refrain from doing so as well.

In Garcia-Mir v. Meese, decided between the Second Circuit's Filartiga and Kadic decisions, the Eleventh Circuit issued an opinion consistent with some of the prevalent criticisms of the use of customary international law in U.S. courts. Garcia-Mir, which did not include a claim under ATCA, presented the Eleventh Circuit with a customary international law challenge different from the one faced by the Second Circuit in Filartiga and Kadic and the United States District Court for the District of Columbia in Islamic Salvation Front. Garcia-Mir involved an appeal of several consolidated cases brought by Cubans who fled to the United States in the Mariel boat lift.

One of the charges was that U.S. officials had violated what amounted to a customary international norm against prolonged arbitrary detention. In response to a huge insurge in Cuban refugees, U.S. authorities detained the Cubans in federal penitentiaries because U.S. immigration law rendered them "excludable" and therefore removable, but no other country had agreed to admit them. Domestic law failed to protect them because "excludable" aliens have no legal rights in the United States; therefore, the Cubans sought to prove that their indefinite detention in U.S. prisons constituted a violation of international human rights law.

Other federal district court decisions involving Cuban refugees had intimated that a customary international prohibition on arbitrary detention existed, and that the United States had violated it through its actions against the Cubans. In Fernandez-Roque v. Smith, for example, a federal district court stated in dictum that "the various international law principles proscribing prolonged, arbitrary detention of persons are binding on this country and require the same sort of procedural safeguards as the Court has determined below are mandated by the Constitution of the United States."

The district court cited the Universal Declaration of Human Rights, the American Convention on Human Rights, the International Covenant on Civil and Political Rights, and the Protocol Relating to the Status of Refugees for support. Garcia-Mir rejected these prior indications of support for a decision based on customary international law, producing instead a decision that reflected many of the concerns expressed by critics of customary international law.

Although the court did not explicitly deny the existence of an international norm against arbitrary detention, it ultimately found that such a norm was not legally binding in a U.S. court because a "controlling executive or legislative act" on the issue had the power to render the norm nonbinding in the United States. The court found that the requisite "controlling executive act" existed because the Attorney General had acted contrary to the norm against arbitrary detention in deciding to incarcerate the Cubans indefinitely, pending deportation, and that his action as an executive branch official was sufficient to permit departure from the norm.

The Eleventh Circuit added that even if the Attorney General's actions were not sufficient, a controlling judicial decision, such as the one in Jean v. Nelson, which held that "even an indefinitely incarcerated alien `could not challenge his continued detention without a hearing,'" would render the norm nonbinding. The Garcia-Mir court thus carefully avoided an outright disavowal of customary international law while still providing customary international law critics with precedent for their arguments.

The decision advised a narrow interpretation of the scope of international law claims supported by The Paquete Habana and, in so doing, upheld the view espoused by many critics that the judiciary should refrain from basing decisions on international standards. In addition, Garcia-Mir signaled a new warning for plaintiffs of the potential difficulties they could face in attempting to enforce customary international law against U.S. officials.

The United States foreign policy provides a more general example of resistance to the legacy of The Paquete Habana. Ultimately, the legacy of The Paquete Habana centers on a respect for international law and a recognition that the United States should adhere to and protect the integrity of international law. To some extent, such respect is evident in the United States. Federal courts have been willing to hear cases based on international law even when none of the events giving rise to a case occurred in the United States.

Paying credence to international law in U.S. courts, moreover, Congress has codified international law principles in legislation, including ATCA. This express support manifests the United States's appreciation of the relevance of international law. In addition, the United States's willingness to become a party to several human rights treaties further validates the authority of international human rights law in U.S. courts.

Among the human rights treaties to which the United States is a party are the Protocol Relating to the Status of Refugees, the Convention on the Political Rights of Women, the Convention on the Prevention and Punishment of the Crime of Genocide, the Convention Against Torture and Other Cruel, Inhuman and Degrading Treatment or Punishment, and the International Convention on the Elimination of All Forms of Racial Discrimination.

Respect for international law is not, however, as entrenched in the United States as it might seem. Although efforts in the United States do convey some support for enforcement of international rights through the making of treaty law, a closer look at U.S. treaty policy indicates that the United States's commitment to human rights issues is less than firm. Although the United States has provided full support for a handful of human rights treaties, more often it has imposed reservations to those treaties, failed to ratify them for several years, if at all, or refrained from signing them entirely.

Critics of the use of customary international law in U.S. courts can point to weaknesses in the United States's commitment to international treaties, particularly in the field of human rights law, to bolster the argument that courts have no business dictating policy that conflicts with executive branch foreign policy decisions. The theory is that if the President wanted to have the principles reflected in the treaties incorporated into U.S. law, he would sign and submit the treaties to the Senate for ratification.

Likewise, if the Senate wanted to incorporate the treaties into U.S. law, it would sign and ratify them. One therefore might view the United States's failure to sign and ratify treaties as signifying that the principles espoused in the unsigned, unratified treaties are not meant to be incorporated into U.S. law. Furthermore, courts should not be free to make and apply those treaties that have been implicitly rejected by the other branches of government.

Although the resistance to using international law as authority in U.S. courts remains a mere undercurrent at the moment, it does serve to shake the foundation of the underlying principle that U.S. courts are bound by international law. As the resistance gains exposure, courts may begin to question the continued viability of that underlying principle. With the growing prevalence of international human rights cases in U.S. courts, the possible effects of the undercurrents become more consequential, and the threat to the legacy of The Paquete Habana becomes more real.

In spite of the growing criticism of the use of customary international law in domestic litigation, several factors demonstrate that a significant narrowing, or an express prohibition on its use in U.S. courts, is neither immediately inevitable nor advisable. First, paralleling the recent strong movement to prohibit or narrow use of customary international law in human rights litigation is an equally powerful movement to protect it. Academic criticism of domestic use of customary international law, although prevalent, has been met with persuasive, frequent rebuttals by those who support its use. These rebuttals-by some of the country's most notable international law scholars-refute the critics' arguments and resoundingly declare the continued legitimacy and importance of customary international law in domestic courts.

Harold Hongju Koh notes, for example, that the criticism of customary international law "may have superficial appeal for those not well steeped in the fields of international and foreign affairs law" and that the critics' "anti-judicial-activism rhetoric makes for lively and provocative reading.... But even casual reflection compels the conclusion that [those critics] are utterly mistaken."

Koh also notes that "[t]he Framers never suggested... that the federal courts' power to construe customary international law should be somehow subordinated to the concurrent authority of the political branches to define the law of nations."

Similarly, Gerald Neuman points out inherent flaws in critiques of customary international law, such as the critique offered by Curtis Bradley and Jack Goldsmith, and demonstrates that judicial application of customary international law is thoroughly consistent with "the American understanding of democracy."

Furthermore, although the federalism and separation of powers arguments against the use of customary international law are provocative, experts have consistently discredited those arguments and explained that customary international law remains compatible with constitutional principles. Rebuttals such as these, combined with the recent legislative history on TVPA, which specifically preserves the use of customary international law in U.S. courts for norms not individually listed in that Act, suggest that the legacy of support for customary international law remains strong.

Second, although the critics may be correct in noting that significant ambiguities remain in the area of customary international law, those ambiguities do not necessarily defeat the effectiveness and value of using customary international law in international human rights litigation in U.S. courts. Understandably, the argument that customary international law contains great ambiguities could lead to a call for clarity and guidance from the Restatement, or perhaps from some sort of legislation.

From a purely practical perspective, further clarity and guidance on customary international law issues could prove useful for plaintiffs, defendants, lawyers, and judges. From a theoretical perspective, clarification might help codify emerging customary international law trends and reaffirm the enforceability of customary norms in federal courts. A call for precise clarity and guidance regarding customary international law, however, probably would not be successful and might even be destructive. Customary international law is by its very nature indefinable; it is law that treaties or legislation do not clearly define.

Putting forth a very specific definition with firm guidelines for discerning customary norms is not only inadvisable because it inevitably would be under inclusive; it also is impossible due to the continually evolving nature of international law. Furthermore, ambiguities are prevalent throughout many other areas of law. As one international law scholar explained:

> There are, of course, uncertainties and ambiguities in international law, but questions about state practice and community norms are not necessarily more difficult to answer than, for example, questions about due process, equal protection and legislative intent. In purely domestic cases, novel and highly complex technical issues are regularly and successfully addressed. Few international matters are more formidable.

Indeed, part of the judiciary's job is to wade through those ambiguities to make difficult determinations. The related argument that judges lack the expertise required to make informed decisions regarding international law is simply without merit. If ignorance of the law is no excuse for those required to obey the law, it should not be an excuse for those required to decide the law. Judges routinely rule on issues on which they lack expertise.

Instead of succumbing to the view that international law is outside the realm of the judiciary and foreclosing to plaintiffs the right to judicial redress, "[t]he challenge now is to educate both domestic advocates and judges as to the usefulness and applicability of an increasing body of law, so that judges routinely consider international law-based arguments with the same ease they consider constitutional or statutory ones."

Third, although it might be true that some other countries do not grant customary international law significant authority in their domestic courts, it is extremely plausible that because these countries tend to ratify human rights treaties more often than the United States, they consequently do not need to rely on customary international law.

In addition, some other countries do actually demonstrate respect for customary international law in their domestic courts. For example, both German and Austrian courts recognize customary international law and allow it to take precedence over domestic law even if the domestic law is more recent than the customary international law at issue.

Given the United States's questionable record with human rights treaties, enforcement of customary international law in U.S. courts is essential to the United States's ability to maintain an international reputation as a strong supporter of individual liberties and a champion of human rights.

Allowing the judiciary to rule on human rights claims would not sanction broad judicial activism; rather, it would ensure that the judiciary carries out duties for which it shares responsibility.

[I]t is submitted that courts cannot be oblivious to the consequences of judicial decisions that ignore international human rights, and, by inaction or restrictive statutory interpretation, tolerate or permit their violation. In the application of constitutional guarantees and in the interpretation of laws that affect human rights, the Supreme Court in particular can neither restrict nor abandon its special constitutional role as the protector of fundamental human rights. In the words of Justice Thurgood Marshall, in his last dissenting opinion before retiring from the Court, the Supreme Court ought not to "squander the authority and the legitimacy of this Court as a protector of the powerless."

Finally, perhaps critics can take solace in recognizing that there actually may be little harm in allowing the enforcement of customary international law in U.S. courts. If a court upholds a norm that the legislature finds invalid, a controlling executive or legislative act can subsequently render the norm nonbinding. The damage done would be minimal. Critics' concerns about the enforcement of norms against U.S. authorities, and the resulting separation of powers anxieties that enforcement might engender, likely are without basis, as the Garcia-Mir case demonstrated.

Locating a controlling executive or legislative act to render the norm nonbinding probably would present little difficulty, given the broad reading the court in Garcia-Mir gave to a "controlling act." The ambiguity surrounding customary international law thus cuts both ways; it not only enables plaintiffs to assert claims that might otherwise be non justifiable, it also allows courts the room to moderate the ultimate impact of those claims.

In short, although enforcement of customary international law in human rights litigation in U.S. courts is currently under attack from critics, the legacy of respect for customary international law fostered by The Paquete Habana remains defensible. Use of customary international law does force the judiciary to make difficult decisions, but, in spite of the quote at the beginning of this Note, "courts cannot isolate themselves from the great moral issues of the day" and "cannot risk the fate of becoming irrelevant in their crucial role of applying the law as an instrument of justice."

Even more fundamentally, in making his statement about the inapplicability of any type of foreign affairs to his role as judge, Judge Robinson apparently overlooked the oft-quoted maxim from Justice Brennan in Baker v. Carr: "[I]t is error to suppose that every case or controversy which touches foreign relations lies beyond judicial cognizance."

The approaching 100-year anniversary of The Paquete Habana sets the stage for a clarification of the United States's commitment to the principle that "[i]nternational law is part of our law." Clarification becomes imperative with the growing number of United States courts hearing international law claims stemming from both treaties and customary international law norms.

Much evidence supports the strength of The Paquete Habana's legacy, but resistance to the legacy increases as the reach of international law continues to expand. Harnessing that reach and retreating to an isolationist view that shelters courts from making decisions based on customary international law is an unsettling solution, one that would send the United States tumbling backwards into the past as a new century begins.

On the other hand, embracing The Paquete Habana's legacy and reiterating the authority of federal courts to rule on claims based on customary international law would enable courts to carry out their responsibility for protecting the powerless, salvage the United States's reputation for fostering individual liberty, demonstrate an eagerness to participate in global accountability, and move the country confidently into the future.

Bibliography

Alston, Philip and Henry J. Steiner, *International Human Rights in Context: Law, Politics, Morals: Text and Materials.* Oxford: Claredon Press, 1996.

Alston, Philip, "The Commission on Human Rights," *The United Nations and Human Rights.* New York: Oxford University Press, 1992.

Bauer, Joanne R. and Daniel A. Bell, eds. *The East Asian Challenge for Human Rights* Cambridge, Cambridge University Press, 1999.

Bell, Daniel A. *East meets West. Human Rights and Democracy in East Asia.* Princeton, Princeton University Press, 2000.

Bell, Lynda S., Nathan, Andrew J., and Peleg, Ilan, eds. *Negotiating Culture and Human Rights.* New York: Columbia University Press, 2001.

Brownlie, Ian, ed., *Basic Instruments on Human Rights.* Oxford: Clarendon Press, 4th ed., 1995.

Buergenthal, Thomas, *International Human Rights in a Nutshell.* St. Paul, MN: West Publishing Co., 2nd ed., 1995.

Burgers, J. Herman and Hans Danelius, *The United Nations Convention Against Torture: A Handbook on the Convention Against Torture and Other Cruel, Inhumane or Degrading Treatment or Punishment.* Boston: M. Nijhoff, 1988.

Center for the Study of Human Rights, *Twenty-Five Human Rights Documents.* New York: Columbia University, 2nd ed., 1994.

Center for the Study of Human Rights, *Women and Human*

Rights: The Basic Documents. New York: Columbia University, 1996.

de Bary, Wm. Theodore. *Asian Values and Human Rights. A Confucian Communitarian Perspective.* Cambridge: Harvard University Press, 1998.

Foot, Rosemary. *Rights beyond Borders. The Global Community and the Struggle over Human Rights in China.* Oxford: Oxford University Press, 2000.

Goodland, Robert. *Tribal Peoples and Economic Development: Human Ecologic Considerations.* Washington, D.C.: World Bank, 1982.

Gurr, Ted Robert. *Minorities at Risk: A Global View of Ethnopolitical Conflicts.* Washington, D.C.: The United States Institute of Peace, 1993.

Gurr, Ted Robert. *Peoples versus States: Minorities at Risk in the New Century.* Washington, D.C.: United States Institute of Peace, 2000.

Hamalengwa, M., C. Flinterman and E.V.O. Dankwa, *The International Law of Human Rights in Africa: Basic Documents and Annotated Bibliography.* Boston, MA: M. Nijhoff, 1988.

Hannum, Hurst, ed., *Guide to International Human Rights Practice.* Philadelphia, PA: University of Pennsylvania Press, 2nd ed., 1992.

Heinz, Wolfgang. Indigenous Populations, Ethnic Minorities, and Human Rights. Berlin: Quorum Verlag, 1988.

Henkin, Louis and John Lawrence Hargrove, *An Agenda for the Next Century.* American Society of International Law, 1994.

Hitchcock, Robert K. Indigenous Peoples, Multinational Corporations, and Human Rights. *Indigenous Affairs* 2/97:6-11, 1997(b)

International Women's Tribune Centre, *Rights of Women: A Guide to the Most Important Treaties on Women's Human Rights.* New York: IWTC, 1998.

Jacobsen, Michael and Ole Bruun. *Human Rights and Asian Values: Contesting National Identities and Cultural Representations in Asia.* Richmond, Curzon: 2000.

Kent, Ann. *Between Freedom and Subsistence. China and Human Rights.* Hong Kong: Oxford University Press, 1993.

Kimlycka, Will, ed. *The Rights of Minority Cultures.* Oxford and New York: Oxford University Press1995.

Maybury-Lewis, David (1997) Indigenous Peoples, Ethnic Groups, and the State. Boston: Allyn and Bacon.

Pritchard, Sarah, ed. *Indigenous Peoples, The United Nations and Human Rights.* London: Zed Books, 1998.

Sachs, Aaron. *Eco-Justice: Linking Human Rights and the Environment. WorldWatch Paper 127.* Washington, D.C.: WorldWatch Institute,1995.

Sigler, Jay A. *Minority Rights: A Comparative Analysis.* Westport, Connecticut: Greenwood Press, 1983.

Stavenhagen, Rodolfo. *Ethnic Conflicts and the Nation-State.* New York, New York: Macmillan Press,1996.

Thornberry, Patrick. *International Law and the Rights of Minorities.* Oxford: Clarendon Press, 1992.

Turner, Terrence and Carole Nagengast, eds. Universal Human Rights versus Cultural Relativity. Special Issue of *Journal of Anthropological Research* 53(3):267-381,1997.

United Nations, *Human Rights: A Compilation of International Instruments,* vols. 1 (*Universal Instruments*) and 2 (*Regional Instruments*). New York and Geneva: United Nations, 1994.

Van Ness, Peter, ed. *Debating human rights. Critical essays from United States and* Asia. London: Routledge, 1999.

Weissbrodt, David and Penny Parker, *The United Nations Commission on Human Rights, Its Sub-Commission, and Related Procedures: An Orientation Manual.* Geneva: International Service for Human Rights, 1993.

World Bank. *Operational Directive on Indigenous Peoples.* Washington, D.C.: World Bank, 1991.

Young, Elspeth. *Third World in the First: Indigenous Peoples and Development. London*: Routledge, 1995.

Index

I

K

L

M

N

O